SEVEN AT SANTA CRUZ

The Life of Fighter Ace Stanley "Swede" Vejtasa

Ted Edwards

Naval Institute Press
Annapolis, Maryland

Naval Institute Press
291 Wood Road
Annapolis, MD 21402

Library of Congress Cataloging-in-Publication Data is available.
ISBN: 978-1-68247-287-3 (hardcover)
ISBN: 978-1-68247-288-0 (eBook)

♾ Print editions meet the requirements of ANSI/NISO z39.48-1992
(Permanence of Paper).

Printed in the United States of America.

26 25 24 23 22 21 20 19 18   9 8 7 6 5 4 3 2 1
First printing

To Robbie Robinson, Swede Vejtasa,
and Whitey Feightner.
Thanks for taking me under your wings
and making this book possible.

CONTENTS

――――

AUTHOR'S NOTE

This book, largely in Swede's words, is the product of several enjoyable collaborations. In 2010 I wrote a biography of Robbie Robinson, an *Enterprise* dive-bomber pilot (*Leonard "Robbie" Robinson, Waxahachie Warrior*). Robbie then steered me to his friend Swede Vejtasa, a hero at the October 26, 1942, Battle of Santa Cruz. In November 2010 I contacted Swede by phone. I was initially interested in a personalized account of that battle. Over the next couple of years I conducted three in-person interviews with him, the last on the seventieth anniversary of the Battle of Santa Cruz.[1] These conversations led to ever-widening stories about his experiences, and the project expanded into a biography. Following each of our sessions together we spent many phone hours reviewing specific details and clarifying ambiguities. Swede reviewed sections or chapters as they became available.

Swede, in turn, put me in touch with Whitey Feightner.[2] Having flown Swede's wing on the eve of the battle, Whitey was very helpful in choreographing the confusing events of the following day. I interviewed Whitey twice in person and for many hours over the phone. He too read and approved elements of the manuscript. In another phone interview, famed dive-bomber pilot Hal Buell provided his perspective. Accomplished fighter pilots Jack Glass and Bill Hardy enthusiastically offered their memories of Swede. Robbie Robinson, of course, weighed in as well. Swede's published and unpublished interviews and a twenty-eight-page autobiographical essay possess a remarkable consistency, and these have been very helpful in expanding on Swede's views and voice.[3]

In addition to an extensive review of the literature, I twice visited the National Archives to access relevant after-action reports. I found pertinent interviews and documents during two visits to the National Naval Aviation Museum in Pensacola, Florida. Records in some cases provided bureaucratic clarification or factual confirmation of confused or faded memories. In the end, though, while records might verify, trusting them as truth can easily lead historians astray.

Navy Squadrons

The following explanation is intended to clarify squadron letters and numbers for those readers unfamiliar with Navy nomenclature. In 1942 World War II aircraft carriers embarked four squadrons identified by letters related to their tasks or missions and numbered for their carrier, air group, or base. All squadrons began with the letter V to denote aviation heavier than air. Fighting squadrons (VF) flew F4F Wildcats as escorts or as combat air patrol over the fleet. In Swede's case in his *Enterprise* squadron VF-10, the VF indicates fighting and 10 refers to Air Group Ten. Squadrons often carried nicknames such as the Grim Reapers or Black Sheep and typically flew in four-plane divisions each bearing a number, such as Swede's Reaper 7. A dive-bombing squadron flying SBD Dauntlesses was sensibly designated VB followed by the appropriate number. Scouting squadrons generally flew SBDs and were designated VS or VSB for scout bomber. Swede flew *Yorktown*'s VS-5 or Scouting Five. Torpedo squadrons (VT) were the fourth element of the air group flying TBD Avenger torpedo bombers. The addition of an M such as VMSB or VMF indicated Marine squadrons.

ACKNOWLEDGMENTS

I am deeply indebted to my late friend and mentor Angus Cameron, who years ago served as senior editor and executive vice president for Alfred A. Knopf. Angus encouraged me to take up the study of history; I like to think he'd be proud of my follow-through.

Dr. John Williams, a treasured graduate history professor at State University of New York at Stony Brook, contributed greatly to my growth as a historian. I shall always appreciate his faith in me.

I twice visited the National Archives, where Nathaniel Patch lent his expertise to my document quest.

I spent very fruitful hours, accompanied by my brother Ned Scantlebury, in the Emil Buehler Naval Aviation Library at the National Naval Aviation Museum, where Theo Ebert and Joe Ezell provided friendly and capable assistance. They were prepared for me and helped me find almost everything I sought. Bill Addison and Royal Cheney continued in the same spirit the next day. On a more recent visit, Roy Hall scanned photos and offered pilot insights, Jack Coyle found pertinent folders, and Dottie Robinson enthusiastically copied articles for me. I felt very privileged. Thanks to all.

Jim Hornfischer offered sage advice and encouraged me to market this book aggressively. Steve Moore's interest and insights have provided a guiding light on many occasions.

Peter Mersky outlasted my repeated assaults on Naval Institute Press convention and style, revealed my advanced and near-terminal hyphen-deficit disorder, and has been an enormous help in improving the clarity and accuracy of this book. I owe Peter a big debt of gratitude and a new pen.

I also offer thanks to Hampton Sides, whose historiography and writing are inspirational. His thoughtful inscription "Nil desperandum" helped sustain my motivation as this project entered its sixth year.

I would also like to acknowledge Bill Shinneman's continued interest and encouragement.

While I offer some corrections to John Lundstrom's *First Team and the Guadalcanal Campaign*, there is no denying the great value of his work. As I have waded through the confusion surrounding this complex battle, Lundstrom is nearly always the go-to or last word guy.

My father, Ted Scantlebury, inspired this project, and his admonition to "do your homework" has served me well. A naval aviator during World War II and beyond, he too held Lundstrom's work in high regard.

Graham St John kindly read parts of this manuscript and offered many helpful suggestions. Lynn Baca has been a wonderful editor and significantly improved many aspects of this book.

Acquisitions editor Glenn Griffith saw through my first-timer errors and put the manuscript into the hands of folks who provided great improvements. Copy editor Mindy Conner worked miracles streamlining my prose. I offer grateful praise to Emily Bakely for her remarkable fine-tuning.

To John Park, trail partner and faithful, interested listener, large thanks for the laughter you bring. That goes as well for superb teacher and lover of history Bob Hudson. Coach Butch Duncanson's understanding of human nature has long been an inspiration.

My wife, Barbara Rose Johnston, has helped in countless ways, from dealing with my techno rages to editing content to sustaining me with great meals.

Any errors that have survived this scrutiny belong, of course, to me.

ACRONYMS

AA	antiaircraft
ACMM	aviation chief machinist mate
ARM1C	aviation radioman first class
CAG	commander air group
CEAG	commander *Enterprise* air group
CAP	combat air patrol
CinCPac	commander in chief, U.S. Pacific Fleet
CO	commanding officer
ComFair Miramar	commander, Fleet Air Miramar
ComFair Quonset	commander, Fleet Air Quonset, Rhode Island
ComSoPac	commander, South Pacific theater of operations
CXAM	a type of radar
FDO	fighter director officer
FCLP	field carrier landing practice
IJN	Imperial Japanese Navy
LSO	landing signal officer
NAS	naval air station
RIO	radar intercept officer
TF	task force
XO	executive officer
YE	a homing signal and transmitter
ZB	Zed Baker, a homing signal receiver

Introduction

On the good advice of my friend Robbie Robinson, at the time a ninety-year-old decorated veteran of VB-10, I called Swede Vejtasa. Anyone familiar with the Battle of Santa Cruz would recognize the name, so I was a little intimidated by the idea. Swede, then ninety-six years old, had played a significant role in the U.S. Navy's Guadalcanal campaign. Swede was a hero; surely someone had already written the definitive story on the man.

I had certainly been impressed by the story of Swede's famous ace-and-more-in-a-day defense of USS *Enterprise* during the October 26, 1942, battle. But as I read up on Swede's legendary mission I encountered wide-ranging confusion regarding what exactly happened that day. Esteemed historians Samuel Eliot Morison, John Lundstrom, Gerald Astor, Steve Ewing, Peter Mersky, Barrett Tillman, and Eric Hammel have written stirring accounts that bear little similarity to one another. How to explain such a remarkable disunity regarding Swede's performance?

After several phone conversations, one of which lasted an hour and a half, Swede extended an invitation to talk with him in person. I was delighted. In February 2011 I visited his home in Escondido, north of San Diego, for two days of interviews.

Air Group 10's performance during the Guadalcanal campaign had long fascinated me. I now had an opportunity to interview a significant participant in the bloody carrier battle at Santa Cruz. I was eager to hear Swede describe his historic ace mission as well as the rest of his career as a naval officer. Prior to my visit, I cobbled together a ten-page summation of his Santa Cruz combat gleaned from several well-regarded histories. After we concluded an animated five-hour interview session during which we covered his life and career prior to Santa Cruz, Swede agreed to look over what I had written.

The next morning my historian's hubris took a hit. Swede, in his gruff voice, gently informed me, "Ted, this is completely wrong. It's just full of errors."

Like many of his fellow aviators, Swede had researched the historical accounts of the battles in which he had participated. He let me down easy. "You get all this stuff out of books?"

"Uh, yeah," I gulped, wondering how many more minutes he would put up with the likes of this badly mistaken historian. He stayed with me.

"Well, if your sources are all wrong, how can you get it right? I'm positive, of course, because I was there."

"Swede, tell me how it went." I turned on my recorder, and Swede described in great detail how he experienced Santa Cruz and several other remarkable missions.

As Swede disabused me and many esteemed historians of our errors, he also made emphatically clear that he viewed the events on the battle's eve as a criminal injustice. Thus, Swede's remarkable story opens the day before the Battle of Santa Cruz with the Phantom Wild Goose Chase.

CHAPTER 1

"The Admiral Is a Stupid Ass"

The December 7, 1941, Japanese attack on Pearl Harbor heralded a new mode of naval combat that would ultimately decide the outcome of the Pacific war. Instead of traditional battleship confrontations, American and Japanese carrier task forces sent strike groups against targets they could not see. By the autumn of 1942 there had been three punishing carrier battles: Coral Sea in early May, Midway a month later, and Eastern Solomons in late August as the Japanese responded to the August 7 Marine landing on Guadalcanal. Three carriers—USS *Lexington* (CV 2), USS *Yorktown* (CV 5), and USS *Wasp* (CV 7)—were lost in those battles. *Enterprise* (CV 6), "the Big E," had been forced to return to Pearl Harbor for repairs. USS *Saratoga* (CV 3) soon joined her, having been torpedoed for the second time. USS *Hornet* (CV 8) alone stood in the way of Japan's attempt to retake Guadalcanal.

In October, U.S. naval intelligence determined that *Kidō Butai*, a powerful four-carrier Japanese mobile strike force, was again headed for Guadalcanal. The Imperial Japanese Navy aimed for a decisive encounter with whatever banged-up carrier forces the United States could muster, while the Imperial Japanese Army planned for the simultaneous seizure of strategic Henderson Field, home to the marauding Cactus Air Force. Guadalcanal, the "unsinkable carrier," would at last be theirs, and in the process they would exterminate every last one of the U.S. Marines grimly hanging on there. Most important for the empire, victory at Guadalcanal would put an end to the appalling sacrifice of Japanese men and resources disappearing down the stinking sinkhole they called "the Island of Death." Then the mighty *Kidō Butai* could properly resume command of the seas.

3

To meet this latest threat, the U.S. Navy formed carrier Task Force 61 (TF 61); the newly repaired *Enterprise* would link up with *Hornet* already operating near Guadalcanal. Rear Adm. George D. Murray, *Enterprise*'s experienced previous commanding officer (CO), currently flew his flag on *Hornet* (TF 17). Rear Adm. Thomas C. Kinkaid had retained his command of *Enterprise* (TF 16) begun prior to Eastern Solomons and now assumed overall command of TF 61. Overmatched in every category by the mobile strike force reportedly steaming his way, Kinkaid, a nonaviator brought up on cruisers and battleships, had orders to confront and destroy this latest Japanese effort to retake Guadalcanal. On October 24, 1942, TF 61 became a reality when Big E joined with *Hornet*.

The next morning, October 25, did not begin well. Lt. (jg) Bill Blair, one of skipper Lt. Cdr. Jimmy Flatley's VF-10 Grim Reapers, while flying an uneventful combat air patrol (CAP) over *Enterprise*, made the unpleasant discovery that his F4F-4 prop had frozen in high pitch. This not uncommon mechanical quirk left Blair with little to no control of his aircraft as he attempted to land. Blair punched through the barrier, knocked one Dauntless SBD dive-bomber overboard, crumpled three others, and wrecked his own Wildcat in the process. He was very fortunate to walk away unscathed. His sarcastic squadronmates, in recognition of his swift and efficient destruction of five U.S. Navy aircraft, quickly appointed Blair their very own Japanese ace.

Short on the heels of this calamity, a PBY patrol plane located the oncoming Japanese carrier force some 360 miles to the northwest. Mincing no words, the newly appointed commander of the South Pacific (ComSoPac), Vice Adm. William F. "Bull" Halsey, wired Kinkaid an electrifying message instructing him to "STRIKE-REPEAT-STRIKE."

Propelled by Halsey's urgency, Kinkaid, in command of a two-carrier task force for the first time, now had an opportunity to put his own aggressive leadership style on display. First, however, having agreed to Rear Admiral Murray's sensible suggestion that the newly arrived *Enterprise* assume duty carrier status, Kinkaid would have to cool his heels. *Enterprise*'s air operations would be limited to CAP and searches. *Hornet* would launch the strikes.

Setting his course for history's fourth carrier battle, Kinkaid harbored no illusions regarding Japanese capabilities. At Eastern Solomons two months earlier the Japanese had very nearly killed him and his staff in their well-coordinated attack on *Enterprise*. In the battle's aftermath he had seen for himself the charred and torn bodies and had acquired a new appreciation of his own vulnerability. For Kinkaid, the takeaway lesson from the Coral Sea, Midway, and Eastern Solomons carrier battles was to strike the first blow, hit those Japanese carriers before they could get to him. To pull that off, he first had to locate them.

Accordingly, at 2:30 p.m. Kinkaid launched a fan of twelve Dauntless dive-bombers flying two-hundred-mile legs in search of the oncoming Japanese. Having obliged his duty status, Kinkaid followed with a bewildering decision that had far-reaching effects. A half hour later, too soon to hear anything back from his searchers, Kinkaid flouted his carrier's duty status and ordered what remained of his air group to conduct a long-range, long-shot, search-and-strike mission.

No one could comprehend Kinkaid's decision. The status arrangement assigning strikes to *Hornet* made perfect sense. Her experienced air group, which for the past five weeks had been attacking Japanese shipping and strafing enemy barges, troop concentrations, and supplies stacked up on Guadalcanal's beaches, currently sat spotted for launch. No one doubted the group's capabilities. Instead, for reasons Kinkaid never explained, he chose *Enterprise*'s untested Air Group 10 for a strike against an enemy yet to be pinpointed.

Lt. Stanley W. "Swede" Vejtasa (pronounced VAY-tuh-suh) listened in disbelief as Kinkaid's staff outlined the plan. Swede, so named by Lt. Cdr. Bill Burch when Swede was flying a dive-bomber with *Yorktown*'s Scouting 5, wondered why Jimmy Flatley wasn't attending this VF-10 briefing, though he might have guessed.[1] Four days earlier, Flatley had been playing Bull in the Ring, and Bill Blair (of the morning's five-plane debacle) and Ens. Roy "Butch" Voris had both landed on Flatley's right foot, breaking a bone. Now, determined to participate in the next day's expected battle, Flatley was busy rigging his F4F's pedals to accommodate his bum foot.

Swede also noticed that VF-10's executive officer (XO), Lt. Cdr. William R. "Killer" Kane, was nowhere in sight. Swede had his own take on Kane. "Everybody liked the guy. In the air he was confusing as hell. He was vision-impaired. He always had trouble with rendezvous, joining up, or spotting incoming bogies. Killer just wasn't with it. We had to give Killer help showing him where the targets were." With Flatley hanging back, Kane would be in charge.

The disarray struck Swede as very strange. "It seemed that the squadron officers had not been consulted about this strike. And the staff was notorious for not putting out any information at all. I looked up at the chart to see my name as escort. I wondered how my name or anybody else's name got up there. We had never trained as an air group. Nobody knew what to do."

Swede listened in disgust as Kincaid's staff presented the plan. "We knew where the Jap fleet was located. I was doing the calculations on my board. I knew our SBDs had no chance to find the Japanese fleet. They were too far away. No way we were going to have contact.

"I bitched about the mission: 'I got the facts. I got the numbers. I've got my board right here. We couldn't get there.' I threw my board down."

The issue was not simply the distance. This air group was far from being a finely honed fighting unit. Newly arrived Ens. Edward L. "Whitey" Feightner was a great pilot, but he hadn't had the practice time to become familiar with how the other guys flew or how they would react to combat situations. Experienced dive-bomber pilot Lt. (jg) Hal Buell shuddered at the thought of sending the untried strike group out. Just a week and a half prior he had witnessed a very confusing nighttime *Enterprise* Air Group 10 "group grope" over Hawaii that he had stayed well clear of. And that exercise had not involved the fog and stresses of combat.[2]

Ens. Donald "Flash" Gordon further detailed the group's inexperience. "Some of us got four day landings and one night landing before we deployed from Hawaii, and most of us got our eleventh through fifteenth landings on 25 and 26 October during the Battle of Santa Cruz."[3] Compared with Swede's previous combat experience with *Yorktown*'s highly effective air group, these guys were a mess. Sending out this raw strike group on a fool's errand reminded Swede of another fateful decision at Coral Sea, when SBD pilots of Scouting 5 were ordered to fly CAP. Zeros shredded them.

"I will tell that idiot this is mission impossible," Swede thundered and headed for flag plot to confront Kinkaid and his staff. "I knew goddamn well we were going to be in big trouble."

Within earshot of Kinkaid's staff, Swede brazenly remarked that "the admiral is a stupid ass, an idiot," the kind of insubordinate mouthing off that could warrant a court-martial.

"I didn't give a damn if they court-martialed me," Swede recalled. "There was the evidence. I knew I had it right, and he [the admiral] did not. I was surprised no action was taken against me. I was pretty vocal."

Bombing 10's skipper, Lt. Cdr. Jim Thomas, pulled him aside and counseled, "Swede, you're too far out, use more caution. Don't be so hasty. We'll do an out and in."

Swede could appreciate the wisdom in that. They would fly out, drop their ordnance, fly back to the ship, and everyone would be satisfied.

Someone called Swede out: "Are you refusing to make this flight?"

"No, I'll do an out and back," he retorted and wheeled out of the room.

Dumbfounded by the lack of organization and distracted by the confused milling about, Swede failed to note who else was listed for the mission.

Just who was this loud-mouthed lieutenant calling Kinkaid's mission into question? Swede, having turned twenty-eight in July, was older and more experienced than most of his fellow Reapers. He had flown neutrality patrols in the Atlantic since August 1939, and he had already been awarded two Navy Crosses for his bombing and dogfighting in the Pacific. Maybe his fellow pilots knew about those medals; maybe they didn't. Stories got around, though, and as good as Swede's record of bombing enemy transports and helping to sink the carrier *Shōhō* sounded, it was his besting a trio of Japan's top-notch Zero pilots with an SBD that really spoke to fellow pilots. In the deadly business of aerial combat, Swede's was the experienced voice of success. He was the guy they would rely on for the straight scoop. And there in the ready room with the admiral's staff present Swede had boldly declared this mission insane. What must the newcomers think?

Of course, Swede had brashly voiced what every pilot in the room had been thinking. They all used the same plotting board, marker pencil, and little metal computer. Beyond the impossible distance, the unstated issue—the elephant in the ready room—was the near certainty that this mission would extend into the night. Whitey Feightner was likely the only fighter pilot in the strike group qualified for night landings. Swede knew that several of the pilots had never made a single night carrier landing. And nobody wanted to consider deploying another little device they carried: the single-cell flashlight, which generally indicated you were bobbing in the water.

Badly in need of some fresh air, Swede climbed up to the flight deck. Lt. Frederick L. "Fritz" Faulkner, his squadronmate from *Yorktown* days, typically flew with Swede, but there he was up on the flight deck, not wearing a flight suit, moving from plane to plane performing his maintenance officer duties. Anticipating a long mission for the short-legged Wildcats, Fritz was checking the auxiliary gas tanks.

"Swede, what do you think of the auxiliary tank hookups?"

There was little for Swede to endorse. The tanks were unpredictable. "All you had to do was drop your nose for a little speed, and the damn things would tear off."

Swede lingered with his friend up top until the loudspeakers blared, "Pilots return to the ready room." A quick briefing, then it was back up to the flight deck and their planes. Deeply troubled by what he knew to be a hopeless mission, Swede reluctantly buckled into his Wildcat. He had even forgotten to ask Fritz if he was going along.

With Swede's mutinous objections ringing in their ears, the strike group launched. By the time everyone joined up with the group commander it was around 3:30 p.m. Flying at 145–150 miles per hour (mph), it would be 4:30 or later when they reached the end of their search vector. That would translate to a return home at or close to sundown. Any action or delay would necessitate one of those nerve-racking night landings.

Commander *Enterprise* Air Group (CEAG) Richard K. Gaines took nominal charge of five SBD dive-bombers led by Jim Thomas and six TBF torpedo bombers under torpedo bomber XO Lt. Albert P. "Scoofer" Coffin. Typically, the CAG—in this case Dick Gaines—would go up unarmed and tag along as an observer. But Swede wasn't even sure that Gaines had joined the strike group.

"Gaines was not in the ready room, and he was not in the air. I saw his command TBF with its special gas tank sitting on the hangar deck. That's the only plane he flew."

Indeed, if Gaines had not flown that day, that would have been fine with the other pilots. "He was not an aviator," Swede opined. "He possessed no sense of combat whatever. On past operations we never saw him; he disappeared. Nobody paid any attention to him back on the *Yorktown*."

Whitey, on the other hand, was sure Gaines was up with them. Bombing 10's war diary concurs,[4] and Capt. Osborne Hardison's after-action report lends further support: "This group comprised all flyable planes on board and consisted of twenty planes, eight of which were fighters and one the CEAG."[5] Thus it seems likely that Gaines was along. Flying alone, above, and behind the group, Gaines could easily have gone unnoticed by Swede. Or maybe Swede's frame of mind rendered Gaines invisible. Regardless, that made a total of nineteen armed aircraft to attack an unreachable *Kidō Butai*.

Whether or not Gaines was present didn't really matter. Tactical leadership typically fell on squadron commanders, in this case Jim Thomas, Bombing 10's skipper. It would be his job to navigate and provide the base squadron; everyone else flew on him.

Escort duty for the meager force fell to Reaper 7 and Reaper 4. With both skipper Flatley and XO Kane unaccounted for, command of the entire eight-plane escort thus fell to Swede. Taking stock of his resources, Swede was unclear as to who, in fact, now flew under his command. He led Reaper 7 with Whitey Feightner flying his wing. Ens. Ed Coalson and Ens. William "Hank" Leder flew the second section. Swede also knew that Lt. Frank Donald "Don" Miller and Ens. Maurice N. "Wick" Wickendoll flew a two-plane section of Reaper 4. The nagging question was, who was flying the lead section of Reaper 4? Ens. James Dowden may have been up, but that still left the leader unidentified.

Flying this bogus mission was bad enough, and now this confusion was in the air. Swede had come of age as a combat pilot under the tight organization that Scouting 5 skipper Bill Burch had structured on board *Yorktown*. Against that professionalism, this situation was totally screwed up, especially not knowing who was up with him, who he could count on.[6]

Assuming they could actually find the Japanese, a textbook strike would involve the escorting Wildcats, SBD Dauntless dive-bombers, and TBF Avenger torpedo planes in a coordinated attack. With Dauntlesses diving out of the sun, Avengers coming in low from both sides, and F4Fs buzzing around strafing the enemy ship, antiaircraft (AA) fire would be diffused as gunners were challenged first to determine and then to respond to the greatest threat.

Working against such a coordinated attack plan was its complete dependence on the simultaneous arrival of fighters and bombers over their target. And pilots understood how easy it was to get lost or separated in the tropical murk. Once formations broke down, a piecemeal attack enabled the defenses to concentrate their fire. Midway had amply demonstrated what could happen to assets committed separately. *Hornet*'s Torpedo 8, *Enterprise*'s Torpedo 6, and *Yorktown*'s Torpedo 3, all without escorts, had courageously bored in on the Japanese carriers, flying slowly and predictably during their approaches. Zeros and antiaircraft fire annihilated them.

Swede's Reapers would be expected to deflect an experienced Japanese CAP and contribute their strafing to a coordinated bombing and torpedo attack. So many things could go wrong. As it turned out, none of the things they might have feared did go wrong. Their trials would manifest closer to home.

They droned on, Swede still furious with Kinkaid. "How stupid can you be? Sending a whole bunch of planes out into nothing. The raid will last into the night, and we're not going to accomplish anything at night. There's no horizon, no boats, but plenty of clouds. He's sending a barely integrated force into the dark of night to find a fleet that didn't exist."

They hadn't been gone an hour when, hundreds of miles to the north, another American snooper located the *Kidō Butai*. Spooked, the Japanese force turned north, a course change that fully guaranteed no contact would be made. Although apprised of this development, Kinkaid nevertheless elected to maintain radio silence, leaving his now-pointless strike group to their own devices.

One wonders just how the conversation went in flag plot as Kinkaid declined to recall his strike group. Who spoke up for the aviators now needlessly condemned to a dangerous and ultimately lethal exercise? Perhaps Captain Hardison, commanding *Enterprise*, soothed Kinkaid with, "The group will simply fly its search leg, find nothing, and return to the carrier."

The newcomers in the air, guys flying their first combat mission, also pondered the possibilities. *What if Swede's wrong? What if we actually find the Japs? We don't know how to go into battle as a group. Nobody will know what to do.*

Of course, at the end of their search leg they found nothing. Jim Thomas, having changed his mind about conducting an out and back, now directed the group on another seventy-five-mile leg, further distancing them from *Enterprise*.

Whitey Feightner recalled, "Going out 150 miles, there's nobody there, we head east another 75 miles. We can see forever, it's so clear, and we occasionally popped up in hopes of sighting something farther out. Gaines, the group commander, was higher than the rest of us, up behind the bombers, searching the area with binoculars. Jim Thomas decided on another 20-degree turn and another leg at about the time we should have been landing."

Increasingly troubled at the dwindling daylight and gas, Swede asserted some of his experience. "I burped my gun to let Thomas be aware of our turn toward home. Instead, he starts another leg. I got down on top of him, burped my guns again to let him know we need to head home, now." Finally heeding Swede's warning, Thomas bent the group toward Point Option, where *Enterprise* awaited their return.

Relieved to be done with their search legs, pilots anxiously glanced at fuel gauges that were sinking along with the sun. About this time things started getting woolly. A problematic wing tank forced Swede to pump the whole stinking tank by hand, ruining two pairs of gloves and assaulting his senses. Then the afternoon's clear skies gave way to low, scudding clouds. Coupled with the rapidly darkening tropical skies, navigation became a nightmare.

"The weather at this point was hazy with no visible horizon," Swede recalled. "Holding station became difficult due to the poor visibility and the tendency for some pilots to succumb to vertigo." Pilots strained to keep other planes in sight while strict radio silence magnified each man's lonely isolation.

Shortly after sunset things unraveled. Lt. Don Miller made a mystifying decision. Whitey, who was flying nearest him at the time, recalled, "At this point we were all at minimum fuel state, and about fifteen minutes later the leader of the second fighter division dropped out of the formation and opened his canopy and leaped out of his plane. I saw his chute open before we lost sight of him."

Swede only glimpsed what happened. "It was already dark. I was ahead. I noticed erratic movements of Miller's wings, and he shifted from one side of the formation to the other. Then he pushed down. I had no idea who it was. He must have jumped out right as he pushed over."

Wickendoll, Miller's wingman, dropped down, hoping to see what had become of his flight leader. Afterward, Whitey reflected on his first bitter taste of war, no shooting involved. "It wasn't nice to see, but our dwindling fuel meant we had to keep going, so we marked his position on our chart boards and continued. That was the last we ever saw of him."

Miller's engine may have starved owing to one of the frequent faulty gas transfers, or he might have been undone by haze-induced vertigo. Whatever the cause, Miller's loss was a bewildering shock. Nothing for it but to stay cool, fly on, and as a night landing became a certainty, try to recall anything you had ever learned about night carrier landings. Besides crashing.

"We had twelve new pilots in the squadron, most with no prior combat experience, and more to the point, no night landing experience," Swede lamented. "Besides Whitey, I don't think there was one pilot, including me, qualified for night landings. Many had never made any night landings. One pilot had reported only days before leaving Pearl Harbor. As we grouped up in poor visibility conditions, pilots were hanging so close to me their wings were nearly in my cockpit."

The murk stripped away any comfort in numbers. Terrified of collisions, they dropped down low, hoping to get under the clouds and into clear air. For Swede, "It was just like flying into the void. I was real fortunate having done all of those scouting missions, all this dead reckoning by the compass. Magnetic compass and air speed was all we had, but I could calculate pretty good, had a good plotting board, and I knew how to use it. So when we got back to where the carrier was supposed to be, there's no carrier; isn't a damn thing there."[7]

CHAPTER 2

Beginnings

Swede came from pioneer stock. "My father's father, Frank, and wife, Frances Svoboda Vejtasa, were Bohemians from Czechoslovakia. He came from Monrovia and settled in North Dakota as a homesteader. Quite a few Czechs came to Omaha, Nebraska, through Iowa and later settled in North Dakota, which was just being developed despite being in the middle of Indian country. More Czechs kept moving west and eventually got to Circle, Montana. They'd all speak Czech."

Swede's father, John, was one of seven boys and four girls. John was the first to graduate college, a real achievement during those tough times. His degree would serve him well. Swede's mother, Inga Rinnhaugen, came from Norway and was one of five girls in a homesteading family. She and John became acquainted in school. After their marriage John worked for Standard Oil for a time but left that to try his hand at homesteading.

John and Inga's first child was daughter Mildred. Their second child, Stanley Winfield Vejtasa, was born on July 27, 1914, in Paris, Montana. Subsequently, brothers Frank, John ("Stub"), and Eugene and second daughter, Frances, rounded out the family. During World War II all four brothers would serve in the military.

"I was raised in eastern Montana," Swede recounted. "The sheepmen had taken over. Cattle and horses leave a bit of grass when they graze, but the sheep nibble it down until it's bare. There's no grass the next season. It used to be buffalo country. The massive herds used to stop travelers for days. We'd see tracks to their watering holes, and buffalo rings showing where the buffalo bulls had circled to keep foraging wolves away from the females and young in the middle. I saw a few buffalo, but they were rare by then. Indians were still taking some up near the Missouri River Breaks."

Life was challenging. "We had no roads, no running water. And we could only communicate by voice. Transportation was by wagon, sled, horseback, or you walked. This was difficult for my mother; she only walked or rode in a wagon. It was all we had. The winters were really, really tough. When I was eleven or twelve, I went to town and saw my first telephone.

"We were homesteaders, and everybody believed in education. People just didn't have the money to build a school or hire teachers, so what they did for the initial school was to build one of sod. I think it had some tin or metal for a roof. They hired a teacher. I don't know what they paid or what kind of an agreement was made, but he had to live in one section of this sod house and the other section was the schoolhouse where the kids gathered. Well, he lasted less than a week. That just was not for him."[1]

Something had to be done. "So I think parents volunteered for the year. Then parent homesteaders built us another school out of rough lumber and so forth. Out there on the prairie wood was hard to come by. It was a one-room schoolhouse. Anyway that's where I first went to school. It was a building of that rough lumber and a little tarpaper on the outside to keep the snow out. I think one of the things I remember most about that was having to walk, of course, to school, which was probably at least a mile and a half. In those bitter winters we froze our feet and hands at least twice a day. When the weather was bad, we did homeschooling. There wasn't a lot of social life, but when there was a gathering, it was held at the schoolhouse. We never questioned it. I had a reasonable start that way."

Good fortune smiled on Swede's father. "By 1924 I was a ten-year-old. Homesteaders, entrepreneurs, big cattlemen were coming in. They were establishing counties, and they were looking for someone to be county treasurer. The word got around, 'John Vejtasa, he's a college man.' My father didn't have any choice. We moved to the town of Circle. I went to grade school and high school there, probably forty to sixty students."

Depression Days

"A lot of people say the Depression started in 1929, but it felt that way to us by 1925. Things were very difficult for us. Money was short; we could never figure out why. These were times when people killed their stock—cattle and pigs—while people were starving to death. They weren't worth anything. The government was buying livestock and destroying them. Why not provide some of this to hungry folk? It was a tough life for everybody."

Swede fondly recalled his first stirrings for flying. "I like to say that I had an early introduction to aviation. The neighbor lad on those windswept farmlands of eastern Montana used to come by during the haying season and get me to give him a hand. At my age and size at that time I doubt if I was much help, but I guess I must have been good company.

"Young Claire McMahon would load the hayrack while I tried to pack it down, then he would climb up, start the team of horses toward the hay corral and immediately loop the reins over the center post of the rack, and then, with obvious satisfaction, would lie back on the hay and watch the fleecy, white cumulous clouds drift across the clean, blue sky. 'This is just like flying,' he would say, then launch into a discourse on climb, glide, elevators and ailerons, joysticks, props, and other terms common to early aviation that I had never heard before but certainly piqued my interest. Claire must have somehow obtained the books and pubs on early aviation and read well, because I know at that time he had not flown or may not have ever seen an aircraft. However, he had an avid listener, and I could visualize myself skirting those clouds or blasting through in some type of powerful winged craft."

Fantasies are one thing, reality another. "Our reverie was usually interrupted by a loud 'hallo' from the father in the vicinity of the hay corral, who was wondering why the hay wagon was not moving and the horses were so contentedly munching stubble."

It wasn't long before Swede became acquainted with that colorful bit of period Americana, the barnstormer. "They came to the larger cities to give air shows and rides but also often to the smaller towns to pick up a few dollars. These were great occasions, and we listened for the drone of the engine and searched the skies for our first glimpse of the biplane. They were always two-wings in those early days, and mostly surplus Jennies. Hopefully the pilot would find a suitable landing area near the outskirts of the village, but if not, some farmer's field would do nicely.

"Those fellows were an interesting lot with the leather helmets, the goggles, the flight jackets, leather boots, and of course the well-trimmed moustache to add to the mystique. Emerging from the craft after a bumpy landing, the pilot would shove the helmet and goggles back on his head, and after moving a safe distance from the craft he would light a store-bought cigarette before being introduced to the members of the local populace who had rushed to the scene.

"Occasionally our school class could go as a group and get the lecture on nomenclature, flight characteristics, and hear the exploits of that particular pilot. We were spellbound. On one such occasion, my brother and I pooled our meager resources of cash and took a ride in a visiting Jenny. This was heady stuff, buckled in by a safety belt, hair streaming in the wind, eyes watering, and knuckles white from gripping the handholds at the front of the cockpit."

The brothers took it a step further. "We were completely enthralled, and with a new surge of interest, my brother John, who was a genius with mechanical things, built engines from discarded parts at the city dump, constructed wings and fuselages. We never got off the ground, even though we were equipped with the tattered and worn copy of *Popular Mechanics* and the article therein entitled, 'How to Fly.' This was a great disappointment but perhaps a blessing."[2]

Flying in those days had a dark side as well. "The Great Depression years were tough for all of us, but aviation continued to make quantum strides. One development affecting our area was the light monoplane, which was ideally suited to hunting coyotes and wolves. A pilot would carry a backseat gunner with a shotgun loaded with heavy buckshot and would . . . comb the brakes and coulees of the countryside with unbelievable success and proudly display the numerous pelts for the local news photographers. In a short time, the coyote and wolf population was completely decimated—a situation which to me was repugnant and one in which I would not participate."[3]

Beyond his high school studies, Swede enjoyed athletics. "I played football, but there weren't enough students for teams. As was common in those days, we had to play both offense and defense. We weren't very professional. We had no uniforms. I was much better in track. I didn't need much training for running and jumping. I did well in the fifty-yard and one-hundred-yard dashes, but I was not what you call a great athlete."

His father contributed in a variety of ways to their community. "My dad's wages started at $135 a month. Later he became clerk of the district court and held that job for more than fifty years. At one time or another, he had every job in town: treasurer of this, secretary of that, school board, farmers' union; he had jobs everywhere. He was very capable. He had the moxie."

All the same, it was a stretch for Swede to come up with money for college. "I had good teachers in high school, and they urged us to try to improve, to do better, college-level work. I kept my grades up and earned a four-year scholarship to Montana State College."

But that scholarship fell short of paying full expenses. "We didn't have the money to pay the fees, so I had to go to work for a year. I got a good job at a gas station, and next year I went to college."

Swede spent the next two years at Montana State College, and on February 13, 1935, he was initiated into the Phi Eta Sigma fraternity. When he had only a quarter to go in his sophomore year, the administration abruptly canceled all scholarships. Lacking the money to pay even the last-quarter dues, Swede resolved to drop out. But a good friend, the son of the president of Montana Power, and a big man on campus, prevented that. He had asked for Swede's help in drawing sketches of dissected cat parts. "He was a bright lad. He could have done it, but I did it for him." Advised that Swede contemplated dropping out, his friend held up his hands. "Let's go see the dean."

The dean's receptionist stonewalled the brassy sophomores until his friend's last name was mentioned. Relationships established, they were ushered in to see a suddenly available dean, who informed them that scholarship decisions were not his; it would be up to the board.

"Well, then, issue Swede my scholarship. Just transfer mine," his friend implored.

"Oh, we can't do that," came the reply.

The dean conceded that Swede could take his final exams, but he would have to sign a note promising to pay all back fees. With no real intention of paying for their breach of contract, Swede signed the note. The college never did reinstate Swede's scholarship.

Savings from summer grocery store work funded a return to school, this time to the University of Montana. With his Montana State credits fully approved, Swede entered the School of Forestry. Three months on, the dean offered him some work. "It didn't pay much, but a few dollars was good money in 1937."

As part of the forestry program, Swede worked alongside a pilot flying a Ford trimotor. They ferried supplies to Forest Service depots, where Swede kicked out bundles to crews on the ground. "It was a great introduction to flying."

The experience made a lasting impression. "My years at college went swiftly, and I haunted the local airports, admiring the new aircraft, constantly amazed at the broadening field of application for planes."

By winter of that term, war clouds were building in Europe. Anticipating the future need for pilots, the government developed a student aviator program. "If you could pass preliminary training, they'd send you to flight school. They sent Marines around to schools, looking good in their uniforms.

"Lacking funds for flying lessons, I searched for any program that might be open to me. One day on the campus of the University of Montana, I heard that Hub Zemke, a recent graduate, had gone to the Army Air Corps for training at Kelly Field in Texas. This lead was like finding gold. I immediately sent away for information on the requirements and promptly enrolled in the subject classes specified.

"Ready to make my bid, word was passed on the campus one day that a U.S. Marine Corps aviator had landed at the Missoula airport and was available to brief anyone interested in the U.S. Navy Aviation Cadet Program.

"Needless to say, I was at the appointed place in a flash and was most favorably impressed with this dapper young man in a natty uniform, complete with decorations and Navy wings of gold. I fear I took too much of his time, but he was very honest and straightforward. I thanked him and made application for the Navy flight program offered."[4]

Application was limited to college graduates, though, or those who at least had coursework in solid geometry and spherical trigonometry. "There was no solid geometry course at the school, and I was not enrolled in the spherical trig class. I went to see the dean. Three days later, I had no seat but I was in the trig class, and there was a new course in solid geometry. How he handled this I don't know. There were eight students—three were girls—taught by a fine elderly instructor. Shortly I completed the lengthy examination required and was advised that I would receive orders to preliminary flight training at NAS Seattle."

That summer of 1937 Swede returned to his Forest Service work, anxiously awaiting the letter informing him of his appearance date. "I manned a lookout, broke trail, and fought forest fires in the Selway National Forest located in Idaho. Our base was in Montana, and we didn't have any regular communication. One day a guy with a pack train comes in to replenish us. As he was about to leave, he pushed his hat back and said, 'Oh, Stanley, I got a letter for you.' It was from the Naval Reserve Station in Seattle with my come-on date—two days past.

"I didn't want to miss out on this. 'Just wait here,' I told him. 'I'll write a letter.' I discovered I had no paper, no pencil. The cook had a brown paper bag, from which he tore a piece, and somebody had a pencil. I wrote a reply requesting an advance notice of thirty days because it would take that long for mail to reach me. I gave my friend the muleskinner a bit of green to keep his memory fresh and admonished him to get this thing in the mail immediately upon his arrival at the ranger station. He disappeared into the woods scratching his head and muttering, 'I didn't know you could write.' "

This sketchy arrangement bore fruit. "In a month, he comes back. First thing he says, 'I've got a letter for you.' I'm due in Seattle in two days. I just about fainted. I had alerted the boss. I've got to get going. I immediately put my pack on my back, said adieu, and took off at best speed for the ranger station some thirty-five miles away through very mountainous terrain. The next morning, tired and exhausted, I got into my trusty Ford coupe, drove to Missoula, and caught a bus for Seattle, hoping to get some rest. I found my way to Air Station Seattle and arrived one hour before the time set for the interview."

Farewell to Civilian Life

Swede had no idea what to expect. "I walk in. I wouldn't have been surprised had they said, 'There's the door.' I had my working clothes, boots on. All these college guys sittin' there, eight of them, I think, including one sailor in uniform looking like a million dollars. They called me in. The interview went very well. I found the officers most friendly and interested in my life in the woods, lookout stations, and my experience with smoke jumpers. In the open file in front of the chairman they had my pathetic brown paper letter, which was referred to but only as an expression of appreciation for keeping them informed."

They accepted Swede that day. "I joined that group in Seattle and took my preliminary training. There were all these college guys, obviously well qualified. I was not sure how I stood in this group."

Seattle's naval air station in those early days boasted no hard-surface runways, only grass. Each morning it was the duty of the group to chase the pheasants from the airstrip before operations could begin. During his off time, Swede wrote many letters to Irene Funk, his hometown sweetheart, who was, Swede recalled, "known for her academic strengths and outstanding dance skills."[5] In his September 17, 1937, letter to Irene, Swede wrote, "It's a great life here at the station—some seven hundred sailors and marines but we have a lot of fun. The weather here reminds me of a bathhouse on a cold day, and so far I've only got in one hour of flying. They may make a pilot out of me but I'm not so sure."

In the same letter Swede noted the Navy's impact on Seattle. "We all got shore leave this afternoon, so I'll see what Seattle has to offer. All the clubs and burlesque shows run all day and night here while the fleet is in, and there's just hundreds of girls here that sigh and turn on the love light when they see a uniform."

Reflecting on his abrupt transition from forestry to flight training, "I was glad to get out of the brush anyway, where there wasn't much but bears for company. I'll never go back. If I wash out here I don't know what I would do. I know I'm not doing myself much good but I'm having too much fun."

And he anguished over his relationship with Irene. "I always think of coming back to you, but you should have never let me go. Remember, I asked you once. I could have settled down then and been good, but now I can't. I would have come to see you long ago but I never forgot that letter you wrote once. I love you just the same, more than anyone, and I'll come to see you but I'll never be the same—better to you I hope. Love XXXXX Stan."

A few weeks later Swede described his progress in piloting. "We've been flying almost every day. I've got the most time in of all the cadets and I've been shooting landings for two days. I'm having lots of fun in the air but the landings and takeoffs aren't so smooth yet."

Then it was time for transition. "After preliminary training they put me on another list," he recalled. "After a four-month wait I received tickets for a cross-country train trip to Pensacola. I'd never been on a cross-country anything."

Their route took them to Chicago, on to New Orleans, and finally to Pensacola, Florida. "On June 4, 1938, I checked into Pensacola as a flight student, or aviation cadet. I was most grateful for the opportunity that had come my way and approached each day with a resolve to excel. We had the finest training there; it couldn't have been any better. There were five squadrons in the progressive training program providing a most complete and comprehensive preparation for fleet duty as an aviator. In Squadron 1, we flew half a day and went to school half a day; they didn't let up on the education. We covered all Navy and aircraft subjects, financial administration. Everybody griped about it, but it was damned good. We had to memorize all the flags, signaling, Morse code, and then pass tests on all this. We stripped a rotary engine and put it back together. We studied Navy military law and practiced ship and small boat handling. This very practical education lasted for nine months."

Conviction now marked Swede's attitude toward flying. "I think I will always stay in aviation," he wrote to Irene. "It's far better that anything I've ever done so far and it sure beats peddling prunes for twelve or fifteen hours a day. Maybe I'm lazy. We fly three or four hours a day and go to ground school three and think we work hard. One thing about it though, it's too fast a life to be good in for long. I haven't seen one flyer yet that isn't a pretty heavy drinker. There is more liquor consumed here on one weekend than in a whole month in Circle."

In a later letter to Irene, Swede described how the regimen and separation took their toll. "Some boys bust out of here on purpose because their girls quit them when they come here. One was telling me his troubles last night, how it broke his heart when she told him she was going to marry someone else. I feel sorry for anyone that is in that deep. They sure do some funny things." Ever the romantic, Swede closed with, "I love you more every day because I think you are the most wonderful girl in the world. All my love, XXXXXX Stan."

During his training in Pensacola Swede got to know fellow student David L. "Tex" Hill, who would later gain considerable fame with the Flying Tigers. Tex recorded eleven and a quarter victories in China and later added six more with the 23rd Fighter Group in the Pacific.

The last three months of Squadron 1 were dedicated to flying all day long. "We started out with the N3N seaplane made in Philadelphia. We called them 'Yellow Perils on floats,' and when the instructor deemed us ready, we flew our first solos."

A successful solo qualified Swede for Squadron 2, where he continued training with N3Ns and an N2S, commonly referred to as the Stearman. He spent many hours practicing landings, takeoffs, gliding, judgment turns, and some formation work. As Swede put it, "everything you'd need to become an adept aviator."

In Squadron 3 they progressed to flying older but more powerful service planes such as the Vought O3U-1, the SU-1, and the SBU-2. Instruction centered on formation flying, gunnery, both pilot and rear-seat approaches, landings, takeoffs, and rendezvous, or join-up training.

In his March 19, 1939, letter to Irene, Swede alluded to the dangers of his work, "We are still flying nine-plane formations. It may not look so bad from the ground but it's an ordeal to be up among them. Every time I go out I test my parachute straps twice because if there isn't a crack-up in that outfit it will be a miracle. We have about three men that put the whirling dervish to shame up there."

Political considerations crept into his letter. "I see there is a part in the new Naval Appropriations bill regarding cadets. If it goes thru [sic] we will get more pay, faster promotion and better service. I hope it does. I think it comes before the House on April 9th."

That same letter revealed something of how his fellow cadets coped with their rigorous training. "This was a wild weekend for cadets. Most of them come back and put in Sunday afternoon in their bunks in a state of dormant hibernation recovering from the effects of internal alcoholic baths."

A month later, an April 19 letter to Irene detailed more of his training experience. "We sure have been busy this week on gunnery. We only stop long enough to change cockpits and then we go again. It's a lot of fun shooting at a sock with a machine gun. Next week by this time I should be flying patrol boats."

He also mentioned trainee troubles. "There sure are a lot of boys getting busted out lately. Every day I see one or two packing up to go home. My friend from Texas [Tex Hill] I'm afraid is in a bad way too. He busted his final and has to go before the board. He also told me his love troubles."

In Squadron 4, the focus shifted to multi-engine seaplanes. Over the next nine months Swede flew many hours in a Douglas twin-engine PD-1 biplane. And he also took up the PM-2, the P3M-2, and O3U-1 on floats. They worked out in the bay, getting checked out in sea operations. They practiced seaplane launches and recovery and trained in over-the-ocean navigation exercises.

Swede's Squadron 5 instruction stressed practical instrument work while flying planes currently in fleet service or newer models just out. "Instrument work, nobody likes it, always tough, there you sit hooded in the backseat, instructor in the front seat. The hours under the hood in the NJ-1 mastering needle, ball, and airspeed weren't always the most pleasant due to the tendency to succumb to vertigo, disorientation, and resulting illness. But it was valuable training. Because we still had them in the fleet, we flew the TBD, a no-performance airplane. It was so clumsy, no power, we couldn't really maneuver the thing, and it had only one forward-firing gun. It was really fun flying the Boeing F4B, a little old biplane fighter. The saying went, 'You have 750 horsepower in your lap and a feather in your ass.' Everybody enjoyed that. Stripped down with no extra weight or racks, it was fantastic, a marvelous machine. You could do anything with it. We practiced gunnery, formation, and night flying. Despite having been a hunter in Montana, I had a lot to learn with skeet shooting. I was not the greatest. I had to attack it conscientiously."

It was during his Squadron 5 training that Swede met one of the era's iconic pilots. "In Squadron 5 at that time we had one of the really great aviators of the era as an instructor. Lt. William J. "Gus" Widhelm usually flew the morning weather hop and finished off with a display of stunting over the field that had all cadets on the ramp awed with the precision and control of the maneuvers before Gus came in high over the runway and slipped the fighter to a landing. It was my good fortune to see much of Gus in the fleet in the years to come, and we maintained contact until his untimely demise."[6]

A skip-the-rope exercise concluded this phase of training. "They put a rope up on a couple of poles not too far apart. You make your approach in your little F4B. You had to come in high, had to slide down, slip to come in, just before you got to the rope to see how close you could come to the rope without hitting it. Then make your touchdown and around again. It was a great exercise, quite demanding. Everybody liked it; I enjoyed the hell out of it. After passing all the tests again, we then graduated from flight school."

Swede was declared a naval aviator on July 13, 1939. But his satisfaction was marred. In an August 6 letter to Irene he confessed, "I cracked up a fighter the other day. I guess I waited long enough to do it, but I done a good job it seems."

In his last letter from Pensacola, dated August 9, Swede expressed his relief. "We finished flying yesterday and I thought maybe we'd get away today, but we haven't gotten either our orders or wings yet, so it may be a couple of days. Anyway it's sure a good feeling to know I got through here. Not many that started will finish."

Swede, now intent on marrying Irene, continued to counsel his buddy Tex. "My old friend Tex sure has troubles. He has two girlfriends and can't make up his mind which he wants. I always give him the answers though." As was his custom, the topic of love concluded his final letter from Pensacola. "I'll sure be glad to see you again. It's been a long time it seems, but I've loved you more as the days go by."

By this point the government was tweaking the Aviation Cadet Program; graduates were now to be considered ensigns in the U.S. Naval Reserve. On August 11, 1939, Swede was the fifth so designated. "The big day for me came in August of 1939, when we fell in for inspection and were awarded the coveted wings of gold and a commission as ensign, USNR. What a thrill and feeling of satisfaction for a lad from the plains of Montana to be a part of this brave new world!"

Days later the newly minted ensign was assigned to Scouting 5 embarked on *Yorktown*. His new home had been operating in the Los Angeles–

Coronado area during the previous months and was currently docked in San Diego.

On September 1, 1939, within weeks of his August wedding to Irene, Germany invaded Poland, igniting World War II. Swede enjoyed a well-earned thirty-day honeymoon leave, after which the greenhorn aviator departed all things familiar to report to his first squadron assignment.

CHAPTER 3

Naval Aviator

Joining *Yorktown*'s Scouting 5 meant flying dive-bombers rather than fighters. "I wanted fighters, but they didn't have enough openings in fighters to accommodate everybody. They told us, 'You can put in on your first fitness report that you want fighters.' So I started out flying the Curtiss SBC-3, a biplane, cloth and tin. I was the officer responsible for floatation gear. There was a float under each wing in case the plane went in. You could pop the float gear, the plane would float, and then get picked up."[1]

During the fall of 1939, as *Yorktown* underwent an overhaul in Bremerton, Washington, Scouting 5 conducted exercises from shore. Swede saw a lot of his training buddy Tex Hill as they proceeded through qualifications, checkout, and finally carrier qualifications. "We could qualify on any ship that was operating. We had to make seven landings aboard the *Saratoga* [CV 3] or the *Lexington* [CV 2]. On his first try Tex creamed an airplane. It went right over the side. The LSO and air boss convened an informal board of inquiry. In such instances the decision must be made to either continue qualification or recommend that the pilot be dropped. Tex continued and qualified, but he felt real bad that night. He stayed with the squadron until he departed for the American Volunteer Group flying in China."

On November 1, 1939, Swede and a group of young squadron aviators made those seven successful landings on board *Saratoga* off North Island and were declared fit for carrier operations.

Her overhaul completed, *Yorktown* operated for the first three months of 1940 out of San Diego. Auspiciously, at the end of March, Lt. Cdr. William O. "Bill" Burch joined VS-5 as XO. "No time was lost in getting the several new pilots carrier qualified, and we were out almost daily doing the field carrier landing practice [FCLP] until we were considered ready by the landing signal officer [LSO]. Checking my logbook in this early period, I had a memorable familiarization flight with Bill Burch. I recall this hop after all these years, as at the time I was really impressed with the smoothness and precision of control exhibited. My reaction was that this is what I must strive for in all my flying."[2]

In addition to expert instruction, Burch provided Stanley with a new name. "I had joined VS-5 and felt like just one of the guys as I made my entry on the logbook. Burch had some questions regarding the logbook. 'Where's that new officer with the blond hair (referring to me), he's got to be a Swede.' From that time on I never heard my own name."

The newly named Swede took an understated view of one of the scarier training exercises. "Night flying was also something of a new experience, especially when a squadron rendezvous was called for after the initial independent cruising."

The risk of collisions was high during join-ups in the dark, and this dangerous work demanded some youthful hijinks afterward. "Frequently, as there is always a sport in the group, someone would turn off the lights and scoot down to Tijuana for a dive-bombing run on the Molino Rojo, a favorite target in the red-light district. This always generated questions with of course the universal denials.

"Another exercise that called for some expertise was the takeoff by the entire squadron of eighteen planes in formation and landing in formation after the exercises were completed. North Island in those days had a mat that was large enough to permit this type of training. We put on a good show."

The Friday squadron-wide "group gropes" revealed technical shortcomings. "At this time the oxygen system consisted of a bottle of pure oxygen with a tube attached to a pipe stem for the pilot and another for the radioman or rear-seat gunner. How crude in the light of later knowledge! Cruising at some altitude before the group attack, it is little wonder that there were differences of opinion as to who was in position and who was lagging."

On April 2, *Yorktown*, with an additional Marine fighter squadron on board, sailed for Hawaii and participation in Fleet Problem XXI. One of those Marine pilots was 2nd Lt. Gregory Boyington, who would later be known as "Pappy" and become famous for his command of VMF-214, the Black Sheep Squadron. For his exploits Pappy would be awarded the Medal of Honor.

Swede described the tubby, inelegant SBC-3 they flew at the time. "It was not a great airplane, but as a dive-bomber it was strong enough for a 70-degree dive and recovery. We could carry a 500-pound bomb on the centerline, either that or 250s under the wings. There was one forward .50-caliber machine gun firing through the prop, and a radioman/gunner with a single .30-caliber facing rearward. The twin .30s came much later."

In May, *Yorktown* departed Hawaii for another overhaul back in Bremerton. Then it was back to Hawaii before returning again to San Diego, where Swede could get to know his son, Eugene, born July 5, 1940. In late August 1940, after President Franklin Delano Roosevelt decided to maintain the Pacific Fleet at Pearl Harbor, *Yorktown* was outfitted with the new CXAM radar. Then she steamed back again to Hawaiian waters, where the aviators languished.

On January 16, 1941, during an exercise, Swede's fellow Scout Ens. Fritz Faulkner crashed in a manner that left his SBC-3 dangling over the side. The plane sank, but Fritz and his aviation chief machinist's mate (ACMM), J. Ulmer, were rescued. It did not always go that well. Two months later, on March 17, two TBD-1s collided while joining up, killing the crews of both planes.

During the first three months of 1941 *Yorktown* participated in tactical exercises intended to improve fighter direction. Principally, the exercises stressed that CAP fighters needed to attain an altitude advantage over the inbound strike forces; secondarily, they were to meet the attackers as far from the fleet as possible. These points of wisdom were seldom adhered to in the carrier battles to come.

Aside from endless training, there were logistics issues to resolve. "On the beach we trained hard, operating from Ford Island with emphasis on gunnery and bombing. A number of drills were held to test the ability of the squadrons to arm and fulfill assigned missions. I recall the confusion when the chap with the key to the ammunition locker could not be found. And when the bombs did become available, they would not fit our bomb racks. Following the rules of the day, guns could not be kept installed in the aircraft except during gunnery exercises."

Some of the exercises were real head-scratchers. "While operating in Hawaiian waters, the *Yorktown* and her squadrons drilled on a number of occasions with the planes landing over the bow while the ship was backing down. Also we made numerous catapult shots from the hangar deck where the catapults were installed athwartships. I believe the *Yorktown* and the *Enterprise* were the only carriers to be equipped for this unusual landing and launching mode."[3]

After a seemingly unending stint of training in Hawaiian waters, on April 20, 1941, in response to the intensifying Battle of the Atlantic, *Yorktown* departed the all-too-familiar facilities around Pearl Harbor. Her upcoming mission was to escort convoys shipping essential supplies bound for Great Britain. Two days later she secretly broke away from the larger task force. Crewmen painted over the identifying "Y" on the funnel, hung a sign reading "USS *Wasp*" meant to confuse spies, and cleared the Panama Canal for duty in the Atlantic. Short on fuel, she arrived in Bermuda on May 7. The men were permitted to send one message, and for most that meant trying to provide some explanation for bewildered families abruptly left behind in Hawaii. *Yorktown* then began a series of Atlantic neutrality patrols intent on countering German submarines and marauding armed merchantmen.

On May 21 a German submarine torpedoed and sank the American merchantman SS *Robin Moor*. Six days later, President Roosevelt proclaimed a state of "unlimited national emergency."

"We happened to be in Norfolk, Virginia, at the time. We'd completed our Hawaiian cruise, and by early '41 things were heating up in the Atlantic. That's when Gus Widhelm showed up again to take over the formation of a new dive-bomber squadron. He was in my office when the squadron operations officer informed Gus, 'We have you scheduled for fam [familiarization] on Tuesday, practice dive-bombing on Wednesday, and practice fixed gunnery on Thursday, and then we can work in quals [qualifications] the next week.'

Gus took a puff from his cigarette, put his hand on the young officer's shoulder, and said, 'This is Widhelm you are talking to. I am busy this afternoon, but load up my plane with five bombs and a full load of ammo. See that the bullets are dipped in red paint. I will take off with the sleeve and do my fam on the way to the gunnery range. Have the dive-bombing target and crew ready on my way back. By the way, send an observer to verify results.'

"Then Gus was gone, leaving the scheduling officer with mouth hanging wide open. By early afternoon the next day, the word had spread that Widhelm had set a new record for hits on the sleeve and had dropped all five bombs within the minimum error circle at the bombing target on successive runs. Widhelm, the true bon vivant!"[4]

Yorktown's assignment was to assist USS *Ranger* (CV 4) in countering the growing menace of German attacks on transport convoys. On May 31, four days after President Roosevelt proclaimed an unlimited national emergency, *Yorktown* set sail for an uneventful first neutrality patrol, during which Swede's VS-5 cross-decked over to *Ranger.*

"Scouting Squadron 5 made a transfer at sea, exchanging with a *Ranger* squadron that went aboard the *Yorktown*. Most of the day, small boats plied between the carrier laying to, carrying men and gear. Then the planes took off and landed on their new decks. The day was May 23, 1941. This was the only operation of this type in my experience or knowledge ever conducted. We made quite a lengthy cruise down toward Africa and up to the north in the Atlantic."

Gus Widhelm again made Swede's radar. "On a windy, foggy day the air group was airborne waiting for the landing signal when the engine in Gus' craft quit. In his inimitable style, Gus radioed the ship, 'Swing that damn thing into the wind—my engine just quit and I am coming aboard.' All eyes were on Gus as he circled down from eight thousand feet, positioning himself so that everything would be just right as the ship came into the wind. As the ship steadied, the plane hit the deck, engaged an early wire, and came to a smooth stop.

"Gus jumped from the plane, ran to the bridge, and told the skipper, 'Hey, you almost screwed me up. I was afraid you weren't going to get into the wind in time and those whitecaps down there were getting bigger and colder all the time. If you think I was going to land in the water, you are crazy. Hey, have you got a cigarette?'

"I asked Gus about this much later, and he verified it. 'Yeah, a piece of cake—you know we should have some good exposure suits, just in case.' A tremendous feat, I say."

Swede's scouting missions came with instructions to report submarines and all shipping sighted. "All flights were by dead reckoning and required meticulous planning and strict adherence to plotted courses. We had done a lot of this before but with available radio aids in case of emergency, but now there was nothing to fall back on except perhaps a square search."

Swede was fortunate to have more than one mentor. "Three-plane searches were the order of the day, and at that time and since I have been most grateful for the leadership and advice of Lt. Bob Pirie, with whom I and my friend Lt. (jg) Earl Johnson made most of our flights. Bob Pirie was an instructor, a kind and understanding gentleman who took a sincere interest in our training, checking our navigation before takeoff and letting us take the lead on every flight. There is no substitute for this type of learning. If we made mistakes, we were corrected in a kindly manner, and on every flight we were briefed and learned to exercise the fine points of combat search at sea regarding reading the wind, using the cloud cover, conserving fuel, and making accurate observations. In the future this invaluable training would stand me in good stead."[5]

Her first neutrality patrol completed, *Yorktown* put into Norfolk without having encountered any U-boats or armed merchantmen.

During the second neutrality patrol (June 29–July 13) Scouting 5 stayed ashore. "That's when we exchanged their very obsolete SBC-3s for sleek new Douglas SBD-3 Dauntlesses. We only got one or two a week. An intensive training period followed, and we polished all the skills of dive-bombing, gunnery, tactics, and carrier landings. To qualify, I made two landings on the *Wasp*, which was departing for the West Coast."

Yorktown began her third neutrality patrol on July 30 with VS-5 again remaining ashore. Advised to "operate as under war conditions," *Yorktown*'s twelve-day escort cruise passed without incident. A fourth neutrality patrol, from August 15 to August 27, turned out to be another uneventful cruise to Bermuda. Eight days after their return, things escalated. On September 4, the German submarine *U-652* fired two torpedoes at the destroyer USS *Greer* (DD 145) and was in turn depth-charged. Neither attack succeeded.

This high-stakes cat-and-mouse business prompted President Roosevelt to raise the ante. Declaring a policy of "active defense," it was now the duty of the United States to protect freedom of the seas for merchant vessels of any nation. German or Italian warships that entered "American Defensive Waters" did so at their own peril.[6]

Instead of another cruise, Burch's VS-5 was assigned to the U.S. Army's General Headquarters Maneuvers to be conducted at Lake Charles, Louisiana—commonly referred to as the "cow pasture." During the nearly three weeks from September 10 to 30, VS-5 Scouting 5 supported Army ground units. To rapturous reviews they flew reconnaissance, "destroyed" bridges, and attacked their opponent's airdrome and armored forces.

Swede got a lot out of those exercises. "In September our squadron participated in an exercise with the Army in the Lake Charles, Louisiana, area. Again it was my good fortune to make many flights with Bill Burch. Every mission was simulated combat of some sort—search, attacking tanks, vehicle trains, enemy troops, and repelling enemy fighters. On every mission I learned more of the art of handling a number of aircraft, achieving the most advantageous position, executing the attack maneuver, and rendezvousing the group expeditiously. Of real interest to me was the timing and execution of the proper counteraction against attacking enemy fighters. 'Bitching the VF' (surprise attacks flying their dive-bombers, gaining the advantage, and setting up shoot-downs of the more agile fighters) was the name of the game, and I was learning from the master."

While Swede was refining his tactical skills the situation in the Atlantic continued to deteriorate. By the end of September the Navy's mandate had broadened "to patrol, cover, and escort, and to report or destroy any German or Italian naval forces encountered."[7] Germany took that as a direct threat, and on October 17, *U-568* torpedoed USS *Kearny* (DD 432), killing eleven and injuring twenty-two, the first of many thousands of American casualties in an undeclared Battle of the Atlantic. Neutrality was long gone.

On October 26 *Yorktown* sortied from Maine's Casco Bay escorting a convoy dubbed "Cargo." As the ships steamed to the prearranged mid-ocean meeting place, *Yorktown*'s job was to safeguard a clutch of six modern freighters slated for delivery to the British merchant marine. At the meeting place they would exchange the freighters for eight British troop transports (stuffed with more than twenty thousand troops ultimately bound for combat in the Middle East) and escort their new charges safely back to Halifax.

It would be a nerve-racking voyage. Word reached the ship that on October 30 the Navy oiler USS *Salinas* (AO 19), servicing another convoy, was torpedoed but not sunk. The following day, *U-552* sank USS *Reuben James* (DD 245), which was escorting convoy HX 156. She was the first U.S. warship lost in the Atlantic. Of her crew of 160, 45 survived.

Against this news, on November 2 the destroyer USS *O'Brien* (DD 415), escorting *Yorktown*'s cargo convoy to Halifax, reported torpedo tracks. The destroyer USS *Walke* (DD 416) responded with a depth-charge attack with no positive results. Four nervous and stormy days later, the convoy reached safe haven in Halifax.

On November 9 a relieved *Yorktown* crew arrived at Casco Bay. As *Yorktown* headed to Norfolk for her twice-postponed overhaul, Swede flew in to rejoin his air group at East Field, NAS Norfolk.

One of his fellow fliers thoroughly impressed Swede. "One really stellar aviator—Rondo Law, from Utah, was with us for about a year. We were getting our families together in Norfolk. His wife and little boy began their journey across the country to meet him. They were going to live near my wife and young son, Gene.

"I was helping Rondo check out in an SBD. Rondo had that sandbag in the backseat (replacing the weight of an absent radioman/gunner) like he didn't need anybody. Of all the unfortunate, damned things that could possibly happen, he took off, came in, spun in, and was killed. Unfortunately, I had the squadron duty to get word to his wife, now only 150 miles away. I couldn't do this over the phone. I got hold of her dad, and he told Rondo's wife. That was a month before Pearl Harbor."

By December 1941 Swede had banked two and a half years of carrier operations. Though he had yet to drop a bomb or fire a shot in anger, the edgy Atlantic campaign had seasoned him. Swede could rightly consider himself a highly experienced carrier pilot.

Yorktown, meanwhile, was upgraded. Oerlikon 20-mm guns replaced the mostly ineffective .50-caliber machine guns, the CXAM radar was improved, and splinter shields were installed. The need for such revisions was not long in coming.

CHAPTER 4

Pearl Harbor

Japan's devastating surprise attack on Pearl Harbor on December 7, 1941, confirmed lessons learned a little more than a year before. The November 11–12, 1940, British attack at Taranto had served notice that ships at anchor were vulnerable targets for aerial assault. Fully alerted Italian defenses had not been able to prevent the sinking of one battleship and severe damage to two others. The raid had also wrecked a seaplane base and set oil tanks afire.[1]

With news of Japan's attack, Swede's world shifted. "I remember very well the news of Pearl Harbor. We had bad weather in Norfolk; flying had been curtailed for a couple of days. Though the field was new, with nice new runways, there was still a lot of mud around. I was at home in a rental place in Norfolk. We had some rather definite ideas that war with Japan was coming on. The telephone rang, 7 a.m. Some guy on the other end says, 'Get your ass down here. Pearl Harbor has just been bombed. Get down to the squadron.'

"We were still drawing the new SBDs when the Japanese hit us. The *Yorktown* was immediately ordered to the Pacific. In these hectic days we had to install radar and complete our qualifications. This was all done in a hurry."

Swede, happily married to Irene and father to young son, Eugene, began his journey into a boiling Pacific air war. On December 21 *Yorktown* again transited the Panama Canal "disguised" as *Wasp*. Nine days later the air group landed at North Island, San Diego. There, *Yorktown* embarked the 4,798 men of the 2nd Marine Brigade and on January 6 set a course for

Pago Pago, Samoa. That meant crossing the equator and, war's urgencies notwithstanding, a time-honored crossing-the-line ceremony in which shellbacks (those who had previously crossed) initiated first-time polly-wogs. Corporal punishment was liberal, pollywogs had to kiss Neptune's repulsive belly, and rank offered no sanctuary. Swede participated with enthusiasm.

As the crew returned to their normal duties, *Yorktown* was plagued by an alarming series of operational troubles. Four planes were lost to a variety of causes, a seaman second class disappeared overboard, and a refueling ran amuck, resulting in parted lines and a near fouling of the oiler USS *Kaskaskia*'s (AO 27) screws.

With American morale badly in need of propping up, the U.S. Navy desperately sought some military response to the Pearl Harbor disaster. To that end, Adm. Chester Nimitz, commander in chief, U.S. Pacific Fleet (CinCPac), directed Vice Admiral Halsey's *Enterprise* task force, after unloading the Marines, to hit Japanese-held Makin Atoll.

As they trained for the strike, Swede deeply appreciated the qualities now-skipper Bill Burch brought to the squadron. "As far as taking advantage of time and opportunity, there was none better. He'd tell other pilots or squadron leaders, 'Attack us any time. In combat we'd be subject to just that and I want to know how we'll maneuver.' Big arguments arose later in the ready room. 'But you weren't in position for firing.' This was good practice. We always got everything we could out of practice sessions. If it hadn't been for him, the war might have lasted six months longer. He showed great leadership."

Burch taught them to separate during their attacks so the Japanese gunners would be forced to disperse their fire. Ever mindful of the larger picture, Burch emphasized the postattack rendezvous, which provided mutual defensive support and help with navigation back home. He stressed the importance of Point Option—the place the carrier was expected to be upon their return. These survival skills would serve Swede well. On January 8, 1942, Swede was promoted to lieutenant (junior grade).

The February 1 raid on Makin Atoll provided the first opportunity for Swede and his gunner, S1C Frank Barton Wood, to face enemy fire. "Whoever planned that raid had done a good job. Everything fell into place because this was not a really heavy operation, not an all-out fight by any means. Each group of planes had designated targets. So before we took off we knew who we'd be with, who our leader was, where we were going, what our target was, and what we had to hit. It just happened that the Marshalls and Gilberts were not heavily defended at the time. We didn't see any opposing fighters at all; just seaplanes, and they were no problem. It was a good introduction to battle."

Burch got a bomb hit on *Nagata Maru*, a Japanese gunboat, while Fritz Faulkner and Ens. William E. Hall, who would later room with Swede, recorded near misses. They followed up by strafing two Kawanishi flying boats. Antiaircraft (AA) fire did little more than bounce Swede and Wood around a bit.

Pilots conducted relentless searches for submarines and other enemy vessels during the week-and-a-half-long cruise to Hawaii. On February 6 *Yorktown* eased into a shattered Pearl Harbor. Two months had passed since the raid, but the harbor looked as though it might have taken place just the day before. Anyone would have been aghast at the destruction, but Swede had spent a lot of time there and was shocked to see once-familiar facilities in shambles.

"Pearl Harbor, the military bases, and airfields were scenes of devastation such as I had never seen before and could not fully imagine from previous reports received. The sunken ships, the burned hangars and aircraft hulks were visible everywhere.[2]

"Coming in, the first thing you notice is the beached battleship *Nevada* [BB 36]. *Oklahoma* [BB 37] had turned turtle from her torpedo wounds, *California* [BB 44] and *West Virginia* [BB 48] rested on the bottom, and oil was everywhere. Sunken *Arizona* [BB 39] showed a gun tub sticking up out of the water. The seaplane area from which we'd flown was completely devastated. A bit of a mess, all right. Over in the slips area we could see that the battleship *Pennsylvania* [BB 38] had taken a couple of bomb hits. It was a world of damage, and I wondered how they survived as well as they did."

The Japanese had annihilated the American battleship fleet, but they had failed to locate and attack the U.S. Pacific fleet carriers. On the morning of the attack, *Lexington*, *Enterprise*, and *Saratoga* had all been elsewhere. There was no mistaking the raid's strategic message: carriers, not battleships, were going to determine the fate of fleets and more in this new brand of warfare.

Taking in the carnage, Swede envisioned worse scenarios. "What if the Japs had run a third raid? That was on my mind as we came in. On the left you'd see the fuel farm and the oiler USS *Neosho* [AO 23] nearby. All they had to do was drop a bomb or two over there and that whole oil supply would have gone up. That would have set us back a couple of months."

The Japanese attack was not only about ships. To eliminate any aerial resistance the Japanese knocked out Army, Navy, and Marine air facilities. Swede was shocked that, two months after the attack, some remained inoperable. "At Ewa [the Marine Corps air station], one of our first tasks was to sweep the runways to clear expended bullets and shell casings left by aerial strafing. This was an all-hands operation." Eleven days into this Hawaiian stop, on February 17, Swede received orders to report to *Enterprise*'s to-be-formed Air Group 10 when he could "conveniently leave" VS-5 and *Yorktown*. There would be little in the way of convenience for several action-filled months.

Japan, meanwhile, had designs on Port Moresby, New Guinea. Control of that port would allow the Imperial Japanese Navy to sever Allied shipping lanes to Australia and New Zealand. To that end the Japanese had recently developed airfields at Lae and Salamaua, New Guinea, and they launched daily harassment attacks on Port Moresby. The strategic implications of these advanced bases demanded an Allied response.

On March 10 the *Yorktown* and *Enterprise* air groups, deferring to Japanese air activity to the north of New Guinea, prepared to strike the New Guinea airfields and ships from the south. This required overflying New Guinea's towering Owen Stanley Mountains. Doing so in a bomb-laden SBD would be challenging. The TBDs, lugging even heavier torpedoes, would have to navigate their way through the lower passes that skipper Burch had discovered while poring over area maps.

For this mission radioman/gunner Frank Wood again sat behind Swede. They carried a 500-pound bomb on the centerline rack and a 250-pound bomb under each wing. Nasty squalls complicated the weather over the targets. Far more perplexing to the pilots as they dove down through the warmer air was that their windshields and bombsights fogged over, completely blinding their attack.

Patiently searching for holes in the cloud cover, Burch somehow got them looks at the ships below. "Our skipper, Bill Burch, was leading the flight with me on one wing. He put us in perfect position for attack, taking advantage of the sun, cloud cover, wind, and with a planned recovery and retirement away from the land mass and mountain where an expeditious join-up could be made."[3]

They bombed the transport *Kongō Maru* and strafed two Kawanishi flying boats. Last in line to dive, Swede targeted the transports. "This was the big thing. They were setting up a big airfield, and we spotted some big guns." Those transports were loaded with materials needed to bring the airfield and guns to operational readiness.

Swede, too, struggled with a fogged windshield, and the smoke and flying debris further compromised his aim. "After my dive someone told me, 'Swede, you got a hung bomb.' So I made a quick run in front of everybody. The bomb released, and the transport, hit in the forward section, burst into flame. Pretty much an accident."

He reported the ship's AA fire as "erratic and ineffective. They couldn't cover the area they really wanted to. There were a lot of explosives coming up, but I don't know anybody that was hit." Burch's advice to separate during an attack, thus diffusing the defenses, had served them well.

Ens. Samuel J. Underhill was another of Scouting 5's pilots. He had a bachelor's degree from Yale and had attended Harvard Law School. But in 1940 Sam gave all that up, joined the Navy, and earned his wings. Like Swede, Sam was a new father, and the two pilots shared quarters. "I used to give Sam hell every day because I said, 'Why in the hell don't you go do something safe? You can make a contribution. Guys like you got no damn business out here in this business.' Sam replied, 'Oh, I'm gonna do my part.' He was determined to fly."[4]

On this, Sam's first combat mission, his bomb "missed by a mile." Swede's fog-impeded efforts, however, had contributed to the sinking of three enemy ships. Swede wasn't sure of the type, but given the Japanese mission to occupy the north shore of New Guinea, they were likely transports, supply vessels, destroyers, or, at best, light cruisers. For his accuracy and skill in disrupting Japanese merchant marine operations Swede was recommended for the Navy Cross, the Navy's highest honor.

"I didn't hear about that until much later."

CHAPTER 5

Tulagi

After pounding Port Moresby with bombs, the Japanese planned to seize the town, from which their task forces could command supply lanes and land-based bombers could strike Australia at will. First, to protect their eastern flank, the Japanese would need to evict the British from their southern Solomons administrative center in Tulagi, northeast of Guadalcanal. Excellent work by cryptanalysts in Hawaii, however had pieced together the Japanese plan. Since losing Port Moresby was completely unacceptable to the Allies, Admiral Nimitz ordered *Lexington* (TF 11) under Rear Adm. Aubrey W. Fitch to join with *Yorktown* and form a two-carrier Task Force 17. Their task was to check Japanese advances and destroy Japanese ships, planes, and shipping in the New Guinea–Solomons area. To that end, on May 1 *Yorktown* contacted *Lexington* but carried on independently for the next four days.

The next day, shortly after 3 p.m., Swede, with ARM2C Leon Hall behind him as gunner/radioman, was flying patrol with Ens. H. N. Ervin on his wing. In his after-action report Swede wrote that he had noticed a wake, and "in a few seconds the conning tower of a submarine (*I-21*), under way with decks awash, became plainly visible. At this time, I believe we were sighted, as the submarine made a crash dive, leaving a spot of turbulent water. We flew by this spot three times on the up sun side, and on the first pass I saw the submarine at some depth and just ahead of the boil."

Swede carefully figured the sub's course, speed, and location and returned to *Yorktown*, where, without breaking radio silence, he instructed Hall to drop their beanbag communiqué onto the flight deck.

Not long after, a trio of TBDs armed with depth bombs launched and headed to the coordinates Swede had provided. *I-21* was once again on the surface but quickly dove as the TBDs set up their attack. They dropped their ordnance with no conclusive result. Records later revealed that the sub had indeed survived, but *I-21*'s contact report never indicated what type of planes had conducted the attack. Because of that ambiguity, the Japanese did not know that *Yorktown* was steaming a mere thirty miles away.

Swede's vigilance did not go unnoticed. His commanding officer wrote, "Lieutenant Vejtasa was deserving of a commendation for his alertness in sighting the submarine and accuracy of his navigation, which enabled the torpedo planes to locate and attack their objective." Not that anyone knew it then, but Swede's initiative had just opened the Battle of the Coral Sea.

Issues of Visibility

On May 3, Japanese ships were spotted offloading supplies for a seaplane base currently under construction on Tulagi. The next day, *Yorktown*, now seriously short on provisions after more than one hundred days without making port or stopping for replenishment, launched a series of raids intent on disrupting the proceedings. On the first of three raids that day, Bill Burch led VS-5 to the north and then on to Tulagi.

Swede, with Leon Hall again seated behind him, joined "fighters, bombers, torpedo planes, the whole air group. We went in high, 20,000 feet. Damn weather, it was bad right down to the bottom. You could see there were some breaks, too, and you could see some of the ships in the harbor."

As they arrived over Tulagi, Bombing 5 and Torpedo 5 joined them. Strike leader Burch assigned pilots to designated targets among a nest of three ships below. "Skipper led us over in good shape," Swede recalled, and "down we went. I was one of the rear ones. Somewhere on the way down, sights and windshields again fogged over; couldn't see a damn thing. We were blind."

The vexing problem of warm, moist air condensing on windshields, bombsights, anything glass still cold from their high-altitude approach, blinded them again. Burch described the sensation. "It is like putting a white sheet in front of you, and you have to bomb from memory. If you start down, watching antiaircraft fire, with your sight well fixed, and then somebody puts a sheet in front of you, you feel sort of bad about it. You try to stick your head out over the side of the cockpit, and aim down the side at the target ship. That's not very accurate bombing."[1]

Swede concurred. "What the hell to do? If you're far enough down, you could try to make a drop or you could try to recover for another attempt. I was high enough so I recovered and dropped my bomb. As I'm pulling away, I dipped down and could see several transports getting under way."

Their group had attacked the Japanese destroyer *Kikuzuki* and claimed four "sure" hits and one probable.

Back on board *Yorktown* following the attack, Burch successfully argued for another strike and, as a result, had barely enough time to down a cup of coffee before *Yorktown*'s efficient deck crews had rearmed and refueled his plane. Aloft again, Burch led his Scouts in an attack on the minelayer *Okinoshima*, which was fleeing the harbor and putting up spirited and accurate AA fire. Burch's gang claimed two hits with an additional probable. Swede, now with ARM2C Lovelace M. Broussard behind him, contributed his bomb to the destruction and headed for some cloud cover.

"I flew into a cloud, and my backseat man started yelling in French. That's when I heard *bdddrrup*. Rounds thudded into my armored seat, pierced my canopy, and shot up my engine. I knew damn well what happened. I'd taken a blast from somebody. I was sure it wasn't AA. I countered immediately, 'cause I know it came from my right rear.

"Here's a biplane, seaplane fighter, an F1M, code-named Pete. Fortunately, Bill Burch had given me many a lesson on countermoves, and I turned hard right into and under the Pete, then hard back to meet him head-on if he scissored, which he did. We exchanged bursts of gunfire, and I could see his tracers coming toward me as he came to bear. His plane was maneuverable as hell. He was apparently a skilled pilot. We scissored three or four times.

"He's coming in. I drop my nose. We're trying to get on each other's tail. I'm trying to out-turn him; I didn't. I pulled up, ready to fire at him. I wished mightily at that time that I had more gun power in my SBD, but the .50-calibers firing through the prop were working well. I sighted on his engine, and I think I hit him. Behind me, Broussard is making that gun chatter. He had the first opportunity to hit him; I wouldn't be surprised if he downed him. I turned back and sure enough, he didn't counter. I turned, got on his tail, and he broke and dove away trailing heavy smoke. I needed to catch him and finish him off. As the Pete sped away, an SBD ahead of me jumped on his tail and sent the plane down in flames."

Thus ended Swede's first dogfight, but the excitement was not finished. As he headed back to *Yorktown*, "Suddenly everything went black for me. 'What in hell . . . ?' My canopy, gun sight, and windshield were black with oil. He had hit me. That oil was thick and kept coming. It looked bad. I recovered, dropped down, and set a course back to the ship. I'm thinking, 'I'm not going down in the middle of the Jap fleet, I want to get away.'

"I headed for Guadalcanal and figured I'd have to ditch somewhere along the way. My SBD chugged along as I used my gloves to try to clear my windshield. Then I see an SBD right nearby. Skipper Burch signals the course back to the *Yorktown*, and I flew straight in. He had things all set up for me coming in. I could barely see him, but the LSO was ready for me, and I came on in. I landed and taxied forward. They put me on the forward elevator, and as we started down the plane's engine froze."

During their return from the second raid Burch had noticed some cargo ships in the harbor and successfully lobbied for yet another strike. Owing to a scarcity of torpedoes, only SBDs flew this raid. Swede exchanged his shot-up Dauntless for a flyable replacement and flew his third mission of the day. Against light AA, they claimed one hit and a few near misses on the Japanese transport *Azumason Maru* and several nearby launches.

"That was the experience of Tulagi." Swede vowed that kind of aerial surprise would not happen to him again.

The seaplane fighter he smoked was listed as an unconfirmed kill. "I got no credit for a kill in my first dogfight in an SBD, but that plane performed like a million bucks."

On May 5, *Lexington* joined up with *Yorktown* to form Task Force 17 under the nominal command of Rear Adm. Frank Jack Fletcher, who in turn assigned operational command over to Rear Adm. Aubrey W. Fitch, a naval aviator.

On the afternoon of May 6, Swede and Fritz Faulkner, who was due to rotate back to the States, were set to hi-line over to the fleet oiler *Neosho*. A survivor of the Pearl Harbor raid, the "Fat Lady" would transport Swede and Fritz, along with five enlisted men, back to Pearl Harbor en route to San Diego and VF-10. Their gear had already been transferred.

Swede recalled the moment. "We were on the flight deck. The *Neosho* signals, 'Get those pilots aboard. We're gonna back away.' Bill Burch says, 'I know you guys are anxious to get off here, and they're waitin' on you and all that. But it looks like we're gonna have some action in the next couple of days. We need all the pilots we can get, and all the experience we can get. And you two are the most experienced pilots in the squadron. How would you like to stay here?'"

Swede spoke for them both. "'Say no more. I'm here.' I didn't want to get aboard an oiler anyway. Not only was it a bad ride, but you gotta stand watches. They steam at ten to twelve knots. Instead, we stay aboard, our gear comes back, and they break *Neosho* off. I was not disappointed at the time because I felt a strong attachment to the squadron and would much rather return with the group. So, of course, I was there for the search and strike on the *Shōhō*." Swede's decision presaged fateful consequences for the oiler *Neosho*, the destroyer escort USS *Sims* (DD 409), the Imperial Japanese Navy's carrier *Shōhō*, and three first-team Japanese pilots.

CHAPTER 6

———

Battle of the Coral Sea

The shocking Doolittle raid over Tokyo and the recent impudent raids on Tulagi were distracting Japanese strategists from their designs on New Guinea and Australia. The Imperial Japanese Navy was spoiling for a decisive clash. Alerted now to the presence of the carriers *Yorktown* and *Lexington*, Vice Adm. Takagi Takeo sought an American comeuppance. In addition to the light carrier *Shōhō*, Takagi had at his disposal Pearl Harbor veterans *Shōkaku* and *Zuikaku* under the command of Rear Adm. Hara Chūichi. The experienced combat pilots embarked on those three carriers, accustomed thus far to having their way in the war, were eager to demonstrate their superiority over their American counterparts.

On May 7, Japanese search planes reported a carrier and escorts to the south. In fact, a Japanese scout had found and falsely identified the flat-decked *Neosho* as a carrier and upgraded the destroyer escort USS *Sims* to a light cruiser. Accurate ship identification played no favorites; both American and Japanese pilots, keen to spot capital ships, sometimes convinced themselves that they had when they hadn't.

Elsewhere that same morning, Swede was again flying wing on skipper Burch. "The *Shōhō* strike came up very suddenly. We had been out on an early morning search, and we had seen nothing. An Army Air Corps B-25 pilot searching near Rabaul reported a carrier and a convoy of some twenty ships or more. For once I'd say the admiral did the right thing. He didn't wait one minute to prepare for a strike. The staff gunnery officer, Cdr. Walter G. Schindler, who would go on to become Admiral Fletcher's staff gunnery officer during the Battle of the Eastern Solomons, informed the skipper, 'I'd like to go along in the backseat.' Burch said, 'Swede, you take him.' So I did. I hurriedly checked Schindler out on the use of the radio and the rear-seat gun before takeoff, and we were off."

Swede described the flight out. "The weather in the Coral Sea was miserable, with fog, rain, and strong winds. However, this did not pose such a great problem as we had been operating for months under similar conditions. We executed a running join-up, climbing all the way. We go up to 22,000 feet and headed north, where the weather was much improved. All I was thinking of, I guess others were too, that damn gun sight fogging up. The skipper, he was a shrewd one, he was watching the clouds, winds, ships' movements, positions they were taking."

And here, Bill Burch's recollection diverges from most histories of the battle, which portray a bombed and badly damaged carrier Shōhō when VS-5 arrived on the scene. "The Lexington group should have been fifteen minutes ahead of us, but they made their dive-bomb attack just ahead of me. There was a little mix-up. I watched them attack. I thought it was all of their bombing group. The Jap carrier Shōhō was maneuvering heavily, and I only saw one hit. The carrier then turned into the wind to launch her planes. I immediately called Joe Taylor, who had our torpedo planes, and told him we were going in. He asked me to wait because it would be at least five minutes before he could arrive on the scene. I told him I wasn't going to wait because the carrier was launching planes and I wasn't going to let them get off. As you know, a carrier into the wind is a dead pigeon. It simplifies your dive-bombing."[1]

Swede described their attack on Shōhō. "I watched Burch drop at 2,500 feet. I saw the big bomb detach from the rack on the skipper's plane taking what seemed to be a slight arcing trajectory and plunge into the carrier deck almost amidships followed by a tremendous blast with smoke and fire shooting out from the sides of the vessel. You talk about a concussion. All I could see was debris and everything, just blowing in all directions. I thought to myself, how in the hell did that carrier stand that? I had dropped too, and my gunner/photographer Schindler says, 'Yes! You got a hit.' As a matter of fact, out of fourteen drops we had twelve hits. If ever there was a perfect attack, this was it."[2] Shōhō suffered an avalanche of ordnance. Burch continued, "There is no doubt we hit it too much, but she had about seven planes in the air and was launching the rest of her fighters. It seemed best to stop that. I got a hit and I don't think any of the squadron behind me missed. We really laid the bombs in that day. The visibility was excellent, it was very warm, and we had no fogging of sights."

By the time one *Lexington* bomber pilot arrived on the scene, he noted that there was nothing left to drop on. Lt. Cdr. Bob Dixon's report was famously succinct: "Scratch one flattop." With their prime target now beneath the waves, the Dauntless pilots directed their attention to the escorting Japanese destroyers and cruisers.

Their attack was not unopposed. Swede "noticed a plane coming in from the right, headed for the skipper, not for me. I pulled over in front of him. I fired at him but he was too far away for any effective firing. He saw my tracers so he broke off. I looked back down toward the *Shōhō*. There was a column of smoke still out there, but there's nothing under it. . . . From Burch's bomb to the disappearance of the *Shōhō* took all of seven minutes."

As the torpedo bombers began their runs, Lt. Cdr. Jimmy Flatley and his VF-42 orbited above and observed four Japanese Type 96 fighters, code-named Claude, attacking the retiring TBD 1 Devastators. Accompanied by his divisionmates, Ens. John D. Baker, Ens. Walter A. Haas, and Lt. (jg) Brainard T. Macomber, Flatley dove to intercede. In the ensuing melee, Flatley downed one of the Claudes and attempted to chase down another, then broke off the engagement.

The Japanese also went after the retiring SBDs. Schindler had been busy fending off a Zero and documenting the action with his camera. Images of the attacked Japanese carrier "plowing herself under" would certainly boost morale at home and explode the mythology of an "invincible" Imperial Japanese Navy.

As they made for home a nasty tropical front ramped up everyone's blood pressure. Swede described their trials. "Raining! Foggy! High winds! It was a mess. We were on radio silence again. The ship was not putting out any signals. We had to find that thing by dead reckoning. I tell you we were all tucked in close to the skipper. He was a good one, and all the rest of us were good on instruments because we had been doing searches for over a year. I was timing our return, and almost at the exact moment, I looked down and there was the *Yorktown*. I could see it through the fog right below us." Once again Burch had seen them through.

Finding *Yorktown* was one thing, getting back on board in the murk was another. "Of course we had a procedure that you had to follow for breaking up and landing, in which you came around as the air group, went in two echelons, some pilots went ahead, and from then on, we made timed turns. All on time, get your altitude, which might start at a thousand feet and go down to five hundred and then even less, everything a timed turn because we couldn't see a thing. So we did that, and we had practiced that enough so it really wasn't that difficult. And of course the landing signal officer had to use night wands because you couldn't see him without those wands. They had the lights on the deck, too, and this was early afternoon." He didn't know it, but Swede's trap concluded his last flight with Bill Burch.

The Japanese fleet carriers *Shōkaku* and *Zuikaku*, however, remained at large. Stung by *Shōhō*'s loss, bent on revenge, and now convinced by the *Neosho* sighting that he finally had an American carrier in his sights, Rear Admiral Hara launched a full strike. He dispatched thirty-six Aichi D3A dive-bombers (later that year code-named Vals and described as such below), twenty-four Nakajima B5N torpedo bombers (later code-named Kates and described as such below), and eighteen Zeros. The impressive strike force found and attacked the hapless *Neosho* and *Sims*. Three bombs in quick succession put *Sims* under with great loss of life, while *Neosho* suffered severe damage from seven bomb hits, eight near misses, and a shot-up Val dive-bomber that crashed onto her deck. Somehow *Neosho* remained afloat. Her survivors and those from *Sims* would endure four horrific days adrift on the oil-soaked derelict, terrified that the ship, which was listing at times to 30 degrees, would sink at any moment. Reflecting later on his lucky decision to stay on *Yorktown*, Swede could only shrug. "A quirk of fate."

It didn't take long for an infuriated Vice Admiral Takagi to apprehend the misidentification on which he had wasted his main shot. Around eight in the morning, in another identification error, Hara's scouts reported they had finally located the American carriers. Instead they had discovered British-born Rear Adm. John Crace's cruiser support group composed of the Australian cruisers *Australia* (HMAS 84) and *Hobart* (HMAS 63),

U.S. cruiser *Chicago* (CA 29), and three American destroyers. Fletcher had dispatched Crace's flotilla to confront the Japanese Port Moresby invasion group off to the northwest.

By midafternoon Japanese Mitsubishi Type 1 land attack planes armed with torpedoes and Mitsubishi Type 96 land attack planes armed with bombs made their appearance over Crace's force but failed to produce a single bomb or torpedo hit. Despite his lack of air cover, Crace's force downed four of the attackers. The next attack came at the hands of Australia-based U.S. Army bombers whose pilots had misidentified Crace's petite fleet as Japanese. Fortunately, that attack was no more successful than the Japanese raids had been, and Crace's group continued undamaged, praying for skies free of planes bearing meatballs *or* stars.

Ignoring the fact that his fatigued pilots had just returned from a grueling and futile seven-hour strike mission, Hara assembled his best pilots, including three lieutenants and three lieutenant commanders, for another last-chance raid. Specifically selected for their night-landing experience, they mounted a modest strike force composed of twelve Val dive-bombers and fifteen torpedo-laden Kates. Given the long distance involved, there would be no fighter escort.

Assuming that Crace was screening the American carriers, Hara sent his weary pilots on a 280-mile flight intent on finding Crace and those carriers. Much closer at 190 miles, but hidden in the murk, *Yorktown* and *Lexington* steamed undiscovered. At the end of their search leg the Japanese found nothing, jettisoned their ordnance, and made for home.

Around dusk American radar interpreted the unescorted, now weaponless, strike group as an incoming raid. Jimmy Flatley was ordered to join up with Lt. Cdr. Paul Ramsey's VF-2 for the intercept. Despite the overcast and fading light, accurate vectoring connected the fighters with their quarry. Ramsey's Flying Chiefs shot down seven of the bombers. Flatley's fighters joined in and claimed two more.

The remaining Japanese aviators were thoroughly dispersed by the intercept and further disoriented in the murk. The conditions and darkening skies prompted Flatley to instruct his wingman, Ens. John D. Baker, to guide his section home using his Zed Baker. Hal Buell described the YE-ZB (Zed Baker) homing system, in which a rotating radio signal–

sending device broadcasted a different alphabetical letter every 30 degrees as it rotated. In his book *Dauntless Helldivers* Buell explained:

> In the corner of each pilot's board was a compass rose. When preparing flight data before starting a search, the pilot filled each slice of the pie with letters designated for the YE that day. Limited to a range of about thirty-five miles, this device gave a returning pilot a reasonable margin of error. He could change his homebound heading to conform to the letter signal being received if he was off course. YE was especially helpful when normal visibility was reduced by clouds or weather and was sufficiently accurate to prevent a plane from missing the task force completely. If you were returning from a 250-mile search jaunt into enemy waters, or a long strike mission, the first faint Morse code dots and dashes in your earphones were as beautiful as a symphony.[3]

YE would guide John Baker and company back to *Yorktown*.

Confusion at Home

Rear Adm. Thomas C. Kinkaid, a fifty-four-year-old Annapolis graduate on board his flagship USS *Minneapolis* (CA 36)—"Minnie" to her crew—was in command of the screening attack group, composed of sister cruisers USS *New Orleans* (CA 32), USS *Astoria* (CA 34), USS *Chester* (CA 27), and USS *Portland* (CA 33). From his perch on board *Minneapolis* Kinkaid observed one of the strangest episodes in carrier operations.

On their respective returns, the Japanese attack force and Wildcat interceptors alike were forced to navigate a gusty, rainy front that dropped right down to the water, visibility close to nil. In the deepening dusk, Kinkaid watched as some of the planes lining up to land on *Yorktown* exhibited strange behavior, one showing lights and blinking in Morse code with a hand-held Aldis lamp, then crossing to port over the carrier's bow.

Swede had a much closer vantage point. "I'm up on the flight deck as Flatley's CAP planes are coming in. Here's one coming up the starboard side; that guy's in trouble—he's supposed to be taking a wave-off on the port side. I could see another one behind him. Someone's in trouble.

"I could have touched the goddamn wing. On the side is the biggest meatball you ever saw. Of course, I dropped my chalkboard right there, my mouth wide open. For Christ's sake, a Jap plane, planes are in the pattern. Two Jap dive-bombers. So I go around the starboard side. I thought, 'Nothing is going to prevent those guys from strafing this deck.' We've got planes on deck, gear, planes are gassed, all kinds of stuff that can burn.

"Quite a ways back I saw another plane coming in, coming down at a perfect angle. 'Damn,' I thought, 'he's gonna land.' The LSO was just standing there, not giving any directions with his wands. This plane kept coming. He had his hook down, and I couldn't see any daylight between his plane and the deck. But he raised up and came right by me. I saw the pilot there, goggles, down flight suit on, right in front of me. As he headed off, the guns on the portside catwalk start going off." Their impulsive gunnery resulted in some unintended damage. Swede continued, "One of our pilots, Lt. (jg) Walter Haas, was still trying to get aboard. Friendly fire shot the hell out of him but didn't drop him. He came in with five wounds."

John Baker, Flatley's wingman, was in line to land when *Lexington* and Kinkaid's *Minneapolis* opened up as well. Baker quickly exited the area to avoid the AA. In so doing he apparently lost his bearings, and worse, he'd set his radio to send but not receive. He was too close to the fleet to engage his homing gear, and the blacked-out fleet effectively rendered Baker lost. For far too long, squadronmates heard his plaintive pleas for direction. Then he was heard no more. This loss hit Flatley hard. By a freak coincidence, *Lexington*'s Lt. (jg) Paul Baker also failed to return that night.

Swede and the others who witnessed the event were baffled, and the Japanese pilots certainly had to wonder how they had very nearly landed on an American carrier. A few minutes later, radar blips and radio chatter indicated orbiting aircraft just twenty-five to thirty miles away. The disoriented Japanese pilots had mistaken *Yorktown* for their own home base.[4]

Admiral Takagi's morning strike force had wasted itself on an oiler and a destroyer escort, and the evening's impulsive raid had sacrificed eleven planes and aircrews with no damage done to U.S. carriers. In the process he had lost a significant piece of his torpedo counterpunch. The next day the surviving Japanese carrier bomber pilots would have to be on top of their game. Meanwhile, despite the proximity of the carrier forces to each other, both sides declined a moonlit night attack.

Mistakes Were Made

The Americans had things go mostly their way on May 7; the next day went very differently. A little before 7:30 a.m. on May 8, a Japanese scout plane reported one American carrier group 163 miles away from Rear Admiral Hara's carriers. Shortly after 9 a.m. *Shōkaku* and *Zuikaku* began launching a combined attack force of eighteen fighters, thirty-three dive-bombers, and eighteen torpedo planes, totaling sixty-nine aircraft. At nearly the same time *Yorktown* sent aloft six of Lt. Cdr. Charles R. Fenton's VF-42 Wildcats, seven of Burch's SBDs, seventeen of Lt. Wallace C. Short's VB-5 Dauntlesses, and nine Devastators of Lt. Cdr. Joe Taylor's Torpedo 5. *Lexington* added fifteen SBDs, twelve TBDs, and nine escorting Wildcats, all overseen by CAG William B. Ault. The slightly larger American strike force came to seventy-five aircraft.

In defense of his task force, Rear Adm. Aubrey Fitch had issued a command decision that was hotly disputed among the air group pilots. He would augment his four-Wildcat CAP with SBD Dauntlesses. The thinking went that the Scouting 5 SBDs not currently en route to attack the Japanese task force could intercept "sluggish" Kate torpedo bombers as they closed low on the water. Having flown the attack on *Shōhō* the day before, Swede would fly this CAP.

Swede was highly critical of the idea. "The SBDs were arranged around the carriers, eight on each carrier's bow, instead of sending them on the attack. This was so bad. This was a terrible mistake, and a lack of consideration on the part of the staff, committing thirty-two SBDs to anti–torpedo plane patrol and almost nothing to attack the enemy. A morning search found the Jap force, but they had nothing to attack it with. We could have sent forty or fifty against the Japanese fleet; taken those guys out."

Besides weakening their offensive punch, Swede, like noted dive-bomber pilot Hal Buell, saw no sense in flying SBDs as interceptors.[5] Designed for dive-bombing, an SBD's aerial weaponry consisted of two forward-firing .50-caliber machine guns whose volume of fire was restricted because they fired through the propeller. A radioman/gunner manned a pair of defensive rear-facing .30-caliber machine guns. Far better suited for dive-bombing Japanese carriers into the Pacific depths, as Midway later demonstrated, the SBDs, nicknamed "Slow but Deadly," were seriously mismatched against the highly experienced Japanese pilots flying agile A6M2 Type 00 fighters, better known as Zekes or Zeros. And those Kates weren't as sluggish as advertised.

Around 7:30 a.m. Swede, flying an SBD, angrily took up his slot in the morning's CAP. The day before, he had performed brilliantly as a dive-bomber pilot. Today he would have to channel Bill Burch's training and fly as a fighter. Burch, meanwhile, commanded the *Yorktown* strike force headed for the Japanese carriers.

Roughly one hundred miles north of Swede's ill-conceived CAP, Burch and his seven Scouting 5 Dauntlesses located and attacked *Shōkaku*. Cloud cover protected her sister carrier *Zuikaku*. Again, fogged sights and wind-shields hampered the attack. A thoroughly confounded Burch noted, "We bombed from memory." While they claimed hits, in fact they had not scored. Shortly thereafter, Bombing 5 arrived on the scene and delivered two hits and several near misses. The resulting damage prevented *Shōkaku* from launching aircraft, although planes could still land. A third bomb hit by Cdr. William B. Ault's division put *Shōkaku* hors de combat. As good as that was for the Americans, the Japanese counterblow was on its way.

Ambushed

Shortly after 11 a.m. *Zuikaku*'s Zeros located Task Force 17 under clear skies and swept down on *Yorktown*'s ill-fated Dauntless CAP. The historical record of the ensuing events is far from clear. Gerald Astor in *Wings of Gold* wrote that Swede put "three Zeros in the Coral Sea." Robert Cressman in *That Gallant Ship* wrote simply that "Vejtasa scored hits on a particularly aggressive antagonist who came at him, head-on." John Lundstrom wrote in *The First Team* that "Scouting Five claimed four Zeros shot down, one to Lt. (jg) Stanley W. Vejtasa (later a renowned ace with Flatley's Fighting Ten). The Japanese, however, lost no fighters in this combat."[6]

Swede recalled his experience during the devastating Japanese attack. "I was tail-end Charlie of eight SBDs, flying on *Yorktown*'s starboard side, wondering 'what in the world am I doing here?' We knew an attack was coming, and we were on double alert. We should have been up high in the direction they were coming. No, we're way off to the side where there isn't gonna be a damn thing. Because of getting shot up at Tulagi, I'm watching 'cause they're not going to get me today, not if I could help it."

For his part, Swede had long practiced flying his bomber as if it were a fighter. "During our checkout phase I'd had a lot of dogfights in the SBD. I did this on purpose, no matter the plane, anybody that wanted to dogfight—fine. I don't believe that about dogfighting there was anything I didn't know." That brand of confidence was about to be severely tested against Zero pilots anxious to avenge *Shōhō*.

"Trying to be especially alert and remembering the many lessons by Bill Burch, I was looking over my shoulder—watching my six—as well as keeping the rear-seat gunner alert. All of a sudden I see this bright glint in the sun. I saw the Zeros coming in fast on our tails, power-diving and driving hard from perfect position. They're coming. Damn, there's a whole bunch of 'em, all Zeros. I yelled into my mike, 'Attack from the rear.' Nobody heard me. I turned underneath, countering the first fighter. I glanced up. Already three of my planes were on fire. On the first pass they hit four, actually knocked all four of 'em down."

Ens. Kendall C. Campbell and radioman ARM3C Franklin Delano Richeson were the first to go down in this slashing attack, quickly followed by Ens. Edward B. Kinzer and Lt. (jg) Earl Johnson, the friend Swede had goofed around with as they crossed the equator. Sam Underhill, the roommate Swede so respected, made the fourth. Their backseat partners, ARM2C Leon Hall (who had sat behind Swede over Tulagi), S1C Charles S. Bonness, and ARM3C Woodrow A. Fontenot, were lost as well.

"Those Zero pilots were damned good. I countered by turning in on the one that shot down my partner Sam Underhill. I hated to lose that boy. He was a good lad." Grieving would have to wait. A Zero, firing his 20-mm cannons, came back for Swede.

"Dogfights," Swede observed, "are exacting as hell, you can't believe the concentration. This was fast, and it was tough. This guy was an expert at dogfighting. I counted on all my training and experience."

Though the Zeros could easily outmaneuver the comparatively clumsy SBDs, Swede praised his own aircraft. "The SBD was a super plane. It didn't have the guns, didn't have the maneuverability, but it was strong, built well, and responded well. You could pull or jerk the hell out of it. It performed, everything worked well on it. It held plenty of gas, and the engine made it responsive."

"But that Zero pilot was a clever son of a gun; he gave me a bad time. Two more Zeros joined, one fore and the other aft. If I turned toward one, the other one had me. And they were shooting."

Their deadly contest swirled across the sky.

"My backseat guy, Frank Wood, he had to be thrown in every direction. I was flying violent maneuvers, skipping, losing altitude, gaining altitude when I could. I didn't have enough power in the SBD to gain. I was always giving altitude to counter these guys.

"I don't know how long it lasted, but you think it's forever. I finally got in a good burst at quite a distance. I hit this dude, and all of a sudden there's a big white blast and smoke—he kinda looked like he stopped in the air. He picked up again; he was on fire and flew into a cloud. At this time I noticed one of our SBDs start a long dive going down at a steep angle, trailing smoke and finally hitting the water making only a small splash, something like a rock entering the water from a near-vertical descent."

Swede was in his own fight for survival. "I was bracketed by the remaining Zeros. Now this other guy came after me. I countered him, and as I came around, he jumped into another cloud, losing altitude. He disappeared. That left me with this last Zero.

"I could counter the one pretty well, well enough. I couldn't get in for a close shot or a tail shot on him. I was very hesitant about pulling up to get a straight-ahead shot. If he's firing, he's gonna hit you. So I'd fire and duck. Pretty quick the third one showed back up. He came up and I watched him coming. He had altitude; he came on. He kept coming, pushed over and came at me from above. For some reason or other he didn't join the other guy in trying to put me in the scissors. He made several attacks, and he pulled up and rolled over, making his runs from above, firing along the way.

"It isn't too hard to counter a guy coming down at you, 'cause you could get under him, forcing him to lose aim. He didn't hit me at all. The other Zero had closed on me, and I was in deep trouble because he was coming up from behind, the other over the top.

"So I countered the one, and he fell off underneath me as the other came down. I used all the altitude I had; I was in a really desperate situation. I tried as much as possible to meet them head-on or turn to give only high-deflection shots. There were many near collisions as they pressed home their attacks, and many times I felt the impact of the air blast as we passed. I pulled up as one came over. I got the guns right on his cockpit and I fired a few rounds, quite a few, and I knew I hit him 'cause I could see pieces flying. The plane gave a puff of smoke, and I wondered at the moment if this was a ruse."

The fight was unrelenting; time became irrelevant.

"I had given up a lot of altitude and speed and was nearly stalled. So I'm gonna have to drop down. I got this guy behind and below me. I don't want him to get on me. So I kicked, used aileron and full rudder—the SBD could take it—kicked the nose down to pick up a little speed.

"The guy I had just shot, he followed me. I didn't do a thing to keep him from hitting me. He came in and he went right under my left wing. I could see the pilot in there. He was on fire, fortunately; that's the only thing that made him miss me. He kept on going. As I fell off behind him I've got only one plane left, this single plane.

"This last Zero pilot didn't give up. He made a turn and he came on, very aggressive. My mouth was very dry, and I couldn't believe what my backseat man had been through. I countered this dude, but he had a little speed on me, and he opened up on me. He got some distance and he made a turn, and he wanted to fire at long distance. I could see what he was working on.

"This guy must be damn near out of ammo. I decided to pull up and shoot a few rounds real quick. This I did. I'll be damned if he *had* ammo. I skidded my plane in an attempt to give him a more difficult angle of fire. I could see his 20-mm tracers coming directly at me. They *crack* as they come by. *Crack, crack, crack.* Not one had hit, but he kept coming."

Then the tactics changed. "I could see as he's coming on, closing pretty rapidly, he was trying to hit me, no question. I moved a little and he would move a little. It's damn difficult to avoid another plane if he's intent on hitting you, colliding with you in the air. But he was trying. He was coming in; I couldn't bring to bear at all.

"I maneuvered to try to avoid him, but he kept closing, closing on me, straight at me. Awful fast. Right at the last moment on my left side it looks like he's going to hit me on my wing edge or right in the cockpit. I lifted that left wing, and I reached down to jerk my elevator all the way back, pull the airplane into a partial stall. He came by, another *crack*, a terrible *crack* as he went close by. I could see him again under my left wing. He's got goggles on, flight suit; he's on fire, burning. As he passed by, something flew off. I thought, my God, it's part of my plane, must be my elevator. The stick was knocked out of my hand, paralyzing my right hand for a second. I couldn't use it.

"He disappeared down. At that time I was able to get hold of the stick, bring it back, and recover the rudder. Then I checked to see if my gunner was okay, and he was. As my hand recovered, I checked out the plane controls: ailerons, elevators, adjustment controls, everything worked. The Zero dove away trailing a bit of smoke. Then, as suddenly as it started, the fight was over. Apparently most of the planes broke off the attack on signal or by time. That ended my dogfight over the Coral Sea."

Swede never saw any of his opponents actually crash, but even if the Japanese record of no fighters lost that day is correct, the point remains that Swede returned in a flyable plane, while those three fortunate Zero pilots, if they did survive, must have endured severe humiliation at being outflown by a dive-bomber. Burch credited Swede with the three.

While Swede outdueled three Zeros, Jimmy Flatley of VF-42 was flying his second CAP of the day. The first had been a do-nothing bore. The second began with him ten miles out from *Yorktown* at two thousand feet expecting to thwart a low-level Japanese torpedo attack, when he was ordered to intercept a Japanese dive-bombing attack up at ten thousand feet. Too late to disrupt them, Flatley noticed Zeros savaging Swede's CAP below him. He dove to help and thought he had downed one. After checking on his carrier, Flatley returned to the area of the previous fight, where he boldly engaged three Zeros. He "definitely winged one" but was badly outnumbered and retired, hide intact. Flatley was someone Swede could respect.[7]

The well-executed Japanese counterstrike paid off. At 11:18 a.m. *Yorktown* absorbed a 250-kg bomb hit. A few minutes later *Lexington* suffered two portside torpedo hits, then two bomb hits and several near misses before the surviving Japanese attackers set course for home.

Swede's dogfight suddenly over, the adrenaline-fueled timelessness gave way to sweaty relief at what he had just survived. He took a look around. "I found myself alone. None of my planes were around. I headed back to the carrier, which had been under attack. Below, the *Lexington* was burning bad, dead in the water. Of course, the *Yorktown* had been hit. I didn't know how bad, but they took me aboard. Then we tried to find out who was aboard and who wasn't." In the attack, *Yorktown* had absorbed one bomb hit and six near misses.

Scouting 5's Dauntless CAP had been shredded. Swede described the atmosphere in the ready room. "We were radically depressed. The enemy had taken advantage of us. We watched friends shot out of the air. There were lots of questions. And we certainly did not feel like we had won any battle at all. We lost four of eight; everybody had seen us get knocked down—quick, I'll tell you. We sat around pretty confused. What had happened? What tactics were employed? It demonstrated the complete stupidity of using SBDs for anti–torpedo plane patrol. And we knew it beforehand. None of the admirals ever admitted making that decision."

Captain Elliott Buckmaster's report to Admiral Nimitz praised the SBD pilots:

ANTI–TORPEDO PLANE PATROL

At 0730, on May 8, 1942, on orders of Commander Air, launched eight SBDs of VS-5 to form an anti–torpedo plane patrol. This patrol attempted to intercept the enemy torpedo planes, but they were too fast for them as the VT planes were making their diving approach when sighted. The patrol was then attacked by a large number of Type 97 and Zero fighters. In the melee that followed, they shot down four fighters confirmed, four more probable and damaged seven others. In the engagement, four of the SBDs were shot down by enemy aircraft and the remainder returned badly damaged by enemy fighter gunfire. This was a splendid example of courage and devotion to duty; although outnumbered, and opposed by faster and more maneuverable aircraft, they were not outfought.[8]

Meanwhile, *Lexington*'s crew, hammered by two bombs and two torpedoes and shivered by several near misses, performed their dangerous jobs and began to get a handle on her fires. *Lexington*'s torpedo blisters had absorbed some of the destruction, but the intense shaking had loosened aviation gas fittings. Eventually a spark ignited the accumulated vapors, producing a devastating explosion, which in turn ignited numerous additional fires around the ship. Flight operations continued as damage control parties vainly struggled to gain control.

Explosions had taken out *Lexington*'s radar and soon thereafter her YE homing antenna. By midafternoon, stragglers from the *Lexington* strike group were searching for their now-silent home base. *Yorktown* assumed control of all radio circuits and called in *Lexington*'s aircraft, air group commander Bill Ault among them. Ault reported that he and his gunner were wounded, lost in the overcast, down to twenty minutes of flying time, and requested directions home. In a dark echo of the previous night's loss of John Baker and Paul Baker, *Yorktown* could hear Ault, and unlike the previous night's heartbreak, he could hear the ship. But *Yorktown* couldn't find him on radar and thus could do nothing for him. *Yorktown* suggested Ault head for the nearest land, to which he replied, "Nearest land is over two hundred miles away. We would never make it." *Yorktown* sadly radioed back, "CLAG you are on your own. Good luck." Ault made his farewell, "OK, so long, people. We got a 1,000-pound hit on that flattop." He and his gunner were never seen again.[9]

Meanwhile, on *Lexington*, as heat and flames threatened the bomb and torpedo rooms, further damage control was deemed too hazardous. Shortly after 5 p.m., with fires blazing out of control, Rear Admiral Fitch leaned over to Capt. Frederick C. Sherman and advised him, "Get the boys off the ship."

Sherman later wrote, "It was heartbreaking, but it seemed to be the only thing left to do. Reluctantly, I gave the order to abandon ship. It was the hardest thing I have ever done. Nevertheless, if we could not prevent the loss of the *Lexington*, saving the lives of her crew was of utmost importance."[10] Then Sherman made it his business to tour every accessible area of the ship searching out possible survivors. Finally, assured there were none, Sherman was the last to slide down the rope and join the thousands of crewmen on rafts or treading water, awaiting rescue.[11]

Swede bore witness. "I stood on the deck of the *Yorktown* and saw the whole thing, saw them abandoning ship with the ropes down; some were just diving over the side. And then they had one explosion that was spectacular, and I thought, 'If only I had a movie camera,' because the explosion occurred beneath the forward elevator, which was blown into the air, turned over in the air two or three times, and came right back down on deck."[12]

Rear Admiral Kinkaid was tasked with rescuing the survivors in the fortunately calm, warm waters of the Coral Sea, and he responded with a smoothly efficient operation. This was dangerous and delicate work, complicated by the threat of ongoing explosions on *Lexington* and the very real possibility of crushing men between ships. Kinkaid's screening ships plucked some 2,685 dispirited souls (92 percent of *Lexington*'s complement) from the sea.[13] A lot of wet sailors could appreciate Kinkaid's management of their crisis; Kinkaid would be awarded the Navy's Distinguished Service Medal.

With the rescue operation complete, Kinkaid ordered the destroyer USS *Phelps* (DD 360) to torpedo the now-useless *Lexington*. Four hits and a dud concluded the issue; *Lexington* sank a little before 10 p.m. Shortly after she disappeared beneath the waves, an enormous explosion punctuated her farewell.

Short on fuel and bedeviled by unwarranted concerns about an onrushing Japanese surface force, Task Force 17 beat a hasty retreat. The next morning the admirals received intelligence suggesting that *Zuikaku* was still in business. Swede and Fritz Faulkner were sent out on a two-hundred-mile sector search to the northwest. "I saw nothing. Faulkner was to the west of me near the end of his search. Fritz saw what he took to be wakes of fast-moving warships. We returned to *Yorktown* and reported that we might have spotted ships. Bob Dixon took another bomb-laden SBD in search of these ships. He found the area, determined the water's disturbance to be a reef east of Australia, and returned to the ship. Faulkner didn't take any heat about that. Rather, his report was taken as a good, solid report under the conditions."

Consequences

In the short term, Coral Sea could be termed an American victory. *Shōhō* had been sunk in a torrent of bombs and torpedoes. Fleet carrier and Pearl Harbor veteran *Shōkaku* had been savaged and would require three months of repairs. Strategically, Japan's plan to seize Port Moresby had been repulsed.

The damage went even deeper than that. The May 8 attack had cost Japan twenty-nine planes: six Zeros, fifteen Vals, and eight Kates. Added to the previous day's losses, this was a disaster. With *Zuikaku*'s plane inventory reduced to thirty-nine planes, no further attacks on the Americans could be contemplated. Worse, the loss of so many aircrews would keep *Zuikaku* out of action until after the Midway catastrophe, where two more operational fleet carriers might have reversed the outcome.

As for the Americans, the loss of *Lexington* had transformed a tactical victory into a defeat. Though the U.S. Navy lost one-fourth of its carrier strength in the clash, the Imperial Japanese Navy came to appreciate that battling the Americans on equal terms was not going to proceed as smoothly as their surprise attack on a sleepy Pearl Harbor. In this, the first of six carrier battles, the U.S. Navy had given as good as or better than it got.

The far-too-many vacant seats in the VS-5 ready room provided stark evidence of the day's events. For Swede and his fellow pilots, the value and personal satisfaction of any aerial victories could not be squared with buddies and squadronmates lost. With the sad loss of Sam Underhill, Bill Hall was assigned as Swede's new roommate. Like Swede, Bill Hall had contributed a bomb to *Shōhō*'s destruction, and he had been credited with downing three Japanese planes with his SBD. Having been shot through both ankles in the process, he would have to wait until he recovered from his wounds before moving in with Swede.

Meanwhile, to the south, hapless, bomb-shattered *Neosho* would drift for four miserable days. On May 11 the destroyer USS *Henley* (DD 391) discovered *Neosho*'s ghastly plight and rescued her and *Sims*' dazed, oil-soaked survivors. After all were on board, *Henley* torpedoed and shelled the mangled hulk. It was not long before *Neosho*, an Osage word ironically translating to "clear water," succumbed to her many assaults. Of the 293 men crewing *Neosho*, 111 survived; only 13 of *Sims*' crew of 252 came through the ordeal.

As the wounded *Yorktown* made her way to Pearl Harbor, Jimmy Flatley reflected on squadron and fighter performance and drafted a useful list of "Hints to Navy VF Pilots." Among them: gain plenty of altitude before contact, use hit-and-run diving tactics, dive out of tough spots and find a cloud, don't rush in but don't hesitate to dive in, beware ruses like fake smoke from exhaust pipes, and stay together.

For contributing to *Shōhō*'s destruction and for outdueling three Zeros the next day flying his SBD, Swede was written up for a second Navy Cross. Although he knew nothing about it, the Navy Crosses for both his bombing and fighter acumen generated some upper-level confusion about just how best to use him in the future. The Navy desperately needed both aggressive fighter pilots and pinpoint dive-bombers. Swede had proven his skill as both, but with fighters now the prime factor in carrier survival, Swede's superior combat maneuvering settled the issue.

As prospective CO of the First Carrier Replacement Squadron, Jimmy Flatley assembled a list of the SBD pilots who had scored victories or flown aggressively at Coral Sea. It takes little imagination to understand why Swede made Flatley's list. Though Swede and Jimmy had gotten to know one another on board *Yorktown*, it is doubtful that Flatley was aware of Swede's standing orders when he approached him about his squadron-to-be. It will be remembered that back in February, Swede had received orders to join the First Carrier Replacement Squadron "at his convenience." Swede quickly made it clear to Flatley that he wanted in. Deflecting rumors of an inside deal, Swede later insisted, "It's BS that Flatley conferred with the skipper to get us into his new squadron. AirPac had the final say about who'd be in the squadron."

Flatley also singled out Lt. Fritz Faulkner, an Olympic-caliber diver intimately experienced with acrobatics. Better still, Fritz was a squadronmate Swede already knew and liked. Another was *Lexington*'s Ens. John "Jack" Leppla, who had been awarded a Navy Cross for downing three Zeros with his SBD.

Flatley's list already amounted to an impressive gathering of talent. Bill Burch, of course, understood the need for these transfers but had to lament the departure of his highest performers and good friends. To a man, these accomplished veterans enthusiastically embraced the opportunity to transition out of their Dauntlesses and upgrade to Wildcat fighters.

"We put into Pearl Harbor aboard *Yorktown*, and I stayed aboard. On the third morning I was asked, 'You gonna stay aboard?'

" 'No, I'm waiting for transportation.'

" 'You better get off, we're getting under way.'

"There were hooches all over the flight deck to house the engineering and construction crews desperately repairing *Yorktown*'s Coral Sea bomb damage."

The rush was on because Joe Rochefort's radio analysts had tapped into Japan's radio code and by falsely advertising a water shortage on Midway had uncovered the Japanese plan to seize the outpost. Admiral Nimitz then set up the most ambitious ambush in naval history. During the first week in June 1942, *Hornet* and *Enterprise* combined to form Task Force 16. A hastily repaired *Yorktown* and her battle escorts formed Task Force 17 and joined with TF 16 northeast of Midway.

The Battle of Midway would cost Japan the Pearl Harbor veterans *Kaga*, *Akagi*, *Sōryū*, and *Hiryū* and completely alter Japan's ability to project naval air power. The U.S. Navy also paid a price at Midway. *Yorktown*, Swede's first carrier home, so heroically repaired after Coral Sea and made serviceable for the Battle of Midway, was twice attacked and badly damaged. While salvage efforts were under way, the Japanese submarine *I-168* torpedoed *Yorktown* and escort destroyer USS *Hamman* (DD 412), sinking them both.

As Midway unfolded, Swede's buddy Gus, adding to the Widhelm mystique, was heard to announce in *Hornet*'s ready room, "Widhelm is ready; now prepare the Japs." Though his bombers never found the carriers, days later Gus boasted that he intended to put his bomb directly down the smokestack of the biggest cruiser they found. And he nearly did just that, placing his bomb just behind the stack of the heavy cruiser *Mogami*.

Also at Midway, Rear Admiral Kinkaid, commanding Cruiser Division 6 (CRUDIV 6), was charged with providing a defensive screen for the carrier task forces. In the event, Kinkaid stood by largely as an observer. *Minneapolis*, his heavy cruiser flagship, never opened fire, and her security was never in doubt.

From his perch during the Midway battle Kinkaid had noticed that, owing to the sluggish torpedo bombers, strike groups were slow to form up. Perhaps unaware that the unescorted torpedo squadrons had been slaughtered, Kinkaid wrote after the battle, "It is of great importance that attack groups launched from a carrier proceed promptly to their objective, complete the attack immediately, and return to base to prepare to launch a second attack as soon as possible."[14] He further advised that each group of planes be equipped with YE-ZB homing equipment so searching aircraft could locate aircraft already attacking enemy ships. Elements of these recommendations would come into play months later at Santa Cruz.

Meanwhile, Swede was en route to the States. "I was aboard a commercial passenger vessel, the *Barnett* (AP 11), with Fritz Faulkner, Jack Leppla, and Jimmy Flatley. We had no details about Midway until we got to San Francisco. We got the real dope when we got to San Diego." On June 15, 1942, Swede, a lieutenant (junior grade) for a brief five months, was bumped to full lieutenant. While that was satisfying, it was the missteps at Midway that defined his mood.

"The loss of the *Yorktown* was a terrible blow to us. Everybody was just struck dumb. We couldn't believe *Yorktown* could be sunk. We wondered how it could have happened with two other carriers there. What the hell had gone on? We weren't looking out for subs. *I-168* made the whole approach with its periscope up. We needed air coverage from the other two carriers. There were no planes around. They could have sent planes from Hawaii. We all wondered, what next?"

CHAPTER 7

———

Intermission

SUMMER OF 1942

Skipper Jimmy Flatley, soon to be wearing a Navy Cross for his aggressive flying and downing of two enemy planes at Coral Sea, began the process of creating a carrier replacement squadron with a core of nine talented veterans. Swede and Fritz brought maturity, experience, and fighter pilot attitude to the group. *Lexington*'s VS-2 pilots Bobby Edwards and Jack Leppla also made the list. Together they had shot down four aircraft during the sinking of *Shōhō* and added three more the next day. Lt. Albert D. "Dave" Pollock from *Lexington*'s air department was the fifth pilot invited. Lt. John C. Eckhardt Jr., Lt. Leroy E. "Tex" Harris, Lt. Frank Donald Miller, and Lt. Macgregor Kilpatrick rounded out the core group. These men knew each other from many encounters in North Island bars as well as shared carrier duty.

Swede was quick to appreciate his new circumstances. "As so often happens in times of crises and dire need, the right man, who may be just a face in the crowd, comes to the fore and meets the challenge. And it so happened this time. Lt. Cdr. Jimmy Flatley, previously unknown to me except by name, was ordered as commanding officer and turned out to be the true leader, the tactician, the man of superior judgments—a man of vision and a true friend."[1]

Swede's relationship with his new skipper was respectful and attentive. "Flatley's greatness stemmed from his leadership and his approach to people. He considered others and their ideas. He had a lot of tact. Jimmy would gladly sit down and discuss your concerns at length. He had a good sense of humor, and he recognized the little things pilots might do and congratulated their improvements large and small."

Flatley and his pilots had to figure out how to meet and defeat highly experienced, battle-tested Japanese pilots flying superior Zero fighters. The Zero's primary advantage was its great agility. Superbly engineered but lacking weighty cockpit armor, the Zeros seemed capable of flying circles around anything else in the air. The armor concession, however, made the Zero and the Zero pilots far more vulnerable to sharpshooting U.S. Navy pilots. Worse, the Zero's lack of self-sealing gas tanks meant they reliably torched or exploded, as many startled victors had witnessed. Some referred to the Zeros as "Zippos—they light every time."

The Zero's two 7.7-mm machine guns and two 20-mm cannons were lethal enough, but the rugged American planes were rightly celebrated for getting pilots and crews back despite incredible battle damage. Swede weighed in. "The Zero wasn't that bad. People talk about how light and fast they were. Those machine guns and 20-mm cannons were bad guns, dangerous. They were a good, strong point for the Zero. But the Zero was not that tough if you didn't get tagged by the twenties."

Zeros, however, exhibited exploitable weaknesses. For one thing, the Zero was designed for operations below 15,000 feet; above that the controls got mushy. Further, the Japanese designers' emphasis on light and nimble created structural limitations; the Zeros could not dive as fast as the heavier American planes. The stronger American aircraft could make radical turns at high dive speeds, something the Zero could not match. After fighting Zeros in his SBD, Swede observed that "the Zeros couldn't handle high g loads. An SBD or Wildcat could."

As information on Japanese aircraft and tactics accumulated, Flatley expanded on his earlier "Hints to Navy VF Pilots." His updated doctrine, "The Navy Fighter," advised pilots jumped by Zeros to dive to evade or find a cloud. Offensively, make slashing dive attacks out of the sun. Don't follow a Zero into a loop. Stick together. Be highly skilled at gunnery. "We trained hard in our F4F-4s," Swede recalled, "formulating new tactics and keeping the edge on in gunnery, working on various patterns for our six .50-calibers."

Bitchin' Jimmie Thach

Lt. Cdr. Jimmie Thach and freshly promoted Lt. Cdr. Edward "Butch" O'Hare had recently arrived at North Island to train VF-12. Both men owned some serious credentials. O'Hare had been awarded a Medal of Honor for shooting down five Japanese twin-engine bombers in defense of *Lexington* back in February. For his part, Thach had downed dive-bombers and shared credit for two other kills early in the war. At Midway, with smart flying and excellent gunnery, Thach added three Zeros and one Kate torpedo bomber to his tally.

Even before the Battle of the Coral Sea, Thach and Jimmy Flatley had put their heads together and brainstormed tactics with which to counter the Zero's advantages. Going into the summer training, Flatley favored six-plane divisions. Thach, on the other hand, pressed for four-plane divisions because he felt that four could more effectively employ his "mutual-support beam defensive maneuver." Events at Midway had made a believer out of Thach when his weaving maneuver had confounded a swarm of Zeros attacking his strike escorts.[2] Flatley later dubbed Thach's defensive maneuver the "Thach Weave."

As Flatley and Thach thrashed out defensive tactics, Swede and his squadronmates refined squadron and group tactics.

"Fritz and I had met the Japanese Zero plane in combat, and it was our job to work with the CO and develop tactics that would utilize any advantages our planes might have over the Zero. We settled on the two-plane section and could work with either two or three sections in a division. The three sections provided the capability of keeping a large enemy formation under continuous attack."[3]

Butch O'Hare had recently relieved Thach as VF-12's skipper. In one of those service intersects, Swede remembered that it was none other than his old friend Gus Widhelm who had taught O'Hare instrument and night flying. Since then, Butch's combat experience had given him plenty to share with his new crop of pilots. Ens. Whitey Feightner, future ace, Blue Angel, and admiral, was one of the new pilots.

"Butch was a real aviator," Whitey enthused, "innovative, a fighter pilot kind of guy. He taught us to look behind when you're shooting, and don't follow 'em down to see what happened; they'll ambush you."[4]

To mixed reviews, Thach hung around to oversee his protégé's progress. Flatley's wife, Dorothy, recalled that Thach could be a delight to be around despite his air of superiority and that no one really minded because he was, indeed, superior.[5] Swede, nine years younger than Thach, cocky, and flushed with success, was less accommodating. "I first met Thach in mid-June when he took over VF-12 across the hangar from us. My impression of Thach was windy, very assertive and windy."

"I was a pain in the ass," Swede acknowledged. "I would jump people. I was always looking for a dogfight. We'd go after Thach's squadron. One day I jumped Thach out of nowhere. Afterward he strode across the hanger and burst into Flatley's office cursing VF-10. He'd picked up my number and, pointing at me, hollered, 'You're ruining our training.' He cussed me out for jumping him. Later, the ops guys would call me when Thach took off, and I'd try to jump him again. We just rode his ass unmercifully. God, he was mad. He tried out a lot of good ideas, but damn, when they don't work, they should be shelved."

Fellow pilots had all witnessed Thach's ranting and raving, but Flatley seemed to know best how to handle Thach's volatility. At a Thach outburst Flatley might calmly suggest, "Time we had a little lunch, don'cha think?" They'd head off for a bite or libation while continuing their discussion of defensive tactics.

Although he acknowledged that the Weave might have held some Zeros at bay, Swede did not share Thach's conviction that his Weave tactic could neutralize Zero attacks. Personally, Swede had no confidence in the maneuver. And having downed three Zeros with an SBD and gained essential insights on Japanese tactics and pilot tendencies, Swede was no armchair critic.

Naturally the tactic became the topic of intense discussion among the pilots. Flatley suggested that they try out the maneuver to see what might be done. Swede went up with his division to attack Flatley's division, all of them combat-experienced pilots. The attackers prevailed. They repeated the exercise. This time newer, inexperienced pilots practiced attacking Swede's defending division. Each time the attacking planes were easy victors.

"One fighter with an initial advantage could shoot 'em all down in two passes. If two of us attacked, we could shoot 'em all down in one pass. The weavers couldn't even see the attacking plane. That's the Thach Weave. It was a total washout. We could never utilize the Weave the way it was outlined. The best pilots couldn't use it effectively. After all that, Jimmy Flatley didn't buy into the Thach Weave."[6]

To settle the matter, Swede issued Thach a written challenge. "'You use your defensive beam maneuver. I'll take two Wildcats and attack you over North Island. I guarantee that I will knock you out of the sky. If you can demonstrate the Weave's usefulness, I'll apologize publicly.' Thach was observed crumpling up the note and tossing it in the waste can. That led to some hard feelings."

Whitey Feightner agreed that the Weave could be broken. "It could work," Whitey noted, "but it took a lot of training and discipline. You could only take the shots in front of you, and that's all. Some said it was too hard to perfect, and very few squadrons got good at it. To break it, we'd start a run, fake, lay on our backs, drop down, and shoot them as they crossed in the figure eight."

The Japanese also figured out how to break the maneuver. Later in the war, the Thach Weave presented a mixed bag for VF-18 pilot Lt. Cdr. Sam Silber. During a New Year's Day 1944 raid on Kavieng, he and his wingman, Ens. Robert Westfield "Bobbie" Beedle, were jumped by eight Zeros. Defensively, "Bob and I were weaving toward each other. It was simple and they were stupid about the whole thing. The Japanese pilots made no attempt to put up any opposition. They just turned away from us and presented nice targets. We were able to down four Zeros between us."

Very satisfying, but there was more to his story. On their next mission over Kavieng a few days later, the two were attacked by eight Zeros as they escorted bombers low over the water. The Japanese had done their homework regarding this weaving business. "It was during the vulnerable part of our Weave maneuver, when we were crossing each other, that Bob was shot down." A few seconds later Silber heard a tremendous explosion and discovered his left wing flap was gone. He was fortunate to make it back.[7]

Knowing the Thach Weave could be broken, Swede worked instead on what he called the Open Section. "One of the things we dreamed up and kept working with, was why should you have one man pinned to his leader so he can't do a thing except follow him and supposedly keep planes off his tail, which he's not going to do anyway? Why not open out, get four eyes instead of two, two planes instead of one, and enjoy complete maneuverability? In bad weather it doesn't work so good. That's one of the limitations, but ordinarily it worked well."[8]

Gunnery

Paradoxically, a new problem arose for the new F4F-4 Wildcats with the addition of two .50-caliber machine guns. The added guns significantly reduced firing time from forty seconds to twenty-four seconds, which left fighter pilots deeply concerned.

In his book *Reaper Leader: The Life of Jimmy Flatley*, Steve Ewing quoted Swede:

> The skipper took great interest in the guns in the F4F-4 and in conference with other pilots, discussed such things as boresighting and plans utilizing two, four, or all six guns at once. We had access to several competent engineers who could figure bullet concentrations, depth of bullet fields and arrive at good scientific solutions to such questions. Then an added question was what the load should be, using tracer, ball and any other rounds available. All of these things were made part of squadron doctrine during the training period.[9]

Whitey recalled O'Hare's advice to "use your ammunition sparingly. We clocked our firing time when all six guns are firing at fourteen and a half seconds. So be selective about how many guns to use; two .50s are enough to bring down any Japanese plane."

While the dangerous business of boresighting could be done on board ship, Swede felt it was best accomplished on shore where they could fire into dirt banks. Wherever boresighting took place, there was often a difference of opinion regarding the optimal distance at which their gunfire should converge. Never assured he would be flying the same Wildcat, Swede recalled, "I wanted my inboards to converge at 750 feet, but the group wanted 900 feet, which is what the squadron adopted."

Reduced firing time demanded superior accuracy; consequently, one-third of their training time focused on aerial gunnery. The focus on accuracy would pay off. "I never missed," Whitey recalled. "I put the pipper on the pilot's head. If I missed, I got the engine or the wing root where the gas tanks were." To improve on that accuracy, Whitey said, "we went in close, point blank."

Typically, newcomers to aerial combat would begin firing far too soon, spraying bullets into empty space. Training focused on developing patience and improving accuracy. When dogfighting, Swede noted, "different forces applied to you and your guns. You had to hold the plane steady, get a good view of the target. He's moving, you're moving, so the closer the better." They applied these considerations to shooting up banners being towed by their intrepid squadronmates. This intensive training and attention to detail would figure large during the events to come.

A year later, in an August 3, 1943, letter to Cdr. F. W. Wead, Flatley provided a glowing assessment of Swede's contributions to VF-10's growth and development. "Swede was outstanding from the beginning. He was a natural if there ever was one. His prowess was evident in all phases of training particularly in shooting and in his ability to make the F4Fs do things very few pilots could make it do. The youngsters that flew in his formation found that following Swede was effortless. As a result, his influence was a tremendous help to me."

CHAPTER 8

——

Developments Elsewhere

As Flatley and his Reapers worked on tactics, the Japanese were constructing an airstrip on Guadalcanal, across Sealark Channel from Tulagi. Should that airfield become operational, the Japanese would command the shipping routes to Australia, an unacceptable state of affairs for the Allies.

On August 7, 1942, *Enterprise* (TF 16), under the direction of Rear Adm. Thomas Kinkaid, covered the 1st Marine Division's hastily organized landing on Guadalcanal. Once the Marines were ashore, the covering carriers *Enterprise*, *Saratoga*, and *Wasp*, short of fuel and protective Wildcats and vulnerable to Japanese land-based aircraft, withdrew to the safety of more distant waters.

The success of the Marines' unopposed landing was soon overshadowed by calamitous events that evening. An undetected Japanese cruiser force shattered two Allied cruiser forces tasked with guarding the invasion beach. In the action, known as the Battle of Savo Island, three Japanese cruisers sank HMAS *Canberra* (D 33) and the U.S. Navy cruisers *Astoria* (CA 34), *Vincennes* (CA 44), and *Quincy* (CA 39). *Chicago* (CA 29) and the destroyer USS *Ralph Talbot* (DD 390) were both badly damaged. The now unprotected transports and supply ships fled before daylight. The Marines, completely on their own, could soon count on regular daytime air raids and nighttime bombardments. The waters near Savo Island were branded Iron Bottom Sound.

On August 8, the day after the Marines landed on Guadalcanal, Flatley's Grim Reapers set sail from San Diego bound for Maui in the Hawaiian Islands. By August 24, Swede and his squadronmates had resumed training.

That same August 24 the Japanese responded to the Marine landing. In the resulting Battle of the Eastern Solomons, the American carriers *Enterprise*, *Saratoga* (CV 3), and *Wasp*, with Vice Admiral Fletcher in overall command, confronted Japan's *Shōkaku*, *Zuikaku*, and *Ryūjō*.

Back on June 30 Nimitz had selected Rear Adm. Thomas Kinkaid for temporary command of the *Enterprise* force (TF 16) until Vice Adm. William F. Halsey, stricken with a severe case of psoriasis, could return. Halsey had not yet returned by August 24, so Kinkaid retained command. *Enterprise* had been assigned as the duty carrier, thus restricting her air operations to fleet CAP and search duties. Nonetheless, Kinkaid, eager to strike the first blow, pleaded with Fletcher to send out his *Enterprise* search/attack group before *Saratoga* could launch hers. Fletcher declined to expose his strike group to a night recovery and reined him in; Kinkaid would stick to searches.

As the battle developed, *Enterprise* endured a savage attack. A cascade of thirty Val dive-bombers inflicted three damaging near misses and three bomb hits in a matter of minutes, killing seventy-four and wounding ninety-one. Kinkaid and his flag plot staff were physically hurled around by the bomb blasts and were very fortunate not to have suffered serious injury. An hour and a half after that pummeling, *Enterprise* shocked her escorts when her rudder suddenly jammed. For a terrifying thirty-eight minutes she was restricted to a highly vulnerable circling pattern. For a time, Big E's very survival was in question.

After the battle Kinkaid saw for himself the grisly carnage of shattered and charred bodies; moaning wounded; and mangled, shrapnel-shredded machinery, decks, and bulkheads—enough to wound any psyche. With *Enterprise* the principal target of the Japanese attack, Kinkaid had been a study in impotence. Vice Admiral Fletcher had overruled him, and Capt. Arthur C. Davis conned his ship. Kinkaid could only stand mutely by, unable to affect the battle's outcome in any way. Perhaps the whole ordeal scarred him, sank deeper into his bones than he or anyone else appreciated. His leadership at Santa Cruz would reflect a man governed more by his fears than by realistic combat assessments.

Meanwhile, on the ground, in the air, and on the water—all around the Guadalcanal hellhole—a seemingly endless and inconclusive series of battles raged, with Henderson Field always the prize. As the months of bitter fighting wore on, the righteousness of American or Japanese ideology mattered not at all. All nationalities suffered equally on the "Island of Death."

By late October, Japan planned a decisive combined Imperial Army and Imperial Japanese Navy (IJN) offensive aimed at finally regaining control of Guadalcanal. This moment in time seemed propitious for the IJN. After all, U.S. Navy carrier presence in the Pacific was close to nonexistent. The Japanese mobile strike force had dispatched *Lexington* at Coral Sea, and a month later at Midway had finished off *Yorktown*. Eastern Solomons battle damage had forced the Big E to retire for repairs. Less than a week later, Japanese torpedoes put *Saratoga* out of action for months. Then, on September 15, the Japanese submarine *I-19* fired three torpedoes into *Wasp*, and she sank that same day. The Japanese had every reason to feel optimistic.

Appreciating this state of affairs, Vice Adm. Nagumo Chūichi sought the decisive encounter that would conclusively shatter the remaining American carrier forces in the Pacific. Japanese landing forces could then finally destroy the tenacious but shrinking Cactus Air Force at Henderson Field, and the *Kidō Butai* could resume roaming the Pacific and Indian Oceans unmolested.

Readiness

Back in Hawaii, the repaired and refitted *Enterprise* embarked her newly formed, and as yet untested, Air Group 10. Already a storied carrier, *Enterprise* had participated in the early raids on the Gilberts, Marshalls, Wake Island, and Marcus Island. She had escorted *Hornet* on Jimmy Doolittle's raid on Tokyo, and at Midway her squadrons sank three of the four Japanese carriers present. She had barely avoided destruction during the punishing Battle of the Eastern Solomons, and now a patched-up *Enterprise* prepared for a pivotal carrier battle that would determine Guadalcanal's fate.

On October 16, 1942, *Enterprise* steamed away from Hawaii's amenities. Flatley's experienced pilots constituted about one-third of VF-10's Grim Reapers; the rest were newcomers. Just prior to their departure, two Reaper pilots died in a midair collision during night training. Replacement pilots Whitey Feightner and Ens. Gordon Barnes had been last-minute appropriations from Butch O'Hare's pilfered squadron.

New guy Whitey Feightner came to the squadron with serious skills and experience. Michael Murphy, a world-champion acrobatic pilot, had taught him the art of flying. In fact, Whitey's first solo came on a trip with Murphy, who revealed during the flight his intention to purchase a new plane at their destination. Murphy thoughtfully gave the controls over to Whitey for a majority of the outbound trip. When Murphy concluded the deal, it became Whitey's task to solo the return leg in that same Ford trimotor. Said Whitey, "It could fly itself." He had earned his pilot's license by 1938, logged some 300 hours in the air, and had flown 30 or more types of planes before joining the Navy. For Flatley, Whitey was a godsend.

It didn't take Swede long to appreciate Feightner's personality and prowess. "Whitey came to us just as we left Pearl Harbor. A fine flyer, and very receptive about combat, he flew in my division and on my wing and responded well. Whatever Whitey had to say was pretty authentic."

Reaper Lt. Dave Pollock did his best to make Whitey feel at home, and Flatley's leadership style greatly eased Whitey's abrupt transfer. Whitey immediately took to Flatley. He "was a philosophical deep thinker, and he really understood tactics," Whitey recalled. "Jimmy was a great squadron commander."

Despite the presence of those experienced aviators, VF-10 was by no means a well-oiled machine. And the lack of group cohesion was not limited to the Reapers. Efforts to integrate fighters, dive-bombers, and torpedo bombers into an efficient air group had not gone smoothly. Hal Buell, now a Bombing 10 pilot, had witnessed one Air Group 10 exercise back in Hawaii and was alarmed at the disorientation and confusion he saw. Wanting no part of that, he kept his distance.[1]

Change of Command

As *Enterprise* sortied from Pearl Harbor, the Joint Chiefs of Staff, with Admiral Ernest King's approval, appointed the aggressive Vice Adm. William F. "Bull" Halsey as commander of the South Pacific theater of operations (ComSoPac), replacing a dispirited Vice Adm. Robert L. Ghormley, who had already voiced his doubt that Guadalcanal could be held.

With Halsey bumped up to theater commander, who would assume the now-vacant command of the task force? Vice Admiral Fletcher had spent long months in Pacific combat, but his perceived lack of aggressive leadership during the Battle of the Eastern Solomons and his need for a well-earned rest mandated a change in command. Among his first actions as ComSoPac, Halsey reversed an earlier plan for Kinkaid to replace Rear Admiral Murray on *Hornet* (TF 17). The position of commander Task Force 61, which would combine *Enterprise* and *Hornet*, stood open.

Like Fletcher, Kinkaid had served in the Pacific from the start, advancing from cruiser command to carrier command. And Kinkaid, awarded a Distinguished Service Medal for his cruiser division leadership during the Battle of the Coral Sea, stood ready. Despite Kinkaid's lack of familiarity with carrier aviation (a so-called black shoe admiral), Halsey settled on him for the command. Rear Admiral Murray would remain with *Hornet*.

Regarding his ascension to TF 61 commander, Kinkaid wrote to his wife, "I am glad it has come out this way because there are a lot of aviators in the offing, and there is some inclination to push them ahead of us ordinary mortals."[2] This disdain for aviators would not play well in the days to come.

As the struggle for Guadalcanal ground on, Japanese convoys, dubbed the "Tokyo Express," regularly steamed down the Solomons "Slot" to reinforce and replenish starving Japanese forces. The Japanese high command, appalled at Guadalcanal's steady drain of men and material, now planned for that long-sought decisive stroke. The Imperial Japanese Army would mount a massive attack to breach the Marines' perimeter, and the *Kidō Butai* would destroy whatever patched-up U.S. carrier forces might appear.

Astute U.S. Navy radio analysts and code-breakers uncovered the Japanese plan. To counter this latest threat to vital Henderson Field, Halsey ordered Kinkaid's Task Force 61 to intervene. Very recently, on October 21, Capt. Osborne Hardison had replaced the highly experienced Captain Davis as *Enterprise* CO. Steaming headlong into a confrontation with a superior Japanese task force, Kinkaid, with a new carrier commander under him, now wore the unfamiliar mantle of task force commander. Final decisions would be his alone.

Kinkaid's appointment as task force commander immediately raised red flags for Swede. "I was curious as to why he was head of the task group. These guys were appointed by the top brass, Nimitz or Halsey. Kinkaid was not an aviator; that seemed strange to me. Our squadron had a lot of new guys, and few if any had night qualified. I had to train these guys. We needed practice, especially night landings. We were ignored. So we went into this completely unqualified."

Hornet, bearing the flag of longtime aviator and recently promoted Rear Admiral Murray and captained by Capt. Charles P. Mason, constituted the other half of Task Force 61. The cruisers USS *Northampton* (CA 26), USS *Pensacola* (CA 24), USS *San Diego* (CL 53), and USS *Juneau* (CL 52); and screen destroyers USS *Morris* (DD 417), USS *Anderson* (DD 411), USS *Hughes* (DD 410), USS *Mustin* (DD 413), USS *Russell* (DD 414), and USS *Barton* (DD 599) rounded out the task force.

Early in the war Murray had racked up critical experience commanding *Enterprise* during the Pacific raids, through the Doolittle raid in April, and into the Battle of Midway. Then Murray fleeted up to rear admiral and took command of *Hornet*'s TF 17. While *Enterprise* underwent repairs for the Eastern Solomons battle damage, Murray and TF 17 had been guarding the approaches to Guadalcanal. The newly promoted rear admiral might have lamented his departure from *Enterprise*, but he now had command of an effective *Hornet* air group, which over the past five weeks had been attacking Japanese ships and ground installations. Flying his flag on board the lone U.S. carrier in the theater, Murray had experienced some freedom of movement and exercised his own style of command. Now, with Kinkaid in charge, Murray's experience and prior autonomy would be held hostage to Kinkaid's inexperience commanding a two-carrier task force. Halsey's impulsive arrangement would very nearly result in a U.S. naval catastrophe.

On October 24, *Enterprise*, screened by the battleship USS *South Dakota* (BB 57); cruiser USS *Portland* (CA 33); new antiaircraft cruiser USS *San Juan* (CL 54); and destroyers USS *Porter* (DD 356), USS *Mahan* (DD 364), USS *Cushing* (DD 376), USS *Preston* (DD 379), USS *Smith* (DD 378), USS *Maury* (DD 401), USS *Conyngham* (DD 371), and USS *Shaw* (DD 373), joined Murray's TF 17. Task Force 61 was a reality.

Steaming southeast to the Guadalcanal-Tulagi area, Admiral Nagumo's *Kidō Butai* included fleet carriers *Shōkaku* and *Zuikaku*, both veterans of the Pearl Harbor raid, and supporting light carriers *Zuihō* and *Junyō*. This heady assemblage, reinforced with two battleship divisions and numerous cruiser and destroyer divisions, tilted the scales steeply against Kinkaid's undersized Task Force 61.

No longer a dive-bomber jockey, Swede's responsibility as a Wildcat pilot was to fly interceptor CAP missions and fighter escort for strike missions. The stubby Wildcat came with some issues. Hydraulic wheel retractors that would eliminate the odious twenty-nine turns to raise the landing gear had yet to make their appearance. Cranking up that gear presented yet another burden for malnourished or malaria-weakened pilots flying out of Henderson Field. To compensate for the weight of the two additional machine guns and ammunition, the heavy automatic-wing-folding mechanisms were removed. This, of course, amplified the workload for busy deck crews forced to manually fold those wings.

But Swede's new weapons platform might better be defined by the differences from his old SBD dive-bomber. The F4F carried no cumbersome bomb. The Wildcat's combined six forward-firing, wing-mounted .50-caliber machine guns dwarfed the potential firepower of a pair of anemic .50-calibers restricted by having to fire through an SBD's propeller. Missing from the Wildcat, however, was a potentially comforting backseat radioman/gunner covering your rear, warning you of threats, fending off or shooting down potential interlopers, or, in better times, celebrating your successes.

Whatever the merits or limitations of his Wildcat, Swede was one of the few seasoned combat veterans in this replacement squadron. He had learned that the keys to survival against the Zero were good flying, good gunnery, and above all good teamwork.

In his November 11, 1942, *Honolulu Star-Bulletin* article, war correspondent Eugene Burns described Swede as he came to know him on board *Enterprise*. "He's got the ingredients that make a natural flier. . . . Foremost, he's all business about this flying. Others may sit around and bat the breeze in the wardroom, not Swede. I've never seen the man eat. But I've always found him, when he's not in the air, in fighter ready room No. 1 always listening to the pilot's phone system, studying maps, watching the talker chalk up information." Burns quoted Swede's twenty-seven-year-old wingman, Lt. Tex Harris, who called Swede "the smoothest flier I've ever seen."

"The more difficult the situation," Burns concluded, "the calmer he calls them. When the advantage is with him, he wades in and slugs. It's hard to reduce Swede to newsprint. He's not colorful, but you know he's the same clear through from his blonde, sandy hair down through his 5 feet 10 to his number 9 shoes."[3]

That was Swede; but so many in the squadron were new and untested. What skills and luck did they bring with them? And what would happen when, late on the afternoon of October 25, Admiral Kinkaid sent them out on an impossible mission?

CHAPTER 9

———

A Phantom Goose Chase Concluded

The Enterprise *attack group returned and was
landed after dark with considerable difficulty as
pilots were not qualified for night landings.*
REAR ADMIRAL KINKAID TO ADMIRAL HALSEY,
NOVEMBER 3, 1942

We return now to the evening of October 25. The *Enterprise* strike group, with Swede as escort leader, had just flown their futile search and were returning to *Enterprise* when Don Miller shocked everyone by inexplicably jumping out of his plane. Swede navigated the group through the murk and darkness to Point Option, only to find Point Empty. Instead of *Enterprise*'s welcoming deck, hot chow, and some badly needed bunk time, a vast, implacable Pacific lay vacant below them. Not a ship in sight. Admiral Kinkaid had vacated Point Option. He had vanished without providing his returning strike group any idea of how to locate their home base. For the scared and drained pilots this was too much. Panic kicked open the door, and chaos strode in.

"That's when trouble broke out," Whitey recalled. "Everyone milled around. Nobody knew what to do at this point. Everyone was fiddling with his YE-ZB homing set. Somebody thought they got a signal, then we went down low."

To that point the Grim Reapers had been shepherding the bombers. Now faced with this appalling crisis, the groups' formations disintegrated, planes going up or dropping down. Trading bombs for longer flying time, the low-flying SBDs released their ordnance. Two of the bombs were armed and exploded on the water; shrapnel perforated a pair of the SBDs, eventually forcing them to ditch.[1]

Swede was incredulous. "What the hell do you do? What's the next action? I had Coalson on one wing and Whitey on the other. I decided to fly straight ahead, which caused others to join on me. What the hell? You're not going to see anything in the dark. The ships won't have lights on. You might find a wake."

Swede steered them west, everyone's nerves on edge. Compass headings meant nothing that night. Fear soaked the cockpits as pilots narrowly focused on maintaining visual contact while flying dangerously tight on one another. Now, in the dark, practically on the water and dodging low clouds, nobody had a plan. "Of course, we were under absolute radio silence," Whitey recalled. "Even in those dire straits, no one ever said a word."

Swede also referenced their radio discipline and further described their isolation. "There was only silence. There was no YE homing device summoning us, no conversation; everyone observed complete radio silence. I don't know if the *Enterprise* had their radar on. I never heard one damn word from them. I just figured we were committed to be lost. To leave us out there at Point Option without any word was criminal.

"But I couldn't focus on that. I'm desperate. The whole group joined on me as I made wide turns searching for clues. I didn't know more than anyone else about what to do. I was just the most experienced pilot in the group."

Then inspiration struck. "It came to me like a bolt out of the blue. That morning, flying endless circles around the fleet, I noticed a propeller-seal oil slick from the *Enterprise*. There was no sea action; it wasn't choppy, so it was easy to see that slick. And I knew a Japanese sub could follow that slick to my ship. So I turned on my lights and started to look for that slick. They had to have been here at Point Option. I dropped down, and everybody joined up behind me, like I knew what I was doing. I didn't know what the hell I was doing. I turned my lights on bright. Whitey turned his on, which gave much better visibility. We flew twelve to fifteen miles, weaving gently, searching for an obscure sheen on the dark water, and there was nothing."

Staying tight on Swede's wing through low-flying clouds, the night suddenly got more frightening for Whitey. "I'm flying on Swede's right wing, wingtips five feet apart, and he starts making a right turn. We were so low only my lights alerted me, kept me from catching my wing on the water." Adrenalin pumping, Whitey quickly adjusted his position to up wing.

Minutes later things took a turn for the better. Swede spotted an oil slick. "I immediately thought, 'That's no salvation, what if it goes the other way? We'd be going in the wrong direction, and we're getting low on gas.' I was greatly relieved to realize that the slick narrowed down, which meant I was following the correct bearing. After Whitey gave me a little room, we straightened out on the slick. Every little while we'd climb up to three or four hundred feet looking for lights, something."

After forty-something apprehensive miles Swede finally made out ships' wakes and then faint deck lights. Whitey recalled, "For some reason, everyone, including Group CO Gaines, followed Swede, and, lo and behold, in about fifteen minutes we found the carrier!" For many of the spent pilots and aircrews, though, finding the *Enterprise* task force did not signal an end to their tribulations.

Found

It now became LSO Robin Lindsey's challenge to correctly gauge each pilot's situation, communicate precisely with his illuminated paddles, and direct these worn-out pilots into safe traps. The bridge signaled that the short-legged fighters, the ship's primary defense and by now flying mostly on fumes, should have priority.

Whitey recollected, "We came straight in. I purposely gave Swede some room by making a few S turns to slow down. That's when Coalson snuck in between us."

Swede, first in line, recalled his brush with death. "Robin brought me in a little bit high. This was unusual. I came on in, caught a wire, and held onto my brake. All hell broke loose on deck. Guys were banging on the side of my plane, jerking the aileron. I looked out on my right to see the whirling prop of another airplane right between my wing and tail. Another guy had landed with me. Coalson had been on my left, but somehow he got under my right wing. I didn't know he was there. Two planes, landing at the same

time? I'm sure that's the only time in history that happened. Whitey Feightner was on my left, and he landed third." Swede lingered on deck just long
enough to watch the last four Wildcats make it safely back on board. His job
done, Swede headed below as the SBDs came in.

Eddie Coalson, whose Wildcat had threatened to chew up Swede's plane,
could celebrate a great first night carrier landing: one he could walk away
from. Back in the ready room, Swede wanted to know, "Eddie, what in the
hell were you doing tonight?"

"Boss," he replied, "if you thought you were going to get away from me,
you're crazy."

"What could I say? We had been in the air over five hours." Swede
laughed in retrospect, but it had been a close thing.

Lindsey later described to Swede his dilemma when he noticed Coalson slip in line. "I knew that plane was there; he wasn't taking any signals.
I don't think he even saw me. I could see he had his lights on. I could see it
was two airplanes coming in. I could give you a wave-off, yeah, you to the
port side and the other plane would probably go ahead and hit the island."
As it was, Swede had smartly caught the number three wire and Coalson
snagged number one.

For those following on, their relief at reaching Big E was shredded by
ensuing events. Bombing skipper Jim Thomas had just landed, and close
behind him was Lt. (jg) Robert "Hoot" Gibson, who recalled what happened
next:

Klaxon horns sound General Quarters. They are designed to scare the hell
out of you. I had just landed on board, released my tail hook from the arresting gear, and applied full throttle to move forward past the protection of the
barrier as the Klaxon blared. Without looking back I knew the plane following me in landing had ignored a wave-off and would land on top of me.
I tried to bend the throttle forward to get one more ounce of power. Ten more
feet would save my life. No luck. Before reaching the barrier the incoming
plane caught a wire, bounced nose-up, smashed its wing into the island
structure, and fell onto my plane simultaneously. The propeller shredded my
plane to the accompaniment of the Klaxon. I didn't have time to release my
seat and shoulder belt.

Ens. Jefferson "Tiny" Carroum was the guilty party. Gibson continued:

> Lindsey had given Carroum a wave-off because he was too close on my
> tail. If there is any one commandment that is drilled into every carrier pilot,
> it is that wave-off signal is supreme. No excuses, no BS, no reprieve for
> disobeying. Except this time, because everyone was worn out.
>
> He took the cut regardless and was landing right on top of me. His propeller
> cut off the rear of my plane like slicing salami and ended up within three feet of
> my cockpit, but fortunately three inches short of my gunner's cockpit.[2]

Carroum and his gunner were also lucky to have survived the incident. And maybe that luck extended to not facing a court-martial for his desperate disregard of Lindsey's instruction to go around. Carroum's indiscretion had been costly; two more SBDs scrubbed from the inventory. Of the five SBDs that had left on the mission, only one remained flyable.

Worse, the delays required for clearing the deck meant that three gas-starved Avengers faced the unhappy prospect of ditching. As scary as night carrier landings might be, pilots truly dreaded a nighttime ditching. But with fuel gauges reading zero, they had no way of knowing when their engines would finally quit. Better to attempt the water landing while they still had some control over their aircraft.

It wasn't simply about landing safely on the water. Everyone knew stories about canopies jamming closed or planes flipping onto their back. And before Jimmy Flatley came up with a harness arrangement, ditching often included a nasty collision with the gun sight, resulting in a lacerated forehead. Even if pilots or crews made it safely out of the plane and into the water there was no guarantee that a destroyer lookout would see them, especially in the dark.

VT-10 exec Scoofer Coffin and crew had made it to *Enterprise*'s wake when his engine quit. Pilots Lt. (jg) Robert Nelson and Ens. George Wilson also faced the terrors of a night ditching. Their worst fears were confirmed when Wilson's turret gunner, S1C Arthur M. Browning, couldn't escape the plane and drowned. The destroyer *Mahan* retrieved Wilson and his radioman, ARM3C Malcolm Neal; the lifeguard destroyer *Maury* plucked Coffin, Nelson, and their respective crews from the water.

Of six TBF Avengers to start the mission, only three—those piloted by Lt. (jg) George L. Welles, Lt. Marvin "Doc" Norton Jr., and Lt. (jg) George Kemper—made it back on board. Carroum had a lot to answer for. In a few weeks, Tiny would come to understand a lot more about the "drink."[3]

Gibson fully recognized his good luck that night. "I was still fortunate to be alive on board ship instead of in the ocean. I suppose most of the men got picked up. I don't know. I have never had the heart to know."[4]

Whitey confronted the deeper, blacker meaning of what he had just survived. "As for us, the implication was clear. We were dead. They had written off the whole strike group. It was one of the scariest days of my life. I flew ten minutes with my fuel gauge reading zero, and it was dark. If not for Swede, we'd all have been swimming."[5]

In his post-action reports Kinkaid never mentioned leaving Point Option. Instead he shifted the focus and declared the strike leader guilty of "excess zeal" and the pilots incompetent. Nor did Kinkaid ever explain his failure to recall his strike group once he knew the Japanese had turned away from any possible contact.

Completely undone by the ordeal, Whitey rode the elevator down and plodded off to bed before Carroum crashed his SBD. Thus Whitey had no real sense of his squadronmates' thoughts regarding this mission gone to hell. None of that mattered; he faced another flight early the next morning. Whitey was a spent, if unfired, bullet.

Whatever relief they might have experienced from their "miraculous" return to *Enterprise* had to be measured against the air group's loss of Don Miller; the Wildcat he bailed out of; four SBDs to ditching, crashes, or exploding ordnance; three ditched TBFs; and Seaman First Class Browning. Oftentimes war's most harrowing experiences had nothing to do with combat.

For many this had been day one of expected combat operations, and no one, especially the new guys, could fathom what was going on. Blair's morning accident had destroyed five aircraft. That afternoon Kinkaid had sent off his "expendable" strike group. During their nighttime return, Coalson landed alongside Swede. Minutes later, Carroum disregarded a wave-off, crashed his plane, and chewed up Gibson's SBD in the process. By any standard, the day was an unmitigated disaster. The Japanese needed only to stand by and watch while the Americans self-destructed.

Fortunately, plane guard destroyers located and picked up most of the ditched pilots and airmen. But news of the successful recoveries was late in reaching their drained squadronmates, who meanwhile had to process a lot of empty ready room seats. Those who made it back to the ship slumped under a crushing, demoralized fatigue, an exhaustion magnified by what they viewed as Kinkaid's apparent indifference to their fate.

A little past eight that night, the *Enterprise* war diary tersely, if inaccurately, recorded the evening's terrors with, "Landed all remaining planes in air, less 2 VT, 2 VSB and 1 VF which landed in the water." The action report, recording intention if not fact, noted:

> At 1520 launched 11 VF (three returned to *Enterprise*), 12 VSB (five VBs took off), and 6 VTB with the Group Commander as an attack group to follow up the search. This group did not make contact. It was late returning to the carrier and experienced difficulty in landing aboard after dark. One VF pilot crashed about 40 miles from the ship on the return trip, cause unknown. Six additional planes were lost as a result of water landings around the ship due to fuel exhaustion or in crashes incident to landing on board. With the exception of the VF pilot first mentioned, no lives were lost.

The report omitted the loss of S1C Arthur Browning and scarcely captured Air Group 10's terror and vain sacrifices.

Journalist Gene Burns completely understated the evening's events. His sole reference: "Many of these fellows had stretched their search this afternoon and had only a little gas left when they were snubbed up on the carrier deck."[6]

Swede was irate. They had lost Miller from the Reapers along with nearly half the strike group's aircraft. But it did no good that night to dwell on what might have been. Focusing on the practical, Swede set out to inventory the air group's resources for the battle everyone expected the next day. To compensate for Blair's morning accident and the loss of Miller and his plane, spare Wildcats that were intended to supplement Guadalcanal's Cactus Air Force were hastily serviced. For one Reaper team, the rush to get the Wildcats operational would have dangerous consequences in the next morning's combat.

For the rest of his life, bitterness colored Swede's memory of that night. "I had to coordinate with bombers and torpedo planes, and the staff had no plan at all. What will we put in the air tomorrow? What do we have to work with? There was no communication with Kinkaid's staff. They ignored us."

The pilots were convinced that Kinkaid had written off his entire strike force. Incredibly, those apparently considered expendable included Swede (twice a Navy Cross recipient); Bombing 10's skipper, Lt. Cdr. Jim Thomas; Torpedo 10's XO, Lieutenant Coffin; and CAG Dick Gaines in the bargain, some of the most experienced pilots in the air group.

As word of Kinkaid's abandonment got around, every pilot had to wonder who next might be deemed disposable. Air Officer John Crommelin recognized the seriousness of the pilots' morale plunge and called those scheduled for the next morning's strike mission into the wardroom. Gene Burns listened as "Uncle John" pulled out all the stops. Crommelin informed his airmen that the forthcoming battle was to protect their way of life and exhorted them to bomb accurately. He praised their squadron leaders and reminded them that their planes could take more punishment than any planes made and still bring them back. "Use them properly as you have been trained, and you will shoot down the bastards in each encounter." Obliquely referencing the evening's disaster, Crommelin then promised that any pilot who made it back into the groove would be recovered. Half a day later, Robin Lindsey would heroically make good on that pledge.

In the midst of Crommelin's impassioned remarks it was announced that everyone but Miller and Browning had been rescued and would be high-lined back on board *Enterprise*. That news elicited a roar of approval from their relieved buddies. When things settled back down, Crommelin went on to describe the strategic picture and made it clear that Air Group 10 had to stop the Japanese. "The Japs are determined to drive us out of the South Pacific. If they get through to Guadalcanal with their carriers tomorrow, the Japs will take it. If Guadalcanal falls, our lifeline to Australia will be menaced." He finished with, "Best of all, we are on the right side of this war. God is with us. Let's knock those Jap bastards off the face of the earth."[7]

The assembled pilots took those words to heart, and the next day, at fearful cost, would act on them. For the moment, the loss of thirteen aircraft that day posed unsettling questions. Newcomers and veterans alike wondered, is anybody in charge? Will there be a plane for me to fly in the coming battle?

Whitey didn't hear Crommelin's sermon. Wiped out from having dodged a night ditching, he was resting in his bunk. Swede was too busy on the hangar deck sorting out the next day's fighter and strike force inventory to hear any of it. Besides, it didn't apply to him. Crommelin's exhortations were directed toward the men chalk-boarded for the next morning's strike force. Since both Swede and Whitey had flown the Wild Goose Chase on this screwed-up day, they would fly the morning CAP.

Swede hustled to make the necessary preparations. "We worked all night. Our people just worked like hell, got everything loaded, and set out the morning search mission."

Ens. Leonard "Robbie" Robinson, a recent VB-10 arrival, was quick to appreciate Swede's experience and direct honesty when discussing aerial combat. Around midnight Robbie drew the unenviable task of flying one of those dark, early-morning search legs and then delivering that same SBD to *Hornet* to replenish that carrier's depleted stock. Robbie, a wannabe fighter pilot, was reduced to ferry driver. "This is pathetic," he griped. It would get far worse.

CHAPTER 10

———

The Battle of Santa Cruz

To say that Oct. 26, 1942 aboard the Enterprise
was a very long day is a masterful understatement.
LSO Jim Daniels, letter to John Lundstrom,
April 18, 1985

The tension was palpable the morning of October 26. Everyone expected the day to bring combat. On the bridge, in the absence of any word from his search planes, Kinkaid remarked to Gene Burns, "Waiting for contact reports adds years." To distract from that anxious waiting, Kinkaid expounded on the differences between World War I operations and carrier combat, which to him were nothing short of astonishing. Airplanes had added a dynamic and far-reaching complexity to warfare. "Now a battle can be won or lost within five minutes. Trying to anticipate every eventuality keeps one awake."[1]

If the previous evening's Goose Chase had drawn no fire, the next day more than made up for it. Apprised that the Japanese fleet had steamed within reach, the pugnacious Admiral Halsey famously ordered his outnumbered forces to "STRIKE-REPEAT-STRIKE." Some say it went "ATTACK-REPEAT-ATTACK." It didn't matter; everybody got the message. For Kinkaid, Swede, Robbie, and Whitey it was to be a day of firsts. This would be Thomas Kinkaid's first overall command of a two-carrier task force. For both Robbie and Whitey, it was to be their first day of bloody combat. And Swede would fly an F4F-4 Wildcat into combat for the first time. It would be a seminal day for the four of them and many, many others.

At 7:40 a.m. on the morning of October 26, *Enterprise* search pilots Lt. Birney Strong and Ens. Chuck Irvine, following up on a reported sighting of Japanese carriers, located the light carrier *Zuihō*. Achieving total surprise, at least one of their 500-pound bombs hit aft, destroying *Zuihō*'s arresting gear. The bold attack took *Zuihō* out of the battle. A shocked Vice Admiral Nagumo immediately ordered *Shōkaku* and *Zuikaku* to launch their strikes. Initially, *Shōkaku* sent off twenty-two Val dive-bombers and twenty-seven Zero escorts to join with eighteen *Zuikaku* Kate torpedo bombers. Nagumo backed that sixty-seven-plane raid with a potent follow-on strike: twelve *Shōkaku* Kates, twenty *Zuikaku* Vals, and sixteen *Zuikaku* Zero escorts. Altogether, the 2 carriers launched a massive 115-plane raid, far larger than anything Kinkaid could assemble.

Unfortunately, Kinkaid's errors in judgment begun the day before continued apace. To begin with, he was late to the game. Gene Burns was on the bridge when searchers reported Japanese battleships. Over the pleas of his staff, Kinkaid hesitated, saying he needed to wait for carrier sightings. An officer in flight control urged, "We ought to send out our attack force now. Those Jap carriers will be sitting behind the battleships. Why in hell do we wait?"[2] An hour later nothing more had developed on the contact.

It was 8:30, a half hour after the Japanese launched, before Kinkaid launched *Hornet*'s first strike force consisting of fifteen Dauntlesses (seven from VS-8 and eight from VB-8) followed by six VT-6 torpedo-laden Avengers. VF-72 supplied eight Wildcat escorts, with Swede's old friend, the incomparable Lt. Cdr. Gus Widhelm, in overall command. A second wave, consisting of eight fighters, nine Dauntlesses, and ten Avengers (armed with 500-pound bombs) launched ten minutes later. On reciprocal bearings, the Japanese strike group overflew Widhelm's force as both strike groups continued on their respective missions. Neither side deviated; there were bigger fish to fry. Gus duly reported the incoming raid.

Flatley's Despair

With the Japanese attack on the way, *Enterprise* finally launched a modest strike force of three SBDs from VS-10 and seven VT-10 Avengers. Jimmy Flatley, flying Reaper 1 and accompanied by Jack Leppla's Reaper 6, would provide escort. On top of that, Flatley had overall command of the strike group. Dick Gaines would again fly an unarmed TBF, his job to observe and photograph the group's mission. Pilots talked disparagingly about that compromised role, but in a stark contrast to their Japanese counterparts, Navy brass did not want air group commanders unnecessarily exposed to combat.

Swede had his own opinion of Gaines, a former fighter pilot. "If you want a good executive officer, get Gaines," Swede reflected. "He was great with paperwork, and he meant well. The nicest guy; just not a great pilot. After action in the Lae and Salamaua raids, Gaines mistakenly returned to *Lexington*, which looks nothing like the smaller size *Yorktown*. He was not familiar with combat and tactics. He was just out of his element."

While strike pilots positioned to take off, a deck crewman held aloft a disturbing sign instructing them to "Proceed without *Hornet*." Why the change in plan? Kinkaid knew contact was imminent, and he was determined to get in the first blow. Back in August, at the Battle of the Eastern Solomons, he had urged Vice Admiral Fletcher to send groups out singly and had been overruled. Now, with no time to waste, Kinkaid rashly changed the plan and ordered his *Enterprise* attack group to proceed independently to its objective, without joining *Hornet*'s two-wave strike group. With this decision Kinkaid consigned his group to a piecemeal attack, seriously diluting the numbers required to overwhelm alerted Japanese defenses.

The pilots didn't know what to think. Experience recommended strength and intimidation in numbers, so why this last-minute deviation from their ready room briefings? Jimmy Flatley's strike group would pay heavily for Kinkaid's impulsive haste.

Shortly after Flatley's departure, Wick Wickendoll, and Whitey who flew wing, lifted off for the morning's second CAP in the hastily serviced spare Wildcats. Once in the air, they joined the dawn CAP still aloft and scanned for bogies.

It was not long before *Enterprise*'s radar picked up the first wave from *Shōkaku* and *Zuikaku*, led by Lt. Cdr. Seki Mamoru. Two months before at Eastern Solomons, Seki had led the carrier bomber attack that badly damaged *Enterprise*; by his estimate, it was time to complete the job. Though Gus had duly alerted *Hornet* to the incoming raid, no one in Flatley's *Enterprise* strike group had monitored that transmission. Minutes later, as Seki's force pressed on toward TF 61, they intersected Flatley's puny force.

The temptation was too great; a dozen or more Zeros broke off from their escort duty and launched a devastating up-sun attack. They focused on the unsuspecting Avengers and Leppla's Reaper 6 escort division. Things happened fast. Torpedo skipper Lt. Cdr. John A. Collett was immediately shot down and killed along with his gunner, AM1C Steve Nadison; ARM1C Thomas C. Nelson managed to survive. Ens. John M. Reed's Avenger was riddled and blew up just after AMM3C Murray "Mick" Glasser was able to bail out. Lt. Marvin "Doc" Norton and Lt. (jg) Richard "Dick" Batten were quickly shot up and headed home.

The lightning attack also tore into Leppla's Reaper 6; he turned into the swarming Zeros and was shot down and killed. Ens. Al Mead and Ens. Raleigh "Dusty" Rhodes worked Thach's Weave to some defensive success, but the two were overmatched and eventually were forced to ditch their ruined planes. They joined Nelson and Glasser bobbing in the warm South Pacific. Only sixty-some miles from home base, they held out some hope for a destroyer pickup.

Flatley, who had been out in front slowly weaving to the right in order to pace the slower bombers, was oblivious to what was happening to his left and behind him. Finally aware of the unfolding disaster, Flatley jumped into the fight and downed one of the attacking Zeros.

As Leppla and his Reaper 6 mates fought for their lives, Flatley faced a cruel combat dilemma. Though his shaken group had been whittled to three SBDs, four TBFs, Gaines' unarmed Avenger, and the remaining four Wildcats of Reaper 1, Flatley's primary responsibility was to navigate his surviving aircraft to the Japanese, penetrate their CAP, and position his stunted force to attack and destroy a carrier task force. That larger mission overrode Flatley's fervent desire to help his disadvantaged squadronmates. Flatley broke off the fight; overwhelmed Reaper 6 would have to fend for itself. Kinkaid had sent out his assets piecemeal, and Flatley's strike force had paid the price. About an hour later the destroyer *Porter* would add to the cost.

Flatley's remnants droned on, utterly shocked at the abrupt loss of half their escort and half their torpedo bombers—good friends suddenly gone. Just what kind of protection could a mere four-fighter escort provide in the face of a fully aroused Japanese CAP? They had just witnessed what a dozen Zeros could do in a split second. As they sweated the ugly possibilities, things got worse. The dispirited force flew into some cloud cover, and the three Dauntlesses disappeared.

As conditions deteriorated for Flatley's group, the sole Reaper 6 survivor, Ens. Willis "Chip" Reding, nursed his riddled plane back to *Enterprise*, where his shocked plane crew counted 192 holes. Lucky for Reding that those Wildcats were tough.

The four Avengers and Flatley's Reaper 1, now constrained by fuel concerns, abandoned their futile search for Japanese carriers. They located and focused instead on the cruiser *Suzuya*. Four torpedo drops and four maddening misses only deepened their frustration. Air Group 10's mission had resulted only in losses and had done next to nothing to degrade Japanese assets. It was time to return home. Normally that would spell relief, but this would be a journey filled with foreboding. When last seen, the group that had jumped them on the way out had been headed straight for Task Force 61.

Meanwhile, Gus Widhelm made a lucky turn and brought his strike group within sight of the Japanese carrier *Shōkaku*, whose radar screens had already outlined the incoming raid. Widhelm's fighter escort, led by Lt. Cdr. Mike Sanchez, had fallen behind and below the strike group, prompting a dozen opportunistic Zeros to intercept Widhelm's unprotected SBDs. As the Zeros worked over the Dauntlesses, Widhelm's radio circuit burned with eloquent cursing regarding that absent bastard Sanchez. Widhelm's and Lt. (jg) Phil Grant's Dauntlesses were shot down. Two others, Lt. (jg) Clayton Fisher and Lt. (jg) Ken White, both of VB-8, retired in distress. In all the confusion, the Avengers got separated.

Widhelm and his backseat man, ARM1C George D. Stokely, ditched, escaped their sinking aircraft, and got established in their gently bobbing life raft. They were well situated to observe what was about to visit *Shōkaku*. Five of Scouting 8's Dauntlesses penetrated the CAP, loosed their 1,000-pound bombs, and converted the fleet carrier to a burning junkyard. Though *Shōkaku* could still steam at thirty-one knots, further air operations were out of the question.

Hornet's second wave had missed Widhelm's turn. Their search for the carriers was in vain, so they returned to the Japanese cruisers they had spotted outbound. The unlucky heavy cruiser *Chikuma* bore the brunt of their attentions and was badly damaged in the attack.

Not long after that, Flatley's missing SBD pilots—Lt. (jg) George G. Estes Jr., Lt. (jg) Henry N. Ervin, and Lt. (jg) John F. Richey—managed to locate and attack the already suffering *Chikuma*. Two of their 1,000-pound bombs landed close aboard and opened a hole in her side. There was some satisfaction to be had in that.

If screaming frustration defined the *Enterprise* strike group's cockpits, it also applied to Swede and his yet-to-launch Reapers. Decidedly drained from the previous evening's debacle and scarce bunk time, Swede again led Reaper 7. But he and divisionmates Lt. Tex Harris, Lt. Stanley Ruehlow, and Ens. Hank Leder still sat on the deck. Swede was seething, utterly furious at this incomprehensible delay.

It had been announced that the Japanese were on their way, and everyone knew it. The only way to neutralize an incoming attack was to intercept with the advantages of altitude and sun at your back, preferably far from the carriers and friendly AA. "The in-bound strike will be overhead in moments," Swede thought, "and we're still just sitting here. What the hell is going on?"

Defending Task Force 61

The infuriating waiting continued. If yesterday they should never have taken off, today they could not get off soon enough. What fresh madness was Kinkaid up to now?

Certainly there were some issues with fighter direction. In what would prove to be a highly controversial decision, Kinkaid had selected Lt. Cdr. John H. Griffin as overall TF 61 fighter director officer (FDO). New to the theater, Griffin had replaced the experienced Lt. Cdr. Leonard J. "Ham" Dow, recently transferred to Halsey's staff. Griffin would be in charge of fighters from both carriers, thus making *Hornet*'s veteran FDO, Lt. Al Fleming, subordinate to him. Griffin had observed stationary fighter directors during the Battle of Britain and more recently had served as head of the Fighter Director School on Oahu. A respected theorist, Griffin had never actually directed fighters, and he had no experience in a dynamic carrier battle. He was too green in the theater to fully grasp the operational situation. By the end of a very long day he would have a lot to answer for.

For Swede at that moment, there was no fighter direction at all. "Outrageous! We just sat there and sat there. We couldn't get off. We knew they were coming. Nobody seemed to be in control. What's the delay? I was ready to get out of the plane, head up to flag plot to see what was going on."

Swede had seen enough command ineptitude at Coral Sea when he had flown that disastrous CAP in his Dauntless. And this morning the fighters, the true interceptors, sat impotently on deck as the Japanese attack headed right for them. Disadvantages were accumulating. They had anticipated an eight o'clock start to their CAP, but it was going on nine before a livid Swede finally lifted off. His job now was to dodge any Japanese Zero escorts and shoot down the torpedo-bearing Kates and dive-bombing Vals intent on destroying TF 61.

"We took off in heavy cloud, could hardly see the end of the deck. When we got off, we were given no instruction. I took off full throttle in a right turn up through the fog. Tex Harris was ahead of me and Stan Ruehlow was behind. The attackers were coming in."

FDO Griffin, meanwhile, in the interest of conserving fighter fuel, had stationed Wick and Whitey, among others, at ten thousand feet over Big E's task force. This positioning denied them any opportunity to meet the threat away from the task force and deprived them of the altitude advantage from which to attack. Adding to their predicament, the early-model CXAM radars of both carriers picked up bogies a mere forty-five miles out, altitude undetermined. Bewildered by the indecipherable radar information, Griffin further compromised his defenses and vectored a portion of his CAP on a fool's errand—an intercept of their own returning search planes. In fairness, radio chatter greatly hindered communication, but no one knew what to think or where to go when Griffin began directing his fighters using bearings relative to Big E's course. Clouds and combat maneuvering, of course, rendered Griffin's directions meaningless and generated rage and frustration among the pilots.

When it became clear that the Japanese had located Kinkaid's Task Force 61, and *Hornet* in particular, Wick, Whitey, and Swede's Reapers raced to aid the embattled carrier.[3] It was not long before Swede found action. "We climbed and climbed, flying on instruments, vectored toward *Hornet*, and at 12,000 feet I broke out of the fog, wing and wing with a Val dive-bomber."

Swede quickly set up a short high-side run and torched the last in line of seven *Zuikaku* carrier bombers. The surviving six continued on toward *Hornet*, where they contributed to a devastating coordinated attack.

As Wick positioned himself to shoot down the last of the attackers, he was shocked to discover his guns were not working. More than a few pilots had agonized over jammed guns that no effort to recharge, jinking to clear the jam, or eloquent cussing could solve. Here the problem was the protective Cosmoline that had not been completely cleared from the machine guns when the spare Wildcats were hastily brought into service. At four thousand feet, the stuff was freezing up the guns. Wick soon understood that he was limited to two guns, maybe. Beyond exasperating, it put him at a serious disadvantage.

Given the circumstances, Wick reversed his section arrangement and took Whitey's wing. Correctly vectored over to bogies this time, they caught up to a line of Vals pushing over. Whitey targeted the last—"He caught fire and blew up"—scoring the first of many aerial victories to come. While Wick's asymmetric gunfire skidded his Wildcat and ruined his accuracy, the absence of fully functioning guns did not rule out a contribution.

Whitey recalled Wick's courage. "We started back toward the ship and flew around a cloud into two Zeros right out in front of us. Well, Wickendoll, brave soul that he was, started after them and went on the attack! That's how we were. You couldn't hesitate in combat."[4]

Elsewhere, Swede, busy keeping an eye out for bogies around *Hornet*, noticed a Val breaking out of the mist. "He was probably looking for our carriers way down below, or looking for his group. He was confused. I cut in and shot that guy down."

At 9:12, the first bomb hit *Hornet*, closely followed by two more. One of the Val pilots, WO Sato Shigeyuki, was wounded by *Hornet*'s AA. Swede watched him circle wide before making his famously photographed suicidal plunge into *Hornet*'s stack. For Robbie, huddled in Scouting 8's ready room, Sato's bomb suddenly made the war intensely real.

Five minutes later, Kates put two torpedoes into *Hornet*, one amidships and one in the engineering spaces, and the battered carrier drifted to a halt. The Japanese attackers departed, having pulled off a superb coordinated attack. Their success had cost them five Zeros, seventeen Vals, and sixteen Kates. During the shoulder-sagging lull before the Japanese follow-on raid appeared, another of war's tragic ironies unfolded.

Torpedo 10 pilot Dick Batten, mauled when Zeros ambushed Flatley's strike force, had somehow gotten his doomed Avenger back to the embattled

TF 61. Owing to shot-up hydraulics he could not release his torpedo before ditching. Batten shut his torpedo bomb bay doors and carefully set his plane onto the water. He and his crew scrambled out of their sinking plane, greatly relieved to watch the destroyer *Porter* now slowing to a stop beside them. Up in the air, one of Swede's buddies, Lt. Dave Pollock Jr., dispatched one of the first-wave Vals. During a pause in the action Dave spied an erratic torpedo circling right for *Porter*, now fully stopped to pick up Batten and his crew.

Whitey watched in amazement as Pollack "peeled off, dove down through a lot of heavy AA, and then zapped away at the torpedo, trying to set the thing off." Pollock's efforts were vain heroics; the torpedo slammed into the Good Samaritan tin can amidships. By horrific irony, that torpedo was Dick Batten's Mark XIII, which had somehow released when he ditched and then circled around to *Porter*. Worse, Batten's torpedo did something that a shocking percentage of American torpedoes did not: it detonated, killing eleven and mortally wounding four more. Gene Burns was watching. "There's a fountain just as the torpedo hits. Then a tremendous puff of smoke, like a railway engine blowing off a smoke cloud."[5]

Blood pressures spiked at the thought of a Japanese submarine operating around the fleet. This should have been a short-lived alarm. Pacific veterans knew, and recent experience had amply demonstrated, that Imperial Japanese Navy Long Lance 24-inch torpedoes did not run in circles; they generally ran straight and true and detonated as designed.

Even though no one yet knew the source of that torpedo, Batten and his crew were less-than-warmly welcomed on the stricken destroyer.[6] Stopping to rescue anybody exponentially magnified a destroyer's vulnerability. Because Kinkaid could not spare an escort for the wounded ship, Batten, his crew, and many others were quickly transferred to the destroyer USS *Shaw* (DD 373), which was then assigned the unhappy task of sinking the now derelict *Porter*. Destroyer commanders learned from this experience to simply slow down as they recovered drenched and grateful pilots.

Robbie's Ordeal

Swede's introduction into the terrors of combat had been progressive, starting with the early raids on weakly defended Japanese outposts on up to the Coral Sea dogfight. Robbie Robinson's entry allowed for none of that. Early that morning he had concluded an uneventful three-hour search in dark skies, then landed on board *Hornet*. He hadn't liked it, but he and Lt. Bill Martin among others had orders to leave their Dauntlesses where they landed to replenish *Hornet*'s combat-depleted dive-bomber inventory.[7] Later that day Robbie and the other delivery pilots would be ferried back to *Enterprise*.

As soon as he had heard the plans for *Hornet*'s strike, Robbie pleaded with Scouting 8's skipper, Gus Widhelm, for a role in the attack. Widhelm was ready to acquiesce when Bill Martin overrode the proceedings and informed Robbie they were not going up. Instead, Robbie's first day of battle was spent caged inside *Hornet* enduring incessant, terrifying attacks throughout an impossibly long day.

While Swede dispatched two Vals overhead, a frustrated Robbie was hunkered down with the *Hornet* pilots in their ready room. As *Hornet* banked to evade bomb threats, the men sat tensed for action but powerless to do anything. The incredible noise was shocking; it was easy to be scared. Robbie's thoughts were turning to religion when, overhead, Swede watched Sato crash his stricken dive-bomber onto *Hornet*. The Val's wing tore off the signal halyards, and the rest of the plane struck part of the stack and bounced off the island in flames. The wreckage penetrated the flight deck and continued on down through to the ready room. Sato's dud bomb ended up spinning at Robbie's feet.

The crash blew a huge hole in the deck in front of them and the doors off the nearby ready ammunition room. Flaming gas and debris threatened to set off a far greater explosion. A Scouting 8 pilot opened a door only to confront dense black smoke. Panic flooded the room. Taking charge, Robbie and Lt. (jg) Jack Finrow grabbed flashlights, pounded men on their shoulders to get their attention, and hollered, "Gangway, gangway, we're getting out of here, follow us." The group split up. Headed to where the smoke seemed thinner, Jack led about six of them down to the hanger deck, where they encountered bodies scattered everywhere. Robbie conducted his group upward through the blinding smoke to the embattled flight deck, where, in the piercing sunlight, they helped pass ammunition.[8]

"I Was Scared as Hell at Times"

By 9:30 a.m. the *Shōkaku* and *Zuikaku* first-wave attackers were done with *Hornet*. As they withdrew, *Hornet* crewmen rigged a tarp on the flight deck forward to shade an improvised aid station. There, Robbie, miraculously unhurt, injected morphine into a stream of wounded men.

A short thirty minutes later the Japanese follow-on strike force found *Enterprise* no longer concealed by rain squalls. FDO Griffin struggled to sort bogies from friendlies on his crowded radar screen and failed to marshal an intercept. Thus, Seki's Vals proceeded with little to no Wildcat interference and quickly scored two bomb hits along with several damaging near misses. The first hit froze the forward elevator in the up position. The second blew the midships elevator down and reduced the hangar deck to a bloody shambles. The near misses opened underwater seams and shivered the entire ship. Seki's highly effective strike cost him his life.

Gene Burns depicted the scene in his memoir:

> Here come the Japs. Our AA and 5-inchers drown out everything, but not your fear. I flatten out on the steel deck. God, I'm scared. Admiral Kinkaid is the only man up.
>
> Japs are rocking out of the sky like apples. The ship is gyrating, twisting and bending to avoid. I get up to see the attack. For the first time, I'm uncontrollably angry at the Japs. Maybe it is because I am so damn scared. The ship rocks as if from an earthquake. We're hit! I watch a plane waddle 30 feet over the side with the heavy shakes. We must be hit hard. Smoke rolls out of the deck. Near misses are falling all around us. A column of water is higher than the signal bridge. Tons of water.[9]

LSO Robin Lindsey and his assistant Jim Daniels felt personally targeted as the bombs hurtled down at them. A pair of those near misses threw both of them into a water-filled gun tub just under and aft of the LSO platform.

Daniels recalled that "the two bombs exploded some thirty to fifty yards aft, lifting E's stern and her four screws clear of the water, shaking her like a wet puppy. It seemed like I spent an hour face down in that gun tub. Dive-bomber near misses by the Vals splashed tons of water onto the flight deck and into the after port gun tubs some sixty-five feet above the water line. Lindsey and I were covered with water."[10]

Through all this, Gene Burns was present on the bridge. Then the bombing stopped. During the lull, and knowing another attack was incoming, Kinkaid told Burns, "You're the most favored civilian alive. You're seeing the greatest carrier duel of history. Perhaps it will never happen again."[11] Both men were fortunate to have survived that bombing, and there was more to come.

The Japanese strike on *Hornet* provided a tutorial on how to pull off a coordinated attack. Fortunately for Kinkaid, the follow-on attack on *Enterprise* looked more like the Americans' piecemeal approach. Lt. Imajuku Shigeichiro's sixteen *Zuikaku* torpedo-bearing Kates fatefully arrived twenty minutes behind the Vals.

As the Japanese attack shaped up, Swede's Reaper mate Hank Leder took notice, announced, "Enemy aircraft nine o'clock low," and pointed to a formation of Kates at 11,000 feet headed for *Enterprise*. With a three-thousand-foot altitude advantage, Swede promptly recognized the ideal fighter attack situation. As the Kates split to attack *Enterprise* from each bow, Swede's Reaper 7 and Dave Pollock's Reaper 2 dove in for the intercept. "There were maybe a dozen, flying in Vs of three in close formation. It was easy to see them; they had just broken out of some cloud and were ready to enter a big cloud over the *Enterprise*. That's when we followed them, closed on them."

Swede and Leder pressed their attack amid a shower of brass casings from their guns. Leder's targeted Kate exploded. Swede followed the others, a tight, wingtip-to-wingtip V of three Kates with a fourth on their left, into a cloudbank.[12]

"We had practiced with Flatley for months about just how to manage a situation like this one. We had to control our dive speed, join their formation at close range, and shoot them down. There was no room to maneuver. In the fog, I'm supposed to shoot down four Kates. I was scared as hell at times. But I got right under them; what we learned to do."

To conserve ammunition Swede cut out his outboard guns. "So I was firing with four guns and they were very adequate. By putting the pipper on the tail or wing stub, one short blast—we were using armor-piercing, tracers, and incendiary shells—the thing would burn right away. Their tanks were not protected, so they would catch on fire, and once on fire you could go on to the next plane."[13]

Swede continued, "I'm fifty feet behind four of them in heavy fog. I got under their tails to avoid the rear-seat gunners. First, I went after the single Kate on the left. I blew him apart and he pitched forward. I expected the V to break, but they didn't. Then I went after the number two man; he pitched forward and blew up. I shifted to the leader, again careful to keep below him in order to stay out of the gunner's field of fire. When I hit him he pitched up and back, and I thought his wing was going to hit me. The last slowed down, and I flamed him. My reactions were automatic. The whole thing was over in ten seconds." Meanwhile, Dave Pollack and Lt. Bob Holland of VF-72 engaged the remaining Kates and downed one; the rest jettisoned their torpedoes and fled. The battle was far from over, however; the other half of Imajuku's force was lined up to attack from starboard.

Six Japanese bombers had fallen to Swede's guns so far that morning. Increasingly concerned with his dwindling ammunition and fuel, Swede broke into the clear and took a quick look around. Off to his right, *Enterprise* was twisting, turning, fighting off the Kates now coming in on the starboard bow. As he turned to see if *Enterprise* could take him on board, out of the cloud from the left, another Kate very nearly collided with him.

"His wing was practically in my prop. I could see the pilot and his two crewmen. I followed him toward the *Enterprise* and turned in behind him, again under the tail. I fired a burst and set him on fire. I had my pipper on his wing root where the fuel tank sits, but he didn't blow and continued heading for the *Enterprise*. I considered cutting off his tail with my prop if he got in position to drop his torpedo. I kept figuring he'd release his torpedo as he got lower over the water, but he never did. Finally, he caught a wingtip in the water and cartwheeled."

His fuel and ammo situation now near critical, Swede turned off to the left to avoid the outgoing AA. That's when another Kate "flew over the top of me real close. Why hadn't I been looking? I almost had heart failure. All he had to do was drop down and fire his forward machine guns and I was a goner. Instead, I'm on his tail, and he's climbing. The *South Dakota* was gonna open fire. I'll see if I have anything left to get this guy. I switched on all my guns, and I had a few rounds. I set him on fire. I'm sure he's gonna dive onto the *South Dakota*, but she and AA cruiser *San Juan* began firing, putting up a withering fire. You could walk on the smoke from the AA.

"I tore some pieces off that Kate, and he caught fire but didn't explode. He never faltered, didn't go down. He was losing altitude, but he had to be alive because he corrected his dive very noticeably. At this point, with my ammo gone, I meant to cut off his tail with my prop as we had discussed in our training. As I closed, I flew into the fire stream. My plane was full of smoke. Jesus, you talk about a blast, a plane like that with a whole stream of fire blowing back. I was within fifty feet and I got knocked to the right. Turned away, hell, it just knocked me away from the plane. I figured, 'Swede, that was a foolish move; you've just put yourself down.'"

The doomed Kate pilot, S1C Takei Kiyomi, grasped that he was flying too fast to drop his torpedo. "He lined up on the *South Dakota*," Swede continued, "but at the last second, deliberately steepened his dive to crash the destroyer *Smith*."

This abrupt sequence misled observers and after-action board members evaluating victories. They were convinced that Swede had peeled away to avoid the antiaircraft fire; the last Kate was listed as probable. Dave Pollock, in his after-action report, corroborated Swede's version, noting that "the *Smith* was the victim of a Jap suicide dive after being set aflame by Lieutenant Vejtasa."[14]

That flaming Kate was a big plane headed for a small ship. "After a fiery crash onto the *Smith*'s forecastle," Swede recalled, "the wrecked plane rolled off the side into the sea, but the torpedo remained, rolling around in the flaming aftermath. The torpedo cooked off and blew the hell out of everything."

Gene Burns witnessed the disaster from *Enterprise*. "Suddenly a flaming Jap plane crashes into the destroyer USS *Smith*, about 150 feet off the port side. Tremendous fires burn higher than the ship. Her guns keep firing."[15]

Despite an explosion that devastated both forward gun turrets and killed fifty-seven of her crew, *Smith*'s engineers kept the ship going. Skipper Lt. Cdr. Hunter Wood Jr. left an untenable bridge to con the ship from aft. From there, he steered her into the massive, foaming wake of *South Dakota*, which washed most of the gas and fire into the sea. *Smith* resumed her station and continued her antiaircraft fire mission, drawing Swede's utmost admiration.

"That destroyer crew was magnificent. The CO, what kind of medal did he get, saving a ship like that?" Swede wondered. So did many others. In recognition of his composure under duress, Lieutenant Commander Wood was awarded a Navy Cross for his skill, presence of mind, and inspiring example of command leadership.

Swede anguished over the incident. Did those last few rounds only wound the pilot? Could better shooting have prevented the loss of those fifty-seven sailors? Perhaps, but eight downed with no ammo replenishment showcased exemplary gunnery. For that last Kate's pilot and crew, as well as those on board *Smith*, Swede's "probable" was a certainty.[16]

While Swede was eviscerating the Kate formation, escorting Zeros shot down Whitey's friend Gordon Barnes. He ditched near the carrier and was bobbing in the water beside his yet-to-sink Wildcat. Whitey orbited over his buddy, hoping to ensure his recovery by the approaching destroyer *Maury*.

Elsewhere, the battle raged on as *Zuikaku*'s surviving Kates pressed their attacks. LSOs Daniels and Lindsey took matters into their own hands. Without hesitation, both jumped into the backs of nearby SBDs and fired twin .30s at the attackers. Daniels vividly recalled, "The torpedo attack developed, some were shot down in their run in, but one came in from dead astern. Our twin .30s made a hell of a racket, but we could see our tracers hitting him and as he pulled up just yards short of the stern he still had his torpedo. Tracers were all over him, and as he released, his under carriage was right in front of our guns in a no deflection shot. He lost his torpedo as he did a slow wingover and crashed into the water."[17]

Over the CAP frequency Swede overheard Flatley's desperation to land his shot-up strike group. Returning *Hornet* strike pilots, now homeless, also sought an operational deck. Fortunately for the *Hornet* pilots returning from their strike, Big E's YE-ZB homing device, so notoriously silent the previous evening, worked to perfection.

By this point in the battle many of the Reapers had expended all their ammunition and were critically low on fuel. While ammo exhaustion could be managed by dodging fights, fuel gauges bouncing on empty could mean lost Wildcats. Swede spoke for most, if not all, when he anxiously requested permission to land. His CAP was ordered to pancake—to land as quickly as possible—in the midst of the attack. As he waited his turn to come on board, Swede made mental notes on what he had observed of some of his squadronmates. And he wondered, who was the Wildcat pilot he had just watched bail out and splash into the water twelve miles northwest of Big E?

Once again, landing on board *Enterprise* required focus, skill, and patience. Swede and his fellow Reapers had eliminated the threat from portside, which allowed Captain Hardison to focus on the developing threat from starboard. He responded by artfully combing a spray of torpedoes. The twisting and turning carrier, however, meant fuel-exhausted planes had to be waved off, resulting in several ditchings. When things calmed down shortly after 11 a.m., Swede landed his Wildcat on a seriously damaged Reaper base.

While Swede got replenished, Whitey, still orbiting the downed Barnes, heard air boss Crommelin sternly order him to pancake—*now*. Reluctantly he banked away to join the last of an anxious bunch of CAP pilots waiting for Lindsey to guide them in. A dynamically plunging deck complicated by a mere three hundred feet of landing space provided a high-stakes challenge for both pilots and LSO. Once on board, bomb holes, a downed barrier, and the huge square cavity near the island formed by the blown-down number two elevator made spotting aircraft a nightmare for the air boss and his sweating plane handlers.

When Whitey finally got in the groove, he marveled at Robin Lindsey's skill in communicating with pilots. "Robin waved me off as the *Enterprise* dodged a spray of torpedoes. Minutes later as I was setting up in a left-hand pattern, the *Enterprise* leaned away in a hard right turn. There were no barricades, and he brought me in easy. Robin was the best."

Apparently Whitey's well-intentioned lingering over Barnes had delayed the CAP replenishment. Ensign Feightner was immediately directed to flag plot, where Admiral Kinkaid rudely condemned his Good Samaritan efforts.

"Kinkaid really laid into me. He marched back and forth for what seemed like ten minutes while he raved, 'Who do you think you are? You endangered everybody.' He told me how bad I was; he went mad for those minutes." The admiral finally showed Whitey the door and turned his attention to more urgent matters at hand.

Relieved to distance himself from Kinkaid's madness, Whitey's thoughts turned to what might have become of Barnes. The destroyer *Maury* had maneuvered in to pick him up, but incoming Kates had forced her to sheer away.[18]

Whitey headed below to the hangar deck, where he confronted the shocking destruction wrought by the second bomb hit. "Water defiled with blood, oil, and bodies floating around sloshed halfway up to my knees. It was a terrible mess. There was confusion on the ship. More attacks were coming, and I could hear shooting. I couldn't wait to get aloft. I didn't want to be aboard ship when it blew up."

Back up on the flight deck Whitey was told, "Here's your plane assignment. Go man this aircraft now! We've got to get some off the deck because others are in the air waiting to recover. The *Hornet*'s going down, and all of its aircraft are coming here."

Enterprise's radar had been perplexing enough earlier; now, the bombs jarring the ship knocked the bedspring antenna out of alignment. Its consequent failure to rotate created a huge defensive blind spot. As Swede made his way across the slanting deck toward his plane, he couldn't help but notice radar officer Lt. Brad Williams high above him lashed to the radar mast, trying to get it going again. Not quite twenty minutes later, it was back in business in time to reveal the incoming *Junyō* attackers just twenty miles out. Brad was still strapped to the mast when it resumed rotating and was treated to a rigorous merry-go-round ordeal atop a wildly gyrating perch as *Enterprise* dodged *Junyō*'s bombers. Finally, above the din of the attack, someone heard his pleas for help. The mast slowed to a halt, and Brad scrambled down to safety, an ignominious finale to a conspicuously heroic performance.

The first three of eight *Junyō* bombers to attack *Enterprise* missed and were shot down. The leader of the next three produced a damaging near miss that opened seams and destroyed the mechanism controlling the forward elevator. The next four bombers all missed. Nine of the *Junyō* dive-bombers got separated in the clouds, lost contact with *Enterprise*, and instead inflicted bomb hits on the battleship *South Dakota* and antiaircraft cruiser *San Juan*. With that, the surviving attackers set course for home.

His plane refueled and rearmed, Whitey powered back up for his second CAP and found immediate action dealing with the retreating *Junyō* attackers. "It was a wild time! We were vastly outnumbered. That's when I engaged a Zero. He began a loop, but I had been taught, rather than try to follow him, to respond with a hard right-hand turn, and sure enough, when he came down out of his loop, there I was, right on his tail. I shot him down. Later on we chased some Kates. Swede saw one go in; it might have been mine. There were planes in every direction; it was a nightmare."

During his replenishment, Swede found that the extensive bomb damage made even getting a drink of water a problem. Fresh water, so essential in the tropical heat, was prioritized for steam production. "In search of water I went forward and then came back through the hangar deck, which was nearly hip-deep in water, oil, bodies, and blood. As I made my way toward the flight deck, one of our docs, Chief Williams, was wounded. He grabbed me—he just wanted to talk—but I had to get back up in the air."

CHAPTER 11

—

A Battle Concluded

little past 11 a.m. the diminished wave of attackers receded into the horizon; suddenly there was nothing to shoot at. As the firing died away, exhausted gunners sagged at their stations. At least for the time being, the phenomenal noise, chaos, and intensity were abruptly gone. Swede, meanwhile, was back up leading this latest CAP, and once again he was fuming. Mirroring yesterday's Goose Chase, Swede did not know who was up with him. Worse, one of his divisions was short a plane, leaving him with seven fighters, not the eight he expected and felt he needed.

Down on the LSO platform, just short of 11 a.m. Robin Lindsey had relieved a tired Jim Daniels, who for the past hour and a half had supervised the landing of more than sixty planes, some badly shot up. Robin took up his paddles to begin the physically demanding and emotionally taxing business of landing a stream of battered, weary, and fuel-deprived fighter and bomber pilots.

The circumstances were anything but normal. Planes were spotted everywhere on deck, one elevator was gone, another elevator was out of service, the CAP fighters needed gas and ammunition, the survivors of the morning's strike were dribbling back in, and *Hornet*'s orphaned aircraft needed a home. Preserving the remainder of Kinkaid's aircraft inventory would demand the best of everyone.

To help make room on the congested flight deck, replenished SBDs had been ordered off to Espiritu Santo. But observers up on Vulture's Row were still hard-pressed to spot any Douglas-fir planking beneath the fighters and bombers parked everywhere. Plane handlers hustled airplanes around the elevator pit, squeezing as many forward as possible, an undertaking further complicated by the forward elevator being stuck in the up position. Those overseeing the proceedings beneath them quickly grasped their enormous vulnerability. A single plane overshooting a cable could provoke a firestorm.

No novice to the business, Lindsey had served as *Enterprise*'s LSO during and since the Battle of Midway. Following the Battle of the Eastern Solomons in August, a letter of commendation testified to Lindsey's caliber:

> As Landing Signal Officer of the USS *Enterprise*, Lieutenant Lindsey took station in the vicinity of the after port 20-mm battery and during the dive-bombing attack opened fire on enemy aircraft with his .45-caliber automatic pistol. Immediately after the bomb struck the starboard after gun gallery, he manned a fire hose and led it to the scene of the fire and assisted materially in extinguishing a very stubborn conflagration. He is considered to deserve special commendation for his gallant and courageous action under fire and his coolness and presence of mind under very dangerous circumstances. The magnificent example set by him was in keeping with the best traditions of the Naval Service.

Swede tried to sum up the qualities that made Lindsey so good. "I suppose the technique, the judgment. Everything was so easy for the guy. It was all right there, what had to be done, handling the pilot, but he was the same way talking with pilots. He got right to the point, never argued with anybody, nothing to argue about, really. He was a genius. He started out in the squadron; it just fell on him that he became squadron LSO."

Just now Lindsey was the right man in the right place, performing like the virtuoso conductor he was. As the deck grew even more crowded with planes, a nervous bridge instructed Lindsey to "put planes in the water." Scuttlebutt had it that continuing to land planes could earn Lindsey a court-martial.

Following last night's Goose Chase, Air Boss Crommelin had promised his shaken pilots, "Tomorrow if you get back to the ship and into the groove, we'll get you aboard." Now, a little past noon, watching Lindsey work to make good on that promise to returning pilots, "Uncle John" recognized "the kid was hot." Daniels later wrote, "Crommelin ordered the 'red flag,' a signal we had a fouled deck and to land no more airplanes, but the ship did not turn out of the wind."[1]

Wisely, Kinkaid chose not to interfere.

As deck space grew increasingly scarce, Daniels made his famous bet with Robin.

> Robin said that he would bring as many more in as he safely could and to hell with the red flag, he would put them all on number 1 wire. This is when I bet him a dime on every airplane that caught the number 1 wire. He played those pilots like a master, slowing them down, easing the tensions by signaling a roger—"everything OK"—then bringing them in slowly, carefully—no wave-offs allowed, until he got everyone aboard. I owed him a dollar for those last 10 aircraft that caught the number 1 wire.[2]

Wildcat pilot Lt. (jg) Jim Billo wasn't so lucky. Eyes glued to his fuel gauge, he endured two frustrating wave-offs before fuel starvation dictated a full-power ditching. It would be days before his sobered squadronmates learned that USS *Preston* recovered him the following afternoon.

Swede provided the finale. "I was the last to land. We had a lot of inexperienced new guys, and I figured it was best to let them in first. I gave the lead to my wingman. I saw how crowded the deck had become, and thought I might have to land on the water. I had complete confidence in Robin and in my ability to control my plane. I didn't realize how little room there was until I came around. There were planes in front and on both sides. But Lindsey brought me in slow and low. Somehow I missed the round-down and hooked that number one lifeline; my plane was chocked in place. At that point, the place went crazy. Everyone—pilots, crew, the whole ship—waved and hollered at what Lindsey had just pulled off."

Lindsey had doubled down on Crommelin's promise to get everyone back on board. With the aircraft Lindsey had secured, the Marines' sacrifices had been upheld. And going forward, those planes would help tip the balance in the continuing struggle for Guadalcanal. In Swede's considered opinion, "Robin Lindsey was the real hero of Santa Cruz."

Hornet's **Desperation**

As the *Junyō* remnants at last faded into the horizon and Lindsey displayed his remarkable skills, the Japanese began organizing yet another strike. Determined to finish off the crippled *Hornet* and, equally important, to find and destroy *Enterprise*, they sent off their exhausted surviving pilots on a series of afternoon raids.

Swede, again flying CAP, maintained a sharp lookout. "We knew there'd be more attacks."

Indeed there were. But misdirection led the latest Japanese raid past an anxious *Enterprise* and back to the ill-fated *Hornet*.

Just as Swede had feared, "About forty-five minutes into the flight, less than an hour, we saw another attack come in. It was a large group, twelve or more Kates, coming as horizontal bombers. I begged the fighter director for permission to attack.

" 'Negative, hold your position.'

"We could see them; we could have overtaken them.

" 'Can I detach three CAP F4Fs for an interception?'

" 'Request denied. Remain on station.'

"I was sick. The cruiser *Northampton*, which was towing *Hornet*, cut loose, leaving the carrier dead in the water. The whole group swept over the *Hornet*, bent left, and disappeared. I was so mad at the control people."[3] As a thoroughly vexed Swede looked on, further bomb and torpedo hits sealed *Hornet*'s fate.

The failure of Swede's CAP to intercept caused a lot of resentment among the *Hornet* pilots, who had no way of knowing that Swede had been directly ordered to keep station over *Enterprise*. In their eyes Swede had simply forsaken their ship. Even more alarming to Task Force 17, for *Enterprise* to continue her desperate air operations, she had to steam into southeast winds, a course that continued to widen the distance between the carriers. To those on board *Hornet* and to her aircrews currently on board *Enterprise*, the expanding distance had the feel of full-on desertion. Behind their bitterness lay some truth. Hours earlier, at 11:35, with the punishing *Junyō* raid just finished, Kinkaid had decided he could tolerate no further risk to the U.S. Navy's last operational carrier in the Pacific and informed Halsey of his intent to retreat. *Hornet* would be left to fend for herself.

On board the powerless *Hornet*, Robbie and his buddy Jack Finrow eventually rendezvoused on the port bow and observed the cruiser *Northampton*'s repeated attempts to tow their listing, wallowing carrier out of harm's way. The appearance of a "Lone Ranger" Val ended the first attempt, and on the second attempt the steel cable parted. A larger cable was made fast, but the incoming Japanese attack Swede had begged to challenge forced *Northampton* to cut away.

As yet another attack unfolded, an armor-piercing bomb sliced through the flight deck not fifteen feet away from Robbie. Its delayed fuse allowed it to continue through the forecastle and through the side of the ship before detonating on the water. Shrapnel blew back up through the forecastle, wiping out two pods of 40-mm guns. Had it not been for that delayed fuse, Robbie would have been killed. That was the day's second near-miss bomb with Robbie's name on it. Black humor would insist that it's not the one with your name on it; it's the one that says "to whom it may concern."

Some of *Hornet*'s wounded along with air group personnel including Robbie and Jack transferred to the destroyer USS *Russell* (DD 414). The two able-bodied pilots carefully worked down rope ladders, slipped into the calm, warm water, and made the easy swim to the single-stacked destroyer *Russell*, whose decks were soon packed with shocked survivors. There was literally no room to move. Locked in place, men needing to pee did so in their pants. Others made it to the destroyer *Hughes*, which was assisting in the recovery. Robbie eventually returned to Bombing 10 with a serious appreciation for what *Hornet*'s survivors endured.

That last raid put to rest any hope for *Hornet*'s survival. By midafternoon she had absorbed two fiery plane crashes on top of numerous bomb and torpedo hits and was listing at 18 degrees. Fearful she would capsize, Captain Mason ordered everyone up from below and gunnery-control personnel off the island. With nothing more he or anyone else could do to save *Hornet*, it was time to abandon ship.

The destroyers *Mustin* and *Anderson* were assigned the odious task of putting *Hornet* beneath the waves. But multiple torpedo shots aimed at doing so included misses and duds, and those that did detonate were ineffective. *Hornet*'s refusal to succumb to this uncontested attack had to have American torpedo pilots wondering if their sacrificial service was not simply decoy work for the proven dive-bombers. An additional four hundred 5-inch shells still failed to sink the furiously burning derelict. The Japanese battle fleet was fast approaching; it was time to leave.

With the last CAP back on board a crowded, bloodied *Enterprise,* Kinkaid's battered Task Force 61, accompanied by the now-purposeless Task Force 17 screening vessels, retired at flank speed. Further investigation revealed that the damage to *Enterprise* was far more serious than the obvious problem with the elevators. In his next day's dispatch to Halsey, Kinkaid detailed the larger picture. The forward gyro was out, and there were fragment holes in her sides. Numbers three and four bomb elevators were out, as were the 5-inch ammunition hoists, seriously compromising both offensive and defensive operations. Further, the forward fifty feet in the hangar deck bulged, three radio transmitters were out, degaussing cables had been cut, and the crew had suffered thirty or more dead and twice that many wounded. Both *Enterprise* and the Pacific war plan were in serious trouble.

VF-10 pilot and later first Blue Angel Butch Voris described the inglorious retreat as "hauling ass."[4] The fact that *Enterprise* at full speed could still produce a rooster tail—a high wake—was indeed a blessing, perhaps the single measure of victory. In the aftermath of a confusing battle, both FDO Griffin and Admiral Kinkaid had a lot to answer for. Griffin took the heat from frustrated and angry pilots. To his superiors, Kinkaid wrote serials worded to obscure or whitewash his leadership failures.

Just Rewards

Meanwhile, an admiring *Enterprise* crew collectively wondered what should be done to acknowledge Robin Lindsey's remarkable accomplishment. LSOs were not typically awarded medals for paddle heroics. With a grateful crew roaring its approval, John Crommelin presented Robin with the torn and bullet-holed *Enterprise* battle flag.

It was a grand gesture, but Lindsey had another reward in mind. He had taken his turn at LSO duty, and now he publicly informed his audience, "I want to get back in the fighter business."

Swede chuckled at the memory. "Everybody, I mean everybody, looked up. 'What do you mean fighter business?'

"'I want to get back. Let somebody else have the job.'

"It wasn't a minute before the whole air group rose up. 'No! Lindsey is *not* gonna get a change of duty.' Lindsey didn't have a chance."

More to the point, what officer in his right mind could justify removing Lindsey's exquisite expertise from that LSO platform? In the event, Captain Hardison rightly recommended Robin for a Silver Star. A fine honor indeed, but nothing would ever trump the *Enterprise* battle flag.

Aftermath

Back in the ready rooms, surviving pilots and aircrews gaped at the vacant seats. Combat victories and personal survival could not assuage the sadness and grief of losing close friends. In a witch's brew of emotions, victorious pilots had to come to terms with having seen their guns and bombs chew Japanese men and their planes into pieces. Downing enemy aircraft made for good copy, but there was no concealing the business of legalized murder. Pilots had seen the faces of those they had killed, witnessed the frantic head swiveling of their doomed victims, observed men engulfed in cockpit flames or blown out of planes. Searing imagery. And every man knew that such a fatal outcome could just as well have been reversed. The previous night Kinkaid's Goose Chase and abandonment had sabotaged morale. This night, tormented survivors confronted grief, loss, and the undisguised brutality of killing. These were not trivial matters.

As Swede and his squadronmates counted and mourned their losses, the Japanese closed on and boarded *Hornet*'s burning hulk. Shortly after 1 a.m., Japanese commanders acknowledged the wisdom of Captain Mason's order to abandon ship. The destroyers *Makigumo* and *Akigumo* each fired two Long-Lance torpedoes, which provided the coup de grâce. This was a godsend for the Americans. *Hornet*'s loss was tragic enough; her capture and subsequent use against American forces was unthinkable.

The strategic value of the Battle of Santa Cruz could be measured by what did not happen. Japanese battleships and cruisers did not bombard the Marines on Guadalcanal. Nor did they reinforce their beleaguered army for the "Last Battle of Henderson Field." For their part, the Marines had broken up the Japanese army's uncoordinated, storm-lashed jungle attack. Three weeks later the Japanese would mount another offensive to secure the "unsinkable carrier." For the present, the Japanese October offensive had been dismantled.

In his position as CAG, Dick Gaines wrote a commendation for Air Group 10. It led off with an enclosure from Captain Hardison, who expressed his "admiration and appreciation of your magnificent performance of duty in the action. Your courage and determination were unbounded. I am proud of you."

Gaines followed up with, "Well done. Our first job has been accomplished with the morale we expected we would have. We were well trained for even greater success had we been given an ideal set-up or, at least a fully coordinated group action. Lessons were learned—we shall profit by them. The unfortunate phases and errors we must take as men."

Swede attended to the more practical. Regarding Dave Pollock's heroic attempt to detonate the renegade torpedo headed for *Porter*, Swede took his buddy to task over what he had observed. "What were you thinking, Dave? No one else has been successful in detonating a torpedo by strafing. We could have lost your plane, or you, for that matter, to friendly fire." And he brought up the matter of Dave's fruitless long-range firing in pursuit of a Kate. "Close on those Kates, Dave. You could have had him."

Was the battle over? Though no one was quite sure of it yet, the shooting part was in fact finished. *Zuikaku*'s air group had been gutted. Admiral Nagumo might have combined *Shōkaku*'s exhausted survivors with *Junyō*'s remnants to fling a last-ditch strike at the Americans in full flight. Had they done so, "Admiral Nagumo could have done us in at Santa Cruz," Swede acknowledged. "All he had to do was launch a strike. We'd have been completely out of business." That outcome, however, was not to be; both sides had shot their respective bolts.

On a day seemingly without end, *Enterprise* put Swede up again for a final, uneventful CAP. By half past five it was time to bring them in. For a bloodied Air Group 10, the curtain had finally closed on the Battle of Santa Cruz.

CHAPTER 12

———

What Does Victory Look Like?

Historians have viewed the Battle of Santa Cruz as a tactical victory for the Japanese and a strategic victory for the Americans. The Americans lost *Hornet*, *Enterprise* was barely operational, and the damage extended well beyond those two carriers. Batten's errant torpedo had sunk *Porter*; *South Dakota* took a bomb hit on a forward turret; *San Juan* absorbed damaging near misses and a hit; and *Smith* was devastated by the crash of Swede's last Kate and the subsequent topside torpedo explosion. Task Force 61's air group losses attributable to shoot-downs, ditching, and operational accidents totaled eighty carrier planes and included twenty-three officers and sixteen enlisted men.

Flatley's Grim Reapers paid a stiff price. With Miller lost on October 25 and eleven pilots unaccounted for, nearly a third of the squadron was killed or missing. John Leppla, Don Miller, Gordon Barnes, Gerald Davis, James Caldwell, and Lyman Fulton were lost. William Kane, Lt. (jg) Jim Billo, Lt. John Eckhardt, and Ens. Merl Long were listed as missing. The Reapers had no way of knowing that Al Mead and Dusty Rhodes had been captured.[1] Their relief that U.S. destroyers had recovered several others could not offset the startling emotional impact of all those empty ready room seats. Against those depressing losses, VF-10 claimed twenty-one aircraft downed (seven Vals, nine Kates, four Zeros, and one VSB) and an additional nineteen probables (ten Vals, eight Kates, and one VSB).

Beyond VF-10's losses, Swede's longtime friend Gus Widhelm and his gunner, ARM1C George Stokely, had also been shot down in the midst of the Japanese fleet. As far as Swede knew, Gus and Stokely were missing, most likely dead. Far from it. As a Japanese destroyer passed close by the pair, Gus, upholding his legendary persona, thumbed his nose at the Japanese crewmembers. Three days later, a Catalina patrol bomber found and rescued the two.

The Reapers were not alone in their grief. Torpedo 10 had begun this battle with fourteen TBFs. Not counting those from *Hornet*, they had been reduced to just two. Their skipper, Lt. Cdr. John A. Collett, had been killed with one of his crew, and it would be days before they knew anything definitive about the twelve crews eventually pulled from the water.

Just as *Hornet* had before her, *Enterprise* now bore the unsought and decidedly unwelcome distinction of singularity. For the next seven weeks she would be the sole operational American carrier in the Pacific.

Nor had things gone well for the Japanese. Lt. Birney Strong and Ens. Chuck Irvine had bombed the Japanese carrier *Zuiho* and put her out of action. And despite the failure of Air Group 10's morning raid, the *Hornet* strike group had pounded Pearl Harbor veteran *Shōkaku*, shutting down her air operations. She and the heavy cruiser *Chikuma* would require months of repairs.

The decimated Japanese air groups had lost 27 fighters, 41 bombers, 30 torpedo attack planes, and 1 recon plane, totaling 99 aircraft and 148 aircrew members. Statistically those losses amounted to a shocking 49 percent of torpedo bombers, 39 percent of dive-bombers, and 20 percent of fighters. The drain on experienced Japanese aircrews that had begun with 90 lost at Coral Sea had continued apace at the Battle of Midway (121 Japanese airmen) and the Eastern Solomons (with 110 more lost). Now, this so-called victory had come at a cost of 148 airmen. Of the 765 carrier pilots who had attacked Pearl Harbor, 409 now survived. Although it was not yet clear, the Japanese tactical victory was actually a stunning defeat.

Postmortem proclamations of victory aside, as *Zuikaku*, the bomb-damaged *Zuihō*, and the battered *Shōkaku* steamed toward the safety of home waters, shaken Japanese admirals had to confront the virtual destruction of their air groups. Early in the war, the number of carriers sunk had defined victories or defeats. While Japan had not lost a carrier at Santa Cruz, the stakes were changing. The Americans would soon appear with many more fast carrier task forces launching better-trained pilots flying vastly improved aircraft. In contrast to the U.S. Navy's policy of rotating aviators back home to train their replacements, Japan kept elite pilots fighting until they perished. These were qualitative losses Japan could not replace. Attrition now defined the bloody contest.

Back on board *Enterprise*, crewmembers scarcely recognized the place as home. Forty-four of the crew were dead. Horribly mangled bodies sloshed around the hangar deck, and scores of wounded required medical help. Quarters had been wrecked and were littered with charred bodies. In some places there were no corpses to remove, only fragments—a severed arm, bits of scalp, a finger, shreds of flesh. One corpse burned to a crisp remained in place for two days, accompanied by the nauseating stench of death. With the junior officers' quarters obliterated by bombs, men stumbled around searching for any place to sleep. Whitey wound up spending several nights under a 5-inch gun mount. Gene Burns, having lost everything, borrowed clothes, moved in with Jim Daniels, and slept on a mattress on the deck. Further complicating this depressing scenario, *Hornet*'s orphans, dazed by the loss of their home base, also wandered around in search of someplace to rest, bitching bitterly about the lack of *Enterprise* CAP cover during the last, uncontested Japanese raid.

If there were American victories, it seemed they were individual. Swede's unprecedented sortie had transformed him into an ace and more in a day, the significance of which was not lost on skipper Flatley. On the margin of Swede's flight log he noted, "Greatest single combat Fight Record in the history of Air Warfare. Congratulations. J H Flatley." In that flight log, under remarks for the mission, Swede noted, "'The Battle of Stewart Islands' shot down (5) Mitsubishi VT planes, (2) Aichi Dive bombers, (1) probable VT jap [*sic*]. Total: 7 confirmed, 1 probable."

Whatever the official tally, Swede knew he had downed eight. Added to that, the surviving Kates were observed jettisoning their torpedoes and scattering in retreat. Having eliminated at least six torpedoes from the Japanese attack formula, Swede's intercept likely spared a beat-up *Enterprise* mortal damage. Flatley spoke for many when he wrote in a letter, "I feel his [Swede's] action of Oct. 26 had much to do, was the primary factor in the *Enterprise* not being hit by a torpedo."[2]

Had *Enterprise* been sunk, an unsupported Cactus Air Force would have been completely exposed to attrition by nightly bombardments from

Japanese battleships and cruisers as well as persistent daytime attacks from Japanese land-based aircraft. It did not require a leap of imagination to envision the Japanese finally overrunning the Marines grimly holding Henderson Field. With Henderson finally wrested from the Marines, the Japanese would have been positioned to sever shipping lanes to Australia and, in the process, trash the Allied Pacific war plan. The strategic import of Swede's intercept went far beyond the number of planes he downed on October 26.

If Swede was a legend coming into the battle, his flying and leadership at Santa Cruz made it clear that his reputation was no fluke. Swede, the reliable one, had pulled off the miraculous on October 25 when he had brought the expendables home from their Goose Chase, and he had arguably saved *Enterprise* from destruction the next day by downing six Kates. Among the witnesses, there was little doubt that Swede had staved off a stunning defeat.

As for a victory at Santa Cruz, no admiral on either side dared to claim it. For most, personal survival was victory enough.

Flatley's Dilemma

As *Enterprise* and her exhausted crew steamed toward the safety of Espiritu Santo, Flatley began the difficult task of dissecting the battle at Santa Cruz. Whitey alluded to the challenges inherent in Flatley's undertaking: "Pilots were spread out all over the ship. The bombing had devastated officers' country, and it was many days before people came around asking for after-action details. There was no organized recapping of the Battle of Santa Cruz. Nobody officially questioned us pilots until a week or ten days later while we were on Espiritu Santo. Four young lieutenants (jg) flew up on a plane, called us in individually, and asked us what we remembered about the battle."

That disorganization notwithstanding, Flatley had a lot to work out. First, he had to explain the disastrous Goose Chase, something he did not personally experience. Then he had to reconstruct his own shattered escort mission. The loss of fellow Reapers and several of the bombers he was sent to protect weighed heavily on him. And it fell to him to write letters home attempting to console grieving next of kin. As he struggled to work through these issues, his broken foot continually reminded him of life's lesser challenges.

A mere five days after the battle, Flatley hobbled up to flag plot and submitted his twenty-nine-page report. This sharply focused, purposeful document critiqued Air Group 10's performance before and during the battle. It was filled with experience-driven, sensible ideas that might serve everyone concerned, from pilots on up to admirals. Flatley had produced a seminal document from which to understand and *mis*understand the Battle of Santa Cruz.[3] His pointed criticisms would not go unnoticed.

In one section of his report, Flatley, a man who did not take awarding medals lightly, made his recommendations. He recommended Flash Gordon, who downed two Kates, for a Distinguished Flying Cross. Credited with a Val and a Kate and a fruitless attempt to destroy Batten's torpedo, Dave Pollock was recommended for a Navy Cross. Flatley's recommendation for Swede's heroics, however, would generate a bizarre controversy.

Lieutenant Stanley W. Vejtasa, U.S. Navy, as leader of a flight of four fighters on combat patrol in defense of his carrier, the USS *Enterprise*, on the morning of October 26, 1942, in the vicinity of the Santa Cruz Islands, did, courageously, and with great skill and daring, and with complete disregard for his own safety, in the face of strong enemy opposition and often times in the midst of heavy AA fire from own ships, shoot down five enemy torpedo planes, two enemy dive bombers in a single flight, and one more probable enemy torpedo plane. His determined and aggressive action in attacking a squadron of eleven enemy torpedo planes resulted in the actual destruction of five and the probable loss of one.

Three more jettisoned their torpedoes at high altitude and fled, and it is felt that the other two were so demoralized that they were ineffective.

This act alone greatly contributed to the fact that his ship escaped serious damage and probable loss. In addition to the above enemy losses, other members of his flight shot down two enemy dive bombers.

Following his description of Swede's performance Flatley added "Comments by Squadron Commander":

The nature of the award to be made to Lieutenant Vejtasa is, of course, left to the discretion of the board of awards. It is felt that he deserves the highest award our country can give to a courageous and skilled pilot who in a single action, contributed so greatly to the outcome of a very important naval engagement, which might well determine the outcome of the Pacific war for naval supremacy. No other incident of a similar nature has been recounted by any warring nation to date in the case of a fighter pilot.[4]

Was Swede awarded a Medal of Honor? He was not. What happened? Skipper Flatley had addressed his full report, which included the Medal of Honor recommendation, to Captain Hardison, whose duty it was to pass or reject such recommendations. Having no prior experience recommending medals for valor, Hardison sought Kinkaid's counsel and approval. A week after the battle, perhaps blinded by this impetuous pilot speaking truth to power, Kinkaid produced and stood by one last incomprehensible decision relevant to the Battle of Santa Cruz.

Hardison responded to Flatley's recommendation with an eye-popping substitution. In his secret dispatch to Admiral Halsey, disputing none of the official record, Hardison essentially plagiarized Flatley's recommendation, writing:

As the leader of a flight of four fighting planes of the Combat Air Patrol from the USS *Enterprise* during the Battle of Santa Cruz on October 26, 1942, Lieutenant Stanley Winfield Vejtasa, U.S. Navy, shot down two enemy dive bombers and then completely disrupted an enemy torpedo plane formation, shooting down five torpedo planes, thereby contributing immeasurably to the safety of the USS *Enterprise* during the engagement. For his exceptional display of flying skill and daring courage, it is recommended that the Distinguished Flying Cross be awarded to: Stanley Winfield VEJTASA, Lieutenant, U.S. Navy.

CITATION

For an exceptional display of flying skill, air leadership, and courage. As the leader of a Combat Air Patrol of four fighters from the USS *Enterprise* during the Battle of Santa Cruz on October 26, 1942, in which his carrier was heavily attacked by large numbers of enemy airplanes, Lt. Stanley Winfield Vejtasa, U.S. Navy, personally shot down two enemy dive bombers and then led his patrol in an attack on a formation of Japanese torpedo planes with such daring aggressiveness that the formation was completely broken and three torpedo bombers jettisoned their torpedoes and fled. Lieutenant Vejtasa himself then shot down five of the remaining Japanese planes. By his skillful and courageous accomplishment in destroying seven enemy planes in a single flight, Lieutenant Vejtasa performed a service of great value to his country. His superb performance of duty was in keeping with the highest traditions of the Naval Service.

The recommendation for a Distinguished Flying Cross shocked everyone. The citation language itself is filled with superlatives: "exceptional display of flying skill . . . and courage," "performed a service of great value to his country," and "superb performance of duty"—all of which imply the highest honor. Why the downgrade? No question Swede had loudly mouthed off, challenging the admiral before the Goose Chase. However irritating Swede's outburst might have been to Kinkaid, Swede had brought the abandoned strike group home, and those seven returned fighters proved crucial to Big E's survival the next morning. A strong case could be made that Swede saved *Enterprise*, and Kinkaid's hide along with her. For most observers, Swede's actions over the course of two days had the look of above and beyond heroism twice over.

Without question Swede's accomplishment had set a new standard for aerial combat and arguably spared the sole operational U.S. carrier in the Pacific near-certain destruction. By devaluing Flatley's recommendation, Kinkaid squandered his opportunity to acknowledge and celebrate Swede's brilliant intercept. And Jimmy Flatley, one of the most experienced and respected squadron commanders in the business, was no pushover regarding medals. Perhaps it is best that there is no record of Flatley's reaction to the news of Hardison's degrading proposal.

When word of Kinkaid's absurdity finally made the rounds, most pilots could not fathom the rejection. Not only was it an insult to Swede and Flatley, a DFC made absolutely no sense. Hal Buell insisted that of course Swede's performance was Medal of Honor worthy. Hadn't Butch O'Hare been awarded the Medal of Honor for downing five Japanese aircraft in defense of *Lexington* back in February? (Japanese records confirmed that four failed to return.) Swede's mission went considerably further than that. This was a no brainer. "And," Buell allowed, "Swede was a good bit better than Butch."[5]

Dave Pollock had courageously braved his own AA in his futile attempt to kill a run-amuck torpedo and had shot down a Kate and a Val. Good stuff in a time of great peril. But if these medals truly affirmed heroic performance under fire, who could reconcile a DFC for Swede with a Navy Cross for Pollock? It was abundantly clear to everyone that Swede's actions were nothing short of Medal of Honor caliber. And what must Pollock have thought when he heard Swede was to be awarded a Distinguished Flying Cross?

Naturally, Kincaid and his staff might have been reluctant to advance the paperwork required to elevate this insulting, loud-mouthed, mutinous aviator to a new national hero. No need for the inevitable inquiries attendant to a Medal of Honor or any bright lights illuminating Kinkaid's leadership collapse. In the event, on May 4, 1943, Admiral Halsey overturned his task force commander and upgraded Swede's DFC recommendation to a third Navy Cross. Swede was a hero. He already wore two Navy Crosses. This was just more of the same. Kinkaid's command deficiencies would be spared public scrutiny.

In the final analysis, Navy bomber and fighter pilots were flying for survival, not medals. Most combat veterans understood the political considerations that affected who got what for doing what. But Jimmy Flatley had put down on paper what every pilot on board *Enterprise* knew to be true. Swede had undeniably surpassed any sensible criteria for the Medal of Honor.

All this would set tongues wagging months later. For now, Kinkaid set course for Noumea.

CHAPTER 13

The Naval Battle for Guadalcanal

As *Enterprise* underwent repairs and officers wrote their reports, the unremitting struggle for Guadalcanal slogged on with no victor in sight. By early November, Navy radio intelligence had determined that the Japanese were again planning something big. The Japanese, assuming the U.S. carrier forces had been done in at Santa Cruz, felt the time was right to recapture Guadalcanal. To do so, Admiral Tanaka Raizō would steam a super Tokyo Express convoy of eleven transports and eleven destroyers down the slot and deliver two battalions of the 38th Division along with much-needed food and ammunition. Vice Adm. Abe Hiroaki, meanwhile, would bombard Henderson Field with the battleships *Hiei* and *Kirishima*. Admiral Mikawa would mop up the next evening with his cruisers. The Japanese carriers *Junyō* and *Hiyō* would be held at a distance. Yet another pivotal battle for Guadalcanal was shaping up.

The Americans were determined to maintain their possession of strategic Henderson Field but needed reinforcements. By nightfall on November 12, Adm. Richmond K. Turner's four-ship reinforcement convoy, escorted by Rear Adm. Daniel J. Callaghan's cruiser Task Group 67.4, had made their deliveries and departed for Espiritu Santo. Admiral Halsey, on short notice, ordered Rear Adm. Thomas Kinkaid, who retained his command of a marginally operational *Enterprise*, to intercept and destroy the Japanese forces intent on bombarding Henderson Field. Fearful of undiscovered carriers and land-based attacks, Kinkaid stationed his task force fully 360 miles south of Savo Island.

Much closer to Savo Island, at 1:45 a.m., Friday the thirteenth opened with a devastating point-blank collision between U.S. and Japanese battleships, cruisers, and destroyers. Observers on shore were left to anxiously speculate which side had prevailed.

The engagement cost the Americans two destroyers sunk and three others battered and powerless, and it left the cruisers *Atlanta* and *Portland* badly crippled. Rear Admiral Callaghan and Rear Adm. Norman Scott were killed in the gunfight. The Japanese had one destroyer sunk and another crippled, and the battleship *Hiei* was left without steering control. That nighttime big-gun battle, however, spared the Marines the bombardment critical to the Japanese battle plan. At daybreak and for the rest of the day, Cactus Air Force and *Enterprise* raids would bomb, torpedo, and strafe the doomed *Hiei*. That evening, after dark, the Japanese abandoned *Hiei*. No Americans witnessed the first Japanese battleship to be sunk by U.S. forces slip beneath the surface.

Last Victory

Long before *Hiei* succumbed, at 10:45 that same Friday morning, *Enterprise*'s radar detected a snooper scouting the task force. Swede's Reaper 7 was vectored out to intercept. At about 11 a.m., Swede and Reaper mates Tex Harris, Chip Reding, and Hank Leder sighted a Mavis, code name for a huge four-engine Kawanishi patrol plane crewed by nine and used for long-range reconnaissance.

Swede described the intercept. "We watched him for ten miles, he's low down. I've got the throttle on full, and my divisionmates are creeping up on me, passing me, they've all got the power on. As we close, I open fire and the others do as well. After an extended bunch of confused runs and an unbelievable number of expended rounds, suddenly, God Almighty, there's nothing but a fantastic burst of smoke and fire. Under the combined assault of twenty-four machine guns he just literally blew up in a bright fire. The shrapnel from the explosion beat up the ocean. He crumpled on the water as the last gas was left burning, a small black cloud floated away. There was nothing left to attend to. The four of us had literally torn the thing apart.

"I always wondered—they had a crew, I think, of about nine people—I kinda doubt if any of those people got out. We expended a lot of ammo there. We didn't have to, but we did. It was an opportunity, you know. No pictures of this, though. We had no cameras in the planes; they came in with the Hellcats and F4U Corsairs much later."

Swede shared the victory with his three fellow Reapers. Then it was back to *Enterprise*. The Mavis intercept had spooked Kinkaid. Worried that he had been spotted, Kinkaid stationed the *Enterprise* task force farther south than Halsey had intended. As a result, Rear Adm. Willis Lee's battleships *Washington* and *South Dakota* could not reach Savo Island in time to prevent the Japanese cruiser bombardment of Henderson Field and environs that night.

In the early morning hours of November 14, the Japanese cruisers *Suzuya* and *Maya* spent more than half an hour pouring 989 8-inch shells onto Cactus. The Marines and anyone else at Cactus would have sworn it was nine thousand. Daylight revealed two burned Wildcats and fifteen perforated by shrapnel. Swede, Robbie, and Whitey had been very fortunate to spend the night on board *Enterprise*.

Escort to Nowhere

The next morning Swede's Reaper 7 was part of Flatley's twelve-fighter escort for Lt. Cdr. James "Bucky" Lee's eight SBDs sent out in search of targets. Robbie, finally taking part in a raid, felt safer knowing that Swede was escorting. Two hours later, however, before any action, that sense of safety disappeared. Harried crews rushing to fuel his plane had failed to top off his auxiliary tanks. Now, on his first combat mission, Robbie watched his fuel gauges dictate a turn around, and it was galling. Thomas signaled him to return to *Enterprise*, but Robbie, having stretched his fuel to the max, knew he would have to land at Cactus.

For Jimmy Flatley, the mission would develop into another maddening exercise in futility. Early in the flight Flatley discovered that the Wildcats' radios had not been tuned to the search-strike frequency, thus denying him the ability to contact Bucky Lee and the SBDs. More troubling, the escorts had not been given a specific target location; nor had they been informed of the option to land at Henderson Field.

Shortly after Robbie detached, Chip Reding and Hank Leder, flying a section of Swede's Reaper 7, peeled away to fend off a pair of menacing Zeros. They pursued the Zeros into clouds, became completely disoriented, and ended up on their own. Minutes later, Flatley's Reaper 1 and Swede and Tex Harris of Reaper 7, busy searching the sky for Zeros, failed to notice the bombers change course. Suddenly they were nowhere to be seen.

After searching in vain for the bombers he had no way to contact, a furious Flatley turned his Reapers back toward *Enterprise*. At Santa Cruz he had failed to protect the torpedo bombers he was escorting and had agonized over abandoning Leppla's outnumbered Reaper division. Here, three weeks later, he could not even locate his charges.

By 11:30, Swede and the rest of Flatley's escort team, minus two, had landed back on board *Enterprise*. An hour later, Chip Reding and Hank Leder caught wires and went limp. They had been five hours aloft, enduring a nerve-racking search for home base. The Dauntlesses, at least, had managed to find, bomb, and damage two of Vice Adm. Mikawa Gunichi's cruisers. Fortunately, there had been no Zero interference.

Shredding Tanaka's Convoy

At 8:49 that same morning, searchers spotted Admiral Tanaka's convoy of eleven transports, cargo ships, and barges crammed with men and equipment. Thinly escorted by destroyers, they steamed blithely down the Slot in broad daylight.

Robbie, having detached in disgust from the strike group, landed at Henderson Field around 11:30. By noon his plane had been refueled and he was flying wing on Hoot Gibson in a joint Navy-Marine bombing and strafing raid on the plodding transports. One of the land-based Zeros sent to cover the convoy managed to shoot off Robbie's antenna mast, blowing it back over his head. Gibson's backseat man, AMM2C Clifford E. Schindele, drove the Zero off. Gibson coolly maintained his focus and accurately placed his 500-pound bomb on a huge transport.

Robbie was right behind him. Not quite three weeks before, Robbie had impotently endured the Japanese mauling of the *Hornet*. How the tides had turned! At the controls of his SBD-3, this time Robbie would be doing the bombing. Imitating Gibson, Robbie accurately "fired" his bomb into the midships area of the same crowded transport. Marine staff sergeant Albert C. Beneke added a near miss to complete the devastation. The transport promptly broke in half, spilling thousands of troops, her crew, and tons of equipment into the sea. Desperately weaving their aircraft, now one thousand pounds lighter, through intense Japanese AA fire and the intervention of Lt. Iizuka Masao's six Zeros down from Rabaul, Robbie and Hoot made their escape. Back at Henderson Field, ground crews labored furiously, refueling with hand pumps and struggling with bombs and ammunition, to rearm successive waves of American planes bent on destroying Tanaka's oncoming convoy.

By midafternoon Swede was flying CAP over *Enterprise* while Jimmy Flatley busily organized an afternoon raid to consist of twelve Wildcats and eight SBDs. Jimmy would serve as strike coordinator, and this time there would be no confusion in directions; smoke pillars from burning ships pinpointed Tanaka's bloodied convoy. Ignoring the Zeros overhead, Flatley coolly assigned targets to the dive-bombers and fighters in an effort to broadcast the destruction. As the Dauntlesses did their work, Reapers Dave Pollock, Fritz Faulkner, and Whitey Feightner, among others, strafed Tanaka's ships and barges.

Whitey recalled the ugly, bloody business of strafing and the effects of his six .50-caliber machine guns. "Those Japanese troops were packed shoulder to shoulder, and we came with our guns blazing, tearing through them. They dove off the ships by the dozens trying to escape the carnage." Later, touring a beached transport they had shot up, Whitey was amazed to see that his rounds had passed clear through the deck and continued on through the thin hull.

Robbie's Fight

As Whitey slaughtered Tanaka's deck-bound troops, Jim Thomas, who had navigated the Goose Chase, was hustling to mount another Cactus attack on Tanaka's unrelenting convoy. He urged Robbie to hurry up and get his plane refueled and rearmed. With Zeros having contested his previous flight, Robbie said that he preferred to wait for a fighter escort.

Thomas, unaware that land-based Zeros were shuttling down from Rabaul to cover the convoy, was incredulous. "I don't believe it. How can there be Zeros? There are no Jap carriers around. We gotta go now," he insisted. "We need the sun to our advantage. We've got to come out of the sun." The conversation escalated, and Robbie boldly declared he would no longer fly on Thomas' wing.[1]

In what historian John Lundstrom would later call "A Tragic Mission," it was late afternoon by the time Thomas got his seven SBDs into the air.

Robbie, now flying wing on his friend XO Lt. Warren Welch, did not like the look of things. "We took off with no fighter cover and got out toward the target now about sixty miles away. Thomas dilly-dallied around up toward the sun, which was now about to set."

Instead of climbing straight to the normal diving altitude of 15,000–18,000 feet, the height from which they could build up speed and have time during the long dive to adjust their aim, Thomas led the seven SBDs to the west, toward the lowering sun. Alarmed by their leisurely climb, Welch's section, including Robbie, Lt. (jg) J. Donald Wakeham, and Tiny Carroum, split off to gain altitude. Ens. Edwin Stevens and an apprehensive Hoot Gibson remained in formation with Thomas. As the detached section of four clawed for altitude, Welch slid his canopy back and shook his fist at Thomas. Indeed, the unnecessary attempt to get up-sun had allowed the Japanese CAP time to set up an intercept.

Welch had got them to 12,000 feet when six Zeros under the command of Lt. Cdr. Kaneko Tadashi flying down from Buin slashed in and quickly shot down three of the four unescorted Dauntlesses. Warren Welch and Donald Wakeham and their respective rear-seat men, ARM1C Harry Claude Ansley Jr. and ARM1C Forest Glen Stanley, were shot down and killed. Tiny Carroum, with ARM3C Robert C. Hynson Jr. behind him, disappeared from view.

And Robbie was in serious trouble. "I could hear my gunner, ARM3C Joseph G. Teyshak, firing until hits from the Zero jammed his guns." Almost simultaneously, another Japanese pilot, WO Mori Mitsugu, made a head-on pass, and rounds thudded into Robbie's engine. In turn, Robbie triggered his two forward-firing .50-calibers and watched his bullets make hits on Mori's Zero, which dropped sharply away. Emulating Swede's prowess, Robbie, flying an SBD, had just downed a Zero.

But one of Mori's guns had set Robbie's engine on fire, and the rear Zero's bullets were now eating into his left wing. Robbie abruptly side-slipped down and away, presenting every appearance of being shot down. Mori, in the midst of his own plunge toward the sea, looked on, convinced he had downed Robbie's dive-bomber.

Robbie's quick reaction, however, extinguished the fire and, to his amazement, restarted his engine. The pursuing Japanese pilot, PO2C Motegi Shigeo, stayed with Robbie and was riddling his plane. "I could hear rounds hitting the armor behind my head, and I watched my instrument panel getting shot to pieces."

Repeated evasive maneuvers failed to shake the relentless Motegi. As Robbie made one last effort to climb into a cloud, Teyshak announced, "We're gettin' company." Having expended all his ammunition, Motegi boldly flew up alongside them. In a rare display of chivalry, Motegi smartly executed a roll, saluted Robbie, and turned for home.

While Robbie was flying for his survival, Zeros were also roughing up Thomas' section of three. Hoot Gibson received the most attention; he was thoroughly shot up and barely made it back to Guadalcanal. In the melee Jim Thomas and Ens. Edwin Stevens managed to elude the preoccupied Zeros and bomb and strafe the transports before hightailing it to Cactus.

Robbie limped back to Guadalcanal; never had Henderson Field looked so good. There, Teyshak's shrapnel wounds and a tally of sixty-eight bullet hits and more than three hundred exit and shrapnel holes testified to their close call.

This day, in his first taste of combat, Robbie had successfully bombed one of Tanaka's transports. On his second "tragic" mission he had shot down one of the two Zeros attacking him, evaded the other, and brought his ordnance home for another mission. Some would call that distinguished flying. Robbie had clearly joined Swede and Whitey as high performers in the bloody business of air combat.

Robbie's Dauntless was declared no longer airworthy and was cannibalized for useful parts. The scavenged remains appeared later as a convincing prop in the movie *Guadalcanal Diary*. The name on Robbie's SBD cowling? "Zero Bait."

CHAPTER 14

On to Guadalcanal

As *Enterprise* withdrew to Noumea for additional repairs, Air Group 10 shifted operations ashore to reinforce the seriously depleted Cactus Air Force. Marine fighter and bombing squadrons VMF-223, VMF-224, VMSB-231, and VMSB-232 were down to twelve Wildcats, eleven Dauntlesses, three P-400s, three P-39s, and a lone F4F photography plane.[1] Air Group 10's additional SBDs, TBFs, and F4Fs would prove crucial to Cactus' survival.

Whitey recalled their arrival that afternoon at Guadalcanal. "It was pretty grim. We couldn't land at the main field, so they sent me off to the 'cow pasture' (Fighter 1) to land. The guy in front of me caught a wheel in the mud and flipped over onto his back. Seeing that, I landed on the beach." As Whitey carefully set his plane down, Japanese shelling augmented an already impressive adrenaline rush.

Swede found it "remarkable how they managed to keep Fighter 1 repaired, as every day it got beat to hell. When we arrived, there were airplane wrecks all over. You couldn't tell what was operational or not."

With reinforcements at hand, Lt. Col. Harold "Indian Joe" Bauer, CO of Cactus Fighter Command and a double ace, wanted his piece of Tanaka's transports. As Bauer prepared to take off, Flatley hopped up on a wing, said a few words, and waved his friend off, planning to continue their conversation that evening. Bauer strafed Tanaka's wrecked convoy and shot down a Zero before being shot down in turn. How it had happened was something of a mystery.

Swede commented, "Bauer was a good friend of Jimmy Flatley. He was loud; I never saw him in action. When he disappeared, his squadron came

131

in—no Bauer. He had flown tail-end Charlie. The Japs would often follow in the dark and pursue our pilots. The records never showed what happened, but his mates think that's what happened. He was known to be very aggressive, but I didn't see any of it myself."

That evening as the Air Group 10 pilots mingled, Robbie wanted to know about Swede's part in the battle. His response, "I was elsewhere," said it all. The next day would find Swede a lot farther elsewhere.

In the meantime, after dark in the waters north of them, Tanaka was hoping to salvage something from the debacle. He ordered his four remaining transports to beach themselves.

Just before midnight another savage battleship gunfight took place that provided a spectacular pyrotechnic display for Japanese and American observers on shore. In the exchange the battleship *Washington* salvoed 16-inch shells into *Kirishima* and sank her—the second Japanese battleship sunk in as many days. A Japanese destroyer went down as well. Three American destroyers were sunk, another was crippled, and the battleship *South Dakota* was badly hammered. The Japanese retired, and the Cactus Marines and Air Group 10 pilots were spared another terrifying bombardment.

Swede Down?

For two days following the battle, Robbie substituted an OS2U for his junked Dauntless and flew search-and-rescue missions looking for the many oil-soaked survivors of ships sunk or damaged during the fierce naval battles of the evenings of November 13 and 14. It was a serious challenge to distinguish friend from foe among the hundreds of blackened heads bobbing in the water. One sinking cruiser was so covered in oil that it was impossible to determine her nationality. When Robbie could identify survivors as friendly he simply dipped his plane's nose or dropped smoke bombs to indicate their location to rescuers. On one occasion he strafed a half-dozen menacing sharks before he could vector a rescue plane to the grateful pilot.

On the morning of November 15, while Robbie searched for survivors and Whitey strafed Tanaka's beached transports, the *Enterprise* deck log noted: "At 0910, Lieutenant S. W. Vejtasa, USN, and Ensign W. B. Reding, USNR, took off to fly to Noumea."

Swede wrote in his unpublished memoir, "On November 15 an incident took place that I shall not forget. I was on Guadalcanal and Chip Reding [the sole survivor of Leppla's Reaper 6 shredded at Santa Cruz] and I were directed to return to *Enterprise*, pick up messages, and deliver a packet to Admiral Halsey, who at the time was at New Caledonia."[2]

Swede and Chip had witnessed all kinds of snafus during the previous day's strike escort. Against those frustrations, this short hop to Noumea promised to be a lark. In lousy weather they found *Enterprise* and got a green light to come right in. Swede remembered thinking, "I'll get a bath and good drinking water." Instead, the flight deck officer approached and handed Swede a waterproof dispatch bag for Admiral Halsey. He pointed out a different pair of Wildcats assigned to fly this abrupt mission, promptly turned away, and was gone.

Swede and Chip were quickly aloft.

As we left the ship, we completed our navigation, checked the wind and sea, and proceeded on what seemed to be a simple mission. The weather was threatening with low overcast, strong wind, and poor visibility. No problem. New Caledonia is a big island, just a simple hop across the strait toward d'Entrecasteaux Reefs near the north tip of New Caledonia, and then head south. When the time came to sight the reefs north of the island there was nothing below us but waves and saltwater. We checked our navigation and found nothing wrong—headings were correct. I decided at that point to fly to what would be the center of the island, and if nothing was sighted to make a ninety-degree right turn and fly till we came upon the island or fuel was expended. This we did, and we flew at low altitude into the wind headed west.

No luck. "The reefs don't show up, we fly a little farther, another ten minutes, still no reefs." They conferred on radio, expecting to see New Caledonia at any time. "We flew and flew some more, tried radio contact, nobody answers, we're getting low on fuel after four hours in the air." Chip, having gotten separated and lost the day before and now lost with Swede, a renowned navigator, had to be wondering what he had done wrong.

Swede outlined Chip's options. "If you go down first, I'll follow and we'll break out our rubber boats. If I go down first, you can decide what you want to do." They agreed to go down together. They were lost, and nobody else had any idea of their whereabouts either. Best to stick together.

Just then some of that Vejtasa luck showed up. "I noticed a streak of whitecaps, an atoll, then a little island. And on the left, a big island a couple of miles farther. But there was nothing familiar on our charts." Their search for a suitable landing spot revealed natives swimming or fishing offshore and lots of thatched huts and palm trees, but no place to put a plane down.

A slanted beach presented their only option. "Chip, if I don't make it, if I turn over in the sand—you land in the water." Swede carefully let down. His plane bucked a bit, stayed upright, then gingerly braked to a stop in the sand. "'Chip, you can make it,' and he comes in just beyond me."

I got out of the plane and started in the direction of a village we had sighted. There was no one around, however. I knew we were being watched as I saw two lads high in a coconut tree ahead. After six and a half hours in the air on this flight, I was tired, hungry, and very thirsty. Soon I met the village chief coming toward me down the trail. He raised his hand and I did likewise, which seemed to satisfy the greeting. I immediately gave him the signal that I was very thirsty. He clapped his hands, shouted something, and suddenly there were coconuts falling all around me. He took out his machete and cut the tops off a number of them, and I drank with the greatest satisfaction.

My first need was communication of some sort, but I could not make myself understood on this subject. The chief took me to three or four small villages and gave the gathered natives a lecture at each stop. Finally, we approached a better house and a woman came out. I was amazed as she spoke almost perfect English. We talked and I told her of our problem. She told me we were on the island of Ouvea, and they had a radio on the island that could communicate with the lookout tower on New Caledonia.

Things were looking up. "We proceeded to the little tin shed that housed the radio equipment to find the designated operator sitting in the shade smoking the worst-smelling tobacco I have ever inhaled. After the operator looked at the sun, apparently to see if the time was right, he opened the lock and we went in.

"After several attempts, he raised the lookout tower. My elation was quickly deflated when the call came back, 'Identify yourself.'"

Swede replied, "Name Vejtasa, with a name like mine, I need no further identification." Swede then instructed him to get on the phone and contact Admiral Halsey's staff. He had dispatches to deliver.

Having done all that he could do for the time being, Swede "toured the island some more and finally came upon a rather well-constructed house. The gentleman was a French resident and had us stay the night with him, his wife, and two very pretty young daughters. We were most grateful.

"Early the next day, we heard the drone of a seaplane and it circled, we waved and it landed in the lagoon, taxied to the beach, where I embarked. We were off to New Caledonia, some sixty miles yet to the west."

Chip stayed to watch over the planes while Swede went on to Noumea. A waiting jeep delivered him to Admiral Halsey, who graciously accepted the now-late briefs and advised Swede, "We're pretty busy here; my Operations people will take care of you."

Well, you'd think I was king of the island. First they asked me what I wished to do, and I replied that I wanted to make every effort to get those planes out of there. I wanted to take them back to the squadron for compass checking because after all the years of dead-reckoning flying in all kinds of weather, it was most embarrassing to get lost on a flight like that. "Say no more," came the reply. I was turned over to a couple of officers in the local patrol squadron, and the crew immediately hit upon the idea of putting two drums of gas on the bomb racks and flying over to the island. Then they gave me a place to sleep.

The next morning, fitted with extra fuel tanks on each wing and crewed with a half-dozen flight mechanics, a PBY correctly navigated Swede back to Chip and the stranded planes. They had devised special containers so the natives could transport the five-gallon fuel cans some three quarters of a mile away without spilling it all over themselves. To lighten the fighters, mechanics stripped out the fixed guns; others checked out the planes' oil, fuel, and radios. Then they were ready to go.

But could they actually get airborne off that short, sloped beach? To assist that effort, the locals removed stumps and palm fronds, filled holes, and smoothed down the whole surface. "We had a runway."

In order to use this primitive strip, however, both planes had to be moved from where they currently sat back to the start of the runway. The chief got up on a plane and gave another of his long lectures. "Getting the planes back to the far edge of the berm turned out to be no problem as the natives gathered around the craft in great numbers and simply carried them to the designated spot." Sounds straightforward, but Swede sweated out the process, especially when one wheel of his plane got stuck in a soft spot. The enthusiastic plane-lifters might easily damage the rudder or ailerons.

With both planes finally in position, the PBY departed, leaving the fuel tins behind for the natives. "They then cut palm fronds and small logs to be buried in the soft spots. We had worked for two days and I was continually amazed the way these fellows labored. Even the girls pitched in and cut the palms and buried them." All that was needed now was the cool morning breeze essential for a successful takeoff, which delayed their departure until the next morning.

The Frenchman's wife prepared a filling send-off breakfast. After that there could be no more delaying the sketchy beach takeoff. They warmed up their planes and carefully inspected their runway. Despite the sloped beach, Swede confided to Chip, "I think we can make it, but wait until you see how I make out."

They cranked up their engines. Swede gave his full throttle, held his brakes, and sweated that soft sand. Rolling forward, Swede

felt the plane just come up a little bit, easing up, and finally the wheels broke free. I had to get those damn wheels up, cranking all those turns while my throttle was locked forward. Here are those trees coming up. I had put on a quarter flap. I'm airborne. I can feel the lift come on. I'm headed right for a big old palm tree. I'm gaining a little altitude. I put down a little flaps, hoping for better climb and lower stall. I went through the top of a large palm tree, the prop throwing fronds in all directions but I remained airborne. It was close. I made a turn. "Chip, you can make it."

Having seen it done, Chip improved on Swede's liftoff, easily clearing the threatening palm tree. They flew a couple of circles around their helpers, waggled their wings in response to the farewell waves, and flew westward away from Ouvea and toward New Caledonia, where they would rejoin their incredulous squadronmates. Swede dreaded having to explain that navigational gaffe. For Chip, once again it was all about being found.

"We were flying somebody else's planes," Swede explained. "The first thing I faced was good-natured banter. I got those compasses checked, and they were in pretty bad shape. Having not been calibrated in ages, these turned out to be more than 18 degrees off, which on replotting accounted for our distance from the objective. And the charts were way off. The position of the ship when we took off was entirely wrong. We put out a message to get rid of the damn things. I left those airplanes in Noumea. Whose ever they were, they could come and get them."

For Whitey, "It was great to see those guys again. After two days, we thought they were gone; they must have been shot down. The Navy did send out PBYs to search for them. I saw them down near New Caledonia, and we talked about the incident."

In short form, Swede's November 15 flight log noted, "*Enterprise* to Ouvea with Dispatches."

"It was a miracle we got back." Miracle or not, with the help of Ouvea's natives, French residents, and the U.S. Navy, this had to be considered an Allied victory.

Life on the 'Canal

Conditions on Guadalcanal were a far cry from the familiar amenities Air Group 10 enjoyed on board carriers. Whitey described some of the hazards. "They had all the aviators in one big tent, while the Marines had constructed large 'bombproof' bunkers with logs. One night a battleship shell killed nine pilots and aircrew taking shelter in one such bunker. When the Japanese began shelling we'd dive into water-filled foxholes to escape. In the dark, we could hear Japs climbing up into trees. They'd tie themselves to the trees and wait to snipe any pilot coming out of the tent. So each morning the Marines would go out and spray the tops of the trees for snipers."

"Some guys stayed under the wing," Swede recalled, and "some stayed in the cockpit and kept the canopy closed. I tried the dugout several times, but there were creatures, bugs, scorpions in those damn places. The shelling dug some big holes. Most of it landed beyond us or where the Marines were dug in. They kept us awake, killed a few people. Disconcerting as hell, of course. How the Marines managed there I'll never know."

On November 15, while Swede was dealing with his misadventure, his friends Dave Pollock and Whitey had scrambled to meet an incoming raid. Zeros shot up Dave's borrowed Marine Wildcat, creating a propeller pitch problem that forced him to ditch. The sudden stop as his plane hit the water slammed Dave's head against the gun sight. He escaped his sinking plane in a daze and began swimming toward one of the burning transports not far from Henderson Field.

Whitey, with memories of Gordon Barnes' tragic outcome in his head, once again slowly orbited a downed Reaper. Japanese troops noticed and began taking potshots at Pollock. A group of Marines recognized Dave's predicament, bravely paddled out, hauled him onto their inflatable raft, and paddled back, all the while under fire. In a turnabout from Whitey's first unfamiliar days in VF-10 when Dave had looked after him, Whitey lingered at Cactus while Dave recovered.

Scarce fuel was a problem. Whitey remembered "having to hand-pump gas into our planes. We had just enough to go up for brief missions. The one thing we had plenty of was ammunition. We always went up ready for a fight. With afternoon raids every day, and sometimes two, Guadalcanal was a nightmare. We shuttled between Noumea, *Enterprise*, and Guadalcanal. Whenever we left the island, which was a great relief, we left our planes for the Marines."

"They had great mechanics," Swede recalled, "and those guys salvaged everything to keep planes in the air. That was real tough going. There was no radar guidance from Henderson Field, which meant a lot of CAP hours and fewer actual contacts with the Japanese. The guys aboard ship were getting more contact; we contributed by strafing Japanese troop concentrations."

Swede recalled an incident involving Lt. (jg) Gordon E. Firebaugh, known for his night flying. When the Japanese land-based artillery once again shattered their night's rest, Firebaugh had had enough. He resolved to go out and bomb that gunner, nighttime or not. To that end, head-lighted Jeeps at each end of the runway provided enough visibility to get aloft. Gordon dropped his bomb on the gun flashes, and the firing stopped. Returning to the jeep-lit runway, he landed without issue to receive the warm praise of his grateful comrades. Firebaugh later died in a midair collision.

Swede was imperiled by more than distant artillery fire. "There was an awful lot of action right at the edge of the field. I was careful enough to get ahold of a Marine, and I kept him near me. I didn't know where the danger was. Those guys were good."

Strategically, the naval battle for Guadalcanal resulted in an American victory. Admiral Turner successfully landed reinforcements for the Marines against the loss of destroyers and severely damaged cruisers. Two big-gun shootouts denied the Japanese a pair of intended Henderson Field bombardments. The Japanese battleships *Hiei* and *Kirishima* were sunk, Mikawa's cruisers were savaged, and Tanaka's reinforcement convoy was shattered. Big E kept out of harm's way, and Henderson Field remained an American asset.

Colleagues in Harm's Way

As a trusted friend of Jimmy Flatley, Swede often found himself among the power elite on Guadalcanal. "I'd fly in with Jimmy. Gen. Roy Geiger [CO Marine Aircraft Wing] would send his Jeep over to pick us up. I was part of it just because Jimmy and I were close. I was trusted. Then we'd all meet in the tent for a shot and a chat."

On the morning of November 14, the day after Swede's Reaper 7 shattered the Mavis, Lt. Macgregor Kilpatrick along with Bill Blair also downed one of the giant recon planes. "So," Swede continued, "Macgregor and I were invited to join Jimmy and the general. They poured us a drink, but in that heat I couldn't take the shot; it would have killed me. Both of us were happy enough with fresh water. When we slipped out of the tent and dumped it, we stumbled upon thirty cases of whiskey in a nearby tent. We listened carefully as Geiger talked tactics, overall strategy, what we were trying to accomplish, and where ground troops were situated."

Lt. Col. Evans Carlson of Carlson's Raiders fame also hosted Swede. "We stayed with Carlson down near the Matanikau where he had his camp. They had mosquito nets, a big item there. Carlson and Jimmy talked tactics and order of battle, essential to avoid friendly fire incidents." Swede recalled briefly meeting Col. Merritt A. "Red Mike" Edson, awarded a Medal of Honor for his September defense of Bloody Ridge, vital to holding Henderson Field.

Naturally, Swede mingled with some illustrious Marine pilots. "During the heavy fighting on Guadalcanal and the air battles up the island chain, I came to know many of the pilots such as John Smith, Joe Foss, Marion Carl, Bill Jones, and many others who wrote the glorious chapters in the book of aerial warfare for that time and place, which helped so much to turn the tide when pressure was the greatest."

Swede spoke admiringly of Foss' commitment to combat. "I recall being on patrol one day at about 25,000 feet and in the same area that Joe Foss was orbiting with his division. Word came that enemy bombers were approaching at eight thousand feet and had just passed a well-known point of land. I saw Joe roll over and point that Wildcat straight down, and I did the same, the canopy rattling and shaking. Watching for Joe and his division, I saw him pulling rapidly away, and even with throttle open I fell farther behind. I feared for his safety on the pullout, but he made it and flew right through the bomber formation firing with all his guns. The bombers broke, scattered, and turned back, never reaching a drop point.

"After the fracas, I told Joe, 'That was a lot of g's, Joe.' The reply was, 'If the Wildcat can take it, I can.' A bit later we had a look at his plane and found several rows of rivets along the belly of the airplane in holes that were stretched more than a bit."[3]

Swede also had occasion to connect with Marine major Gregory "Pappy" Boyington, the controversial CO of VMF-214, the Black Sheep Squadron. Early in his career, when he was an instructor at Pensacola, Pappy had imprudently slugged a lieutenant. While his superiors were debating the merits of a court-martial, President Roosevelt authorized a clandestine plan to assist the Chinese with planes and pilots. When representatives showed up at Pensacola looking to fill the roster of the newly forming American Volunteer Group, Boyington jumped right in.

"He was there for lunch, gone that afternoon." Swede was convinced that was how Pappy Boyington became part of the outfit subsequently known as the Flying Tigers. "None of the Tigers spoke well of Boyington. He was a liar, a drunk, but I accept all of that."

There was more to the story. "I used to take a group into the airport in Espiritu Santo, and the Marines always took good care of me. When we landed, there would come this Jeep, Boyington at the wheel. 'Get in, Swede.' Eyes straight ahead, he took me to my tent and then to a bar, where he spent most of his time. He had a nice tent, a good bed, a shower. This was special on the beach. 'See you later Swede.' And he'd disappear. I wouldn't see him, but I couldn't have had it better.

"When time came to go back aboard the ship, here'd come the Jeep. 'Get in, Swede.' Never said a word; drove me to where my airplane was, looking straight ahead. 'See you later, Swede.' And again he'd disappear. The guy wasn't all bad. His men sure as hell took care of us there.

"On the 'Canal I made a few flights with him. You never knew what he was going to do in the air. One thing for sure, when you get into the Japs, he went after them. He was a tiger."

Meanwhile, unbeknownst to the beleaguered participants on Guadalcanal, the destruction of Tanaka's reinforcement convoy signaled a shift in Japan's strategic model. Guadalcanal, the Island of Death, had siphoned off far too many critical resources. It was time to cut those terrible losses.

Stress and Demons

There is no predicting how combatants will react to the stresses of combat. Swede had observed pilots on board ship under attack, during aerial combat, and surviving on the 'Canal. "You don't know your ass from thirty seconds when you go into combat. This is completely different. You have to learn how to evade, what your plane can do, what action you can take. In true combat people are shooting at you and you can feel the AA bursts near your plane.

"Some under attack seem to freeze. Next thing you know, they're full of holes. We had a couple like that. One of our pilots at the Battle of Santa Cruz, he'd been at Midway, got lost, not shot down; his group didn't find a damn thing, just ran out of gas. A PBY picked him up. That experience gave him buck fever. Later, there was a plane in front of him but he took no action. He wasn't long in the squadron.

"Other guys immediately knew what to do. They took evasive action, constantly looking for airplanes. Same with AA—a lot of it was behind you; you couldn't worry about it. You learned that stuff, but some guys paid no attention to that kind of thing. They wouldn't become good combat pilots."

On the topic of stress, Swede remembered one guy with "a poor mental attitude." He slept at all times with his .45 under his pillow, even on board ship and at home in the Alameda bachelor officers' quarters. As for Swede, "I harbored no demons; never. I just wanted air action. I never lost a night of sleep."

To Whitey, combat stress was a crapshoot. "People react differently. Some of the meekest, quietest guys were really good in combat, but some of the biggest, most macho guys did the least."[4]

Regarding the business of killing fellow humans, Whitey put it this way: "We shot down planes, not people. As for grieving for our own losses, there was no time to deal with it. It was something that happened every day. You get in a different frame of mind; you get used to the fact that you're going to lose people. I never suffered nightmares, and everybody else was pretty solid."

Kinkaid Relieved

Confronted with Kinkaid's accumulating leadership shortcomings, Halsey had to make some changes. He wrote to Nimitz, "As soon as I can get some flag officers, I would like to send Tom back to the states for a rest. He has done a noble job and has been at it a long time."[5] Halsey endorsed Kinkaid's performance, writing to him that he commanded his forces with "skill and effectiveness. You inflicted great damage upon the enemy in repeated engagements."

Kinkaid's biographer, Gerald Wheeler, also hinted at burnout. "Kinkaid, himself, after almost a year in command and having survived five major operations, was beginning to show signs that he was starting to wear out."[6]

To be fair, during the earlier Battle of the Eastern Solomons *Enterprise* endured a terrifying attack. Kinkaid and his staff had been tossed around, and afterward he had seen the gory consequences of those bomb hits. A mere two months later at Santa Cruz, he was in overall command for the first time and had every reason to be petrified of another Japanese attack. And the Japanese, in scoring two hits and three damaging near misses, did not disappoint. Some weeks later, Kinkaid's apprehensive timidity on November 13 and 14 kept him safe but too far away to prevent the bombardment of Henderson Field.

On November 16 Rear Adm. Frederick C. "Ted" Sherman, an aviator, arrived at Noumea, and a week later, on November 23, relieved Kinkaid as CTF-16. An embittered *Enterprise* air group cheered Kinkaid's departure. Halsey made a follow-up decision; from Kinkaid's relief forward, only aviators would command carrier task forces.

"Long overdue," Swede opined. "King [the CNO] didn't know Kinkaid could be so irresponsible for planning operations. King fired him." That was the last Swede ever saw of Kinkaid.

Kinkaid's December 2 arrival in Pearl Harbor closed out an extensive South Pacific tour. Halsey awarded Kinkaid a new title: commander cruisers, Pacific Fleet. Kinkaid would take charge of Task Force 67, consisting of all South Pacific cruisers still capable of operating at sea. His new job was to write up a plan to counter the Tokyo Express. While this billet better suited his strengths, the new posting undoubtedly felt like the demotion it represented. He rotated back to the States before taking command of the Aleutians invasion force, where his more traditional talents could come into play.

Curiously, Kinkaid had his own medal issues. To ease Kinkaid out of the theater, Nimitz concurred with Halsey's recommendation for a third Distinguished Service Medal. Owing to some undisclosed technicality, the award was never made. Instead, the citation for his Eastern Solomons DSM was expanded to cover Santa Cruz and the naval battle for Guadalcanal.

As Kinkaid made his way out of the Pacific theater, Air Group 10 pilots were astonished to see a skinny and sunburnt Tiny Carroum, who had been declared missing and was presumed dead, step out of a PBY patrol plane. Downed in the tragic mission, he had survived a three-day ordeal beginning when he and backseat man Hynson ditched. They endured a scary and exhausting night bobbing in the dark water. The next morning, as they swam toward an island, Hynson fell behind and slipped under; Tiny was powerless to help. After seventy-three tortured hours in the ocean with no food or drinking water, Carroum made it to land. Islanders helped him evade the Japanese and assisted with his return to Tulagi.

Air Combat off the Rennell Islands

Except for a lone sortie a few days prior to the anniversary of Pearl Harbor, during which no combat occurred, *Enterprise* spent much of December and January undergoing repairs from the bomb damage incurred at Santa Cruz. Air Group 10 appreciated a well-earned respite from fighting, but training proceeded apace with exercises in strafing and shooting up target sleeves. In their off time they could enjoy the relative amenities of Noumea.

Japanese losses during the naval battle for Guadalcanal coupled with the loss of their carrier air groups at Santa Cruz had finally convinced the high command to withdraw. In late January the Japanese began a highly effective, secret evacuation of some 12,000 troops. With the *Kidō Butai* off licking its wounds, the Japanese staged land-based, long-range bomber harassment missions to cover their covert operation.

On January 28, *Enterprise* headed back toward Guadalcanal intent on safeguarding the arrival of another four U.S. reinforcement transports. The next evening, January 29, Japanese Betty bombers carried off an unprecedented nighttime torpedo attack against a column of U.S. cruisers escorting the transports. The attack succeeded in blowing the bow off the heavy cruiser *Chicago*. Her sister ship USS *Louisville* took her under tow, and at daybreak the seagoing tug USS *Navajo* took over the effort.

As the tandem pair made a sluggish four knots, *Enterprise* closed to forty miles. From there Flatley's Reapers could provide a protective air umbrella in the face of expected Japanese efforts to finish off the cripple. Sure enough, just past three in the afternoon, Guadalcanal radioed that eleven bogies, likely out of New Georgia or Kolombangara, were headed toward the *Enterprise* battle group.

As the attack developed, Swede had flown a CAP and was on deck for replenishment. Whitey Feightner, no longer the new guy, was about to improve on his record at Santa Cruz, when he had downed a bomber and punctured a probable Zero. Whitey minced no words recalling his day off the Rennell Islands: "The *Chicago* incident was a fiasco from start to finish. It was early in my four-hour CAP at 22,000 feet over the *Chicago* when I heard, 'Return to ship buster [at best speed]' as everyone feared the raid would focus on the *Enterprise*. About then my wing tank ran dry and my engine quit. I dropped the nose, switched tanks, picked up speed, and the engine caught again."[7]

While Whitey worked to resolve his fuel problem, the other Reapers struggled with their drop tanks. Unless they were completely empty the tanks had a disturbing tendency not to release, and this afternoon only one Reaper was able to successfully drop his tank. Not only frustrating, the hung tanks ruined aiming, reduced speed, and represented a serious fire hazard. The Japanese strike leader quickly sized up the threat from the preoccupied Reapers standing between his flight and *Enterprise*. He abruptly redirected his strike group to break left for an attack on the dead-in-the-water *Chicago*. Their turn put Whitey, lagging because of his engine troubles, in a position of advantage. The rest of the Reapers found themselves in a stern chase.

"Next thing, I'm looking all over for the others, and there are Bettys around me. I nosed over and shot down one and then another. Then I joined up with Flatley while the remaining Bettys formed up and made for the *Chicago*. They were fast and we couldn't catch up. Flatley pulled his nose up and fired a deflection burst at a Betty, which quickly dodged into a cloud. Being a foolish ensign I followed him into the mist to find that he had turned to press a head-on attack. I pressed the trigger and rolled over on my back to avoid him. I couldn't see the results of my gunnery, but Flatley acknowledged the victory with a big thumbs up. He'd watched the bomber plummet into the ocean."

Whitey then witnessed a most unorthodox fighter tactic. Russ Reiserer had damaged one of the Bettys but was now out of ammunition. Not to be undone by this limitation, Russ dropped his tail hook and made repeated attempts to hook the tail fin and flip the bomber into the ocean. Flatley took in the bizarre situation and signaled Whitey, "Go get that one."

"I lined up on his starboard engine and fired my remaining ammo, which set that engine smoking. Time to go home. We later learned he never got home."

Despite an effective Reaper intercept that downed eight, the Japanese nonetheless managed to put four torpedoes into already bowless *Chicago*. In just twenty minutes she rolled over and sank. Before she disappeared into the depths Whitey saw a lot of men waving from her hull. Survivors later clarified that they were not waving but angrily shaking their fists over the CAP's failure to protect their crippled vessel. That sentiment worked its way up the ladder.

Days later, Whitey happened to be on hand when Flatley recommended medals for those helping to down eight bombers, despite being bustered out of position for the intercept. The admiral wanted none of it and lit into Flatley. "You want medals for failing to protect the ship? I want the two of you to shut up. If I hear any more about medals, you'll both be demoted." The admiral's outburst notwithstanding, Whitey was awarded a Distinguished Flying Cross and an Air Medal for downing three Bettys.

By February 9, 1943, the Japanese had completed their covert evacuation, and that same day the Americans declared the end of organized resistance. The six-month campaign for Guadalcanal had cost 29 American ships, 38 Japanese ships, and a total of 1,300 aircraft.

Scouting Squadron Five (VS-5) at Naval Air Station, North Island California in the fall of 1939. This was my first fleet squadron and we were attached to the USS Yorktown CV-5 and flew SBC-3 dive bombers which were bi-planes.

Swede's first squadron (VS-5) on board the USS *Yorktown* (CV 5) in the fall of 1939. As his handwritten notes detail, VS-5 flew soon-to-be or already obsolete SBC-3 biplanes. *Vejtasa collection*

A bomb-rigged SBD Dauntless is readied for takeoff from the USS *Yorktown*. Note the national insignia still contains a red circle in the center, and red and white stripes decorate the rudder. By mid-May 1942, the rudder circles were eliminated along with the red circles in the national insignia, which could and did lead to misidentification of the aircraft's nationality. *Vejtasa collection*

Squadron commander Jimmy Flatley (left) welcomes Swede and Johnny Leppla. Aggressive flyers, Swede and Leppla both had been awarded Navy Crosses at the Battle of the Coral Sea for downing Zeros while flying SBD dive-bombers. As part of Flatley's VF-10, they transitioned to F4F Wildcat fighters during the summer of 1942. *National Archives and Records Administration*

A Navy Cross with two gold stars, a Bronze Star with Combat V, two Presidential Unit Citations, and the Legion of Merit, among other service ribbons, testified to a heroic and accomplished career. Reflecting on it all, Capt. Stanley W. "Swede" Vejtasa had good reason to smile. *Vejtasa collection*

In 1987 Swede was inducted into the Carrier Aviation Hall of Fame. Here Swede accepts his certificate on board the *Essex*-class carrier *Yorktown*, namesake of his first carrier assignment and currently a museum at Patriots Point, South Carolina. Also inducted that year were fellow high performers Ed Heinneman, Rear Adm. John Crommelin, Capt. Art Downing, Adm. J. J. "Jocko" Clark, and Lt. Cdr. Godfrey deC. Chevalier. *Vejtasa collection*

A vibrant Robbie Robinson at age eighty-nine. At Santa Cruz Robinson endured the horrors on board the *Hornet* during her ordeal. In a turnabout during the naval battle for Guadalcanal he shared responsibility for sinking one of Tanaka's transports and shot down a Zero while barely avoiding being shot down himself. His shot-up Dauntless later showed up in the movie *Guadalcanal Diary*. *Photograph by Ted Edwards*

Swede, still using fighter-pilot sign language at age ninety-seven, recounted his Coral Sea combat. Piloting an SBD Dauntless dive-bomber during this engagement, he outflew three Japanese Zeros. *Photograph by Ted Edwards*

CHAPTER 15

From Combat to Commander

Though Guadalcanal was now secure, February 13 was a sad day for Swede and the rest of the Reapers. Jimmy Flatley, their revered leader, was headed off to a new command—air group commander on the new *Yorktown* (CV 10). Too worked up to address the Reapers in person, he had Killer Kane, the new skipper, read a farewell letter.

A period of relative tranquility followed, during which the Navy brass shifted their attention to the next-generation carrier fighter. The British had already adapted the Chance Vought bent-wing Corsairs to their carriers, raising the question of how those same fighters might operate off American carriers. Before his departure from VF-10, Jimmy Flatley had asked Swede, the most experienced pilot available and known as a man with a penchant for truthfully speaking his mind, to test-fly the first F4U Corsair on board *Enterprise*.

Swede described his March 19 assignment. "One Bureau Number 02232, assigned to VF-10, got sent to Espiritu Santo, and they had a big, thick catalog that went with it. This was the test materials, what they want tested, what we should do. I'm not sure how VF-10 wound up with this. Fritz Faulkner, our engineering officer, took the whole thing over. He wrote up the preparations and the final assessment; all I did was fly it and tell him what was going on.

"This was an interesting bit of flying as we were able to test the plane against our Wildcats in the air. The F4U was faster, having a 2,000 h.p. engine, and a supercharger made it better at altitude." There were, however, some nagging issues.

Less than pleased with the plane's performance during his five landings, Swede observed, "It was a bit of an ordeal." The Corsair had a low tail wheel, and Swede found the brakes inadequate. That model, the F4U-1, had fifty-five-gallon wingtip fuel tanks. "Just imagine maneuvering with some three hundred pounds in each wingtip. You don't want weight out there. Think of what would happen if you were unable to purge one or use one and not the other. Now this happened. What the hell do you do?"[1]

Worse, the gun-recharging mechanism was inconsistent, capable of spontaneous gunfire across the deck. With these apprehensions in mind, Swede would be first in line for takeoffs. During landings Swede had to skid the long-nosed fighter just to see the LSO, a counterintuitive distraction that could endanger flight deck personnel. Whitey, assisting Swede in the proceedings, noted that the F4U-1 had a strong tendency to stall out during the left turn into the groove, and the landing hydraulics could ricochet the airplane back into the air. The drawbacks were not limited to these potentially lethal idiosyncrasies. For every hour of flight time, the Corsair demanded a full eleven hours of maintenance, boosting the work requirements of already hustling hangar deck crews. Alarmed by these serious shortcomings, Swede recommended that the Navy restrict Corsairs to the land-based Marines flying out of Espiritu Santo. The Navy's soon-to-arrive Grumman F6F Hellcats would provide the next upgrade.

Years later, Swede praised the subsequent improvements that made the Corsair a favorite with Marine air wings throughout the Pacific. After the war, Whitey assisted Marion Carl at Pax River to adapt the F4U into a functional carrier plane. Modifications included a raised cockpit and pilot seat, altered fuel tanks, improved landing gear, accountable guns, and better brakes. During the Korean War these changes rendered the F4U a formidable carrier weapons platform.

Swede later reflected, "With so much politics and power from Chance Vought, the F4U was going to fly or else. They didn't give a damn about how many people it took with it. Chance Vought never forgave me because we wrote it as it was."

Say Good-bye

On board *Enterprise* on May 27, 1943, Admiral Nimitz stood before the assembled crew and read President Roosevelt's presidential unit citation, the first ever awarded to an aircraft carrier. Shortly after that ceremony

Swede received orders to rotate back to the States. He would never again lay eyes on the heroic *Enterprise*.

By the end of his combined *Yorktown* and *Enterprise* combat tours Swede had played a significant role in two carrier battles. He bombed transports and an aircraft carrier; shot down a Zero floatplane; outdueled three Zeros; and shot down two Val dive-bombers, six Kate torpedo bombers, and a Kawanishi flying boat. These accomplishments all took place early in the war when highly experienced Japanese pilots in their superior aircraft largely defined the rules of engagement. Interestingly, Swede had outflown Zero pilots in an SBD but never had an opportunity take on Zeros in a Wildcat.

Finally, this menace to Japanese pilots and ships and vocal critic of the U.S. admiralty was exiting the Pacific theater. Swede—the indispensable, get-it-done guy, the gutsy pilot who always brought his people and plane back—had flown his last combat mission in the Pacific war, or anywhere else, for that matter.

Swede's was not an insignificant departure. Jimmy Flatley, in an August 3, 1943, letter to Cdr. F. W. Wead, wrote, "In regard to Vejtasa I do feel that he is the best fighter pilot of the war. His status as the greatest fighter pilot cannot be actually substantiated because he had few opportunities for aerial combat. Potentially, he is the best I've seen or heard of." Referring to the Ouvea incident, Flatley remarked, "Six hours and fifteen minutes in an F4F is quite a feat in itself." Flatley encouraged Commander Wead to look Swede up. "I know you would enjoy meeting the guy."

Swede, Whitey, and Robbie had survived those dark, embattled days on and around Guadalcanal, and those shared experiences created enduring friendships. By early summer 1943, Swede, Robbie, and Whitey had all rotated home, each to very different circumstances. By July of that year Robbie was assigned to VB-2 operating out of Wildwood, New Jersey. "The Lousy Squadron," was how Robbie viewed the posting. "The CO was an Academy guy with no combat experience; same for the XO and the operations officer. They were washout fliers sent home early from the war. No veteran pilot wanted to fly wing on an incompetent leader."

Whitey also went east, in his case to Virginia. He would train pilots of the VF-8 fighter squadron for the new carrier USS *Intrepid* air group. His work involved training in the F6F Hellcat, but Whitey too was bedeviled with a lousy commander whose autocratic style clashed with Jimmy Flatley's.

While there were only occasional opportunities to see one another after Air Group 10's breakup, each kept the others' phone numbers. Theirs was a distinguished brotherhood.

From Combat to Commander

Swede's return to the States contrasted sharply with Robbie's and Whitey's experiences. Rather than training replacement pilots, Swede toured Navy bases and air stations all around the country, talking up the war and endlessly recounting his exploits. Though being paraded as a hero helped sell war bonds, the experience left Swede feeling useless.

He could laugh about it later on, but at the time there was nothing funny about Swede's next set of orders making him officer in charge (OIC) of a small boat basin in Annapolis, Maryland. "This is how they want to make the most of my combat experience?" he fretted. "They needed me back home for this?" Frustrated by this absurd turn of events, he told his wife, Irene, that the Navy could "take this order—they know what they can do with it."

He demanded a change of orders, and like many veteran pilots he pleaded, "Just send me back to the Pacific." Sure, it was great to have earned a rest, but not returning to the theater, resuming the fight, felt like bailing on comrades still in harm's way. Maybe there was some survivor's guilt, but having come through intense combat, Swede and the others already possessed the skills to do the job that needed doing. For some, it wasn't simply a desire to return to combat. Robbie, as we have seen, found himself rotated into a poorly led stateside squadron that posed more dangers than the combat he had survived in the Pacific. *Send us back*, they pleaded. Those understandable emotions notwithstanding, wiser minds prevailed.

Instead of the hoped-for return to combat, Swede got new orders to command fighter squadron training at the new air station in Atlantic City, New Jersey, under ComFair Quonset. This assignment, far more attuned to Swede's talents, would last for more than a year.

While a stateside training gig was definitely not his preference, Swede understood its importance. Of course, Swede brought far more than textbook theory to the job. Replacement pilots were eager to listen to a man who had outperformed some of Japan's premier airmen. Swede knew what they would face in combat, what to expect from the Japanese pilots and aircraft, and he knew how to instruct and inspire. Swede was the right man for the job, and he excelled at it.

"I was there longer than I wanted. It was good duty. We provided ground and in-flight instruction including gunnery, rocketry, bombing, and individual combat for pilots of forming squadrons. Many pilots were sent for individual instruction, which was always pleasant and I believe very helpful. I flew with the fighters, taught formation flying and Japanese fighter tactics. About that time we got the new airplanes, the Grumman F6F Hellcats and Chance Vought F4U Corsairs. Among those other than naval officers was Corky Meyers of Grumman Aircraft, who gave a full course including landing qualifications on board carriers in the F6F. There were two British officers who were top-notch pilots, and I learned from them also as they were veterans of much combat in the European theater.

"One of my most interesting experiences was with Col. Tommy Hitch-cock, who was a P-51 pilot in the Army Air Corps and spent much time in England. Undoubtedly one of the greatest polo players of all time and a great athlete, Tommy was a joy to fly with and quickly absorbed our Navy tactics. Over many tours and sessions I flew all the fighters, even with the Army Air Force, working out combat tactics."[2]

The rookie pilots, nervous about combat defense, wanted to hear Swede's thoughts on the Thach Weave. Despite his conviction that the Weave could be broken and could easily generate midair collisions, Swede reluctantly taught the tactic to combat pilot trainees. "A lot of pilots never questioned it; I was afraid to try it. I considered it a dangerous maneuver. I demonstrated for Lt. David McCampbell [the future ace] the fallacy of the Thach Weave. My advice was if you want to use it, it's your prerogative. I don't recommend it."

Despite Swede's lack of faith in the Thach Weave, his superiors appreciated his many contributions to training proficiency. On November 29, 1943, Admiral Durgin spot-promoted him to lieutenant commander. Late the next spring, Swede welcomed a second son, Daniel, born June 3, 1944.

In October 1944 Swede took over as skipper of VF-97, an eight-month assignment that lasted halfway into 1945. Early that spring, Swede and

Robbie got back together for a mission of mercy. Bearing seafood and a bottle of Old Forester, they dropped in on Capt. John M. "Peg-Leg" Hoskins, a man possessed of an illustrious résumé. Among his other accomplishments, Hoskins had commanded USS *Memphis*, which returned Charles Lindbergh and his *Spirit of St. Louis* to the United States. Later, his ship directed the search for Amelia Earhart. Hoskins had served as air officer and executive officer on board *Ranger* (CV 4) during the first year of the war, and after serving in a staff position he had secured the coveted billet as prospective CO of USS *Princeton* (CVL 23). Currently he languished in a hospital bed, his right foot having been blown off during the Battle of Leyte Gulf. Even worse, *Princeton*, his prospective command, had been sunk. Deprived of both his foot and his next command, Hoskins was in serious need of cheering up.

On one visit Peg-Leg told Swede that Admiral Halsey had stopped by and wanted to know how he might bolster his old friend. "Give me command of that ship out my window," Hoskins implored, referring to the newly renamed replacement for the *Princeton* sunk at Leyte. Halsey assured Hoskins he would do what he could. In the meantime, someone convinced Peg-Leg that he would have to pass an absurd test to get his command. Wearing an artificial leg, he would have to make his way up from the ready room to the flight deck in full-dress regalia, sword included, in a specified time. Hoskins feared he would come up short. His worry was unfounded. Halsey had his way, and Hoskins received his coveted command.

In late July 1945 Swede's highly effective pilot training received official notice. His Bronze Star citation read in part:

He was directly responsible for the training of fighter pilots for new and re-formed carrier fighter squadrons. The efficient and able manner in which he discharged his duties, his ingenuity, initiative and sound judgment, industry and untiring devotion to duty are considered to have been a major factor in developing the operational readiness of carrier aircraft fighter squadrons destined for combat service in the Pacific.

The qualities and results achieved by him during this highly important and critical period in our history reflect great credit on himself and upon the United States Naval Service.

Swede was a rising star. Starting in August, and for the next five months, Swede served as commander, Air Group 44. Across the Pacific, meanwhile, a terrifying event was about to terminate the need for further combat training.

Victory over Japan

On August 6, 1945, an atomic bomb obliterated the city of Hiroshima. Three days later, on August 9, a second atomic bomb devastated Nagasaki. Six horror-filled days after that, on August 15, Emperor Hirohito asked the Japanese people to endure the "unthinkable" and lay down their arms.

The atomic bomb was not a complete surprise to Swede. Between scuttlebutt, rumor, and loose lips, "I had a pretty good idea of what was going on. I knew there was a bomb coming; it was just a question of could it be controlled. When they dropped the bombs I knew it would be over. They had some good data on what that bomb would do. The Japanese couldn't continue. I didn't know there were two of them, but it wouldn't have taken long to produce others—they had the material to make more. I spent a lot of time in Japan. Anybody that's exposed to radiation . . . that's powerful, inhumane. I wouldn't want to see any atom-bomb war."

Commanding Officer, VF-17

On board the new USS *Hornet* (CV 12), members of the VF-17 Jolly Rogers were in the process of switching from Hellcats to Corsairs. Their skipper had just left, and everyone wondered who would take over. Swede got the nod and suddenly found himself in charge of some thirty-five to forty fighter pilots.

"In September of 1945 I was reassigned as commanding officer of VF-17 based at Fallon, Nevada. This, again, was a most enjoyable time. Our CAG, Cdr. Bush Bringle, was a fine leader with much recent combat experience, and he worked out a real practical course of training, fitting for the many experienced pilots who were staying in the service intending to make the Navy a career."

Lt. Bill Hardy served as squadron engineering officer. Rising up from the enlisted ranks, Bill had earned his wings flying Hellcats. He flew superbly in the Pacific, most notably during the intense kamikaze raids over Okinawa.

On April 16, 1945, he flew an ace-in-a-day mission. For that remarkable performance Bill was awarded a well-deserved Navy Cross. The war over, "his job now was to keep airplanes flying. He was in charge of repair and maintenance, a big job," Swede recalled.

Hardy described their training regimen. "Swede took each of us up, told us to break right or left, turn 180 degrees, and make passes on him. I got on Swede and he couldn't shake me. He got on me and I couldn't shake him. The exercise was a draw. We couldn't shake each other, and we became good friends over that."

With the postwar demobilization, the Navy hoped to keep the public interested in naval aviation. Faced with a growing Air Force presence and competition for declining postwar funding, Admiral Nimitz listened closely as Navy commander Leroy Simpler suggested an acrobatic flight team. What began as the Naval Flight Demonstration Team would quickly gain renown as the Blue Angels, and VF-10 veterans were heavily involved. Lt. Cdr. Butch Voris led the first group. Whitey Feightner flew with them in the 1950s; Wick Wickendoll, Whitey's former section leader, served for a time; and Dusty Rhodes later served as Angel leader.

Given Swede's history and time spent training fighter pilots, he was considered a shoe-in. Swede, however, didn't care to join the team. "Flatley spoke to me about it. As CO of VF-17, I didn't feel like I was in a position to be considered. I didn't care for routine exhibitions; I just wasn't interested. It was great publicity for the Navy. I supported it but didn't care to participate. I wanted more time to spend with the wife and kids."

The demonstrations were risky business, and the schedule would have seriously complicated his already transient life. Having survived two life-threatening tours in the Pacific, Swede had no desire to further risk his hide in public displays. He would continue his work with VF-17.

"In VF-17 we flew the F4U-4 aircraft, which by this time was well established as a fleet aircraft with combat background. These planes were equipped with a new supercharger, which provided more power and better performance at altitude. I fear I was a bit spoiled, as in late January Cdr. John Smith had come by and let me fly a new F8F-1 Bearcat. I had followed the development of this plane and had met often with the designer, so I maintained an avid interest, hoping to get a squadron as soon as they were in production. This plane was a dream for a fighter pilot, with the performance and handling I had long advocated in a fighter aircraft." Indeed, the Blue Angels chose Bearcats for their high-performance demonstrations.

From May 1946 to May 1947 Swede attended General Line School in Newport, Rhode Island. It was not a productive year. "The stated purpose of the school was commendable, but it did not provide the broadening education I had hoped for. They got the idea from D.C. planners. So many officers had not been exposed to college. The program was a dismal failure. There was too much material, the math was tough on everyone, and they lost me in the first two or three lessons. There were redundant classes on aviation, which pilots often skipped. In the course on electricity, a sharp teacher could lose the class in minutes. I did not fare well in the class; there was no time to pick up the basics, and there was an exam every three to four days." Toward the end of his schoolwork, on May 13, 1947, Irene gave birth to their daughter, Susan.

Concurrently that year, from May 1946 until November 1947, Swede also served as navigator and training officer on board USS *Sicily* (CVE 118). "*Sicily* was a sub hunter. It was a horrible job. I was desperately trying to identify the ship's position; the sun was always covered, there were no stars, what the hell do you do? I tried to pick up radio signals from anywhere to get a bearing. I didn't know where I was half the time. But it did provide a good introduction to modern antisubmarine warfare, coordinating aircraft operations with surface vessel hunts and attacks."

Events then provided Swede another opportunity to do what he most loved. "Due to an unfortunate accident in November of 1947, VF-10's skipper operating off the USS *Philippine Sea* (CV 47) was lost. No senior carrier-qualified pilot was readily available, but a staff officer who had known me on the *Yorktown* said, 'Get Swede' and called me up. 'Do you want to take that squadron?' I left that afternoon."

Thus began a nine-month billet commanding VF-10A, later redesignated VF-92, the Be-Devilers. Their South Atlantic/Mediterranean cruise, deployed to join Vice Adm. Forrest Sherman's Sixth Fleet the following spring, included pleasant ports of call in France, Italy, Greece, and Tunisia.

"This was most opportune for me because the squadron flew F8F-1 Bearcats, which made it possible for me to realize my hope of flying the dream fighter in all phases of training and operations aboard the carrier. I look back on the year of 1948 as being one of the best. We had a great air group and a fine bunch of pilots."

The Bearcat was imposing just to look at. Grumman's latest "cat," after the Wildcat and Hellcat, was a state-of-the-art, high-performance fighter. Given the structural demands of catapult launches and sudden arrests inherent in carrier work, the Bearcats had to be sturdy. Heavier built, clearly durable, yet somehow sleek, this plane represented a serious upgrade in fighter aircraft, and every Navy fighter pilot worth his wings wanted in on that.

The Bearcat did not disappoint. "With the F8Fs we roamed the skies, jumping other aircraft, including the older Air Force P-51s, which were no match for us. We deployed to the Mediterranean for six months and had a great time training and exercising. We met the British Spitfire and bested them. I had a flight in one of their planes in Malta and enjoyed it immensely but remembered my brief flights in the Spitfire Mk V of wartime vintage, which I like much better as it seemed easier to handle and more responsive. That was marvelous duty." It was to be a brief relationship with that beloved fighter; naval aviation was turning to jets.

In June 1948 *Philippine Sea* returned to the United States, where Swede worked up doctrine for carrier-controlled approach landings similar to ground-control approach. November of that year was spent exploring regions of the Arctic Circle testing ships, planes, and equipment in severe cold. Three years into the future, this seemingly off-the-radar training would prove prescient.

The Pursuit of Supersonic

"While I was off doing my fourteen months with Fighting 10, the Navy was busy flying the Phase I D-558-I Skystreak and Phase II D-558-II swept-wing Skyrocket in an effort to break the sound barrier." Over the next two years, from February 1949 until January 1951, Swede served as Bureau of Aeronautics general representative, Western District, at NAS Mojave. Located at Muroc, California, the base had recently been renamed Edwards Air Force Base for Capt. Glen Edwards, killed the year before in a crash of his YB-49 Flying Wing. Swede's vast experience with Army, Air Force, and Allied pilots made him a wise selection for the upcoming work as the Navy liaison officer. Swede would be coordinating with Air Force officers and personnel, integrating Navy–Air Force efforts at a time when elsewhere the interservice relationship was highly antagonistic.

In Washington, D.C., an inter–armed forces drama was building up to what would be dubbed the Admirals' Revolt. On September 18, 1947, the Air Force detached from the Army Air Corps and became a distinct service. That new identity would further intensify competition for increasingly scarce postwar funding. As if to demonstrate the continued need for a robust military, not quite a year later on June 24, 1948, Soviet forces blockaded all road, rail, and water routes into Allied-controlled areas of Berlin. Thus was born the British-American Berlin Airlift, destined to last nearly a year. On March 28, 1949, President Harry Truman appointed Louis Johnson, known for his pro–Air Force views, to succeed James Forrestal as secretary of defense. Despite the ongoing Berlin Airlift and escalating tensions with China, Johnson was ordered to slash defense budgets.

Which service would be hit the hardest? Working in the Air Force's favor was the fact that the only way to take atomic war to Russia's far-flung industrial sites was on board Air Force B-36 long-range bombers. With such targets beyond the reach of Navy carrier bombers, the argument went that naval aviation was limited to tactical rather than strategic missions. To address this shortcoming, the keel had recently been laid for USS *United States* (CVA 58), the Navy's first jet aircraft and nuclear weapons–capable carrier.

Within a month of his appointment, on April 23, 1949, Johnson boldly halted construction of the *United States* while Navy Secretary John L. Sullivan was out of town. Sullivan angrily resigned; naval aviators grew increasingly apprehensive. When Johnson's budget cuts specifically targeted Marine and Navy aviation, the Navy brass feared losing their aviation to the Air Force and the Marines to the Army. Adm. Arthur W. Radford, commander in chief of the Pacific Fleet, returned to Washington to orchestrate the Navy's response.

A revolt was shaping up. By October, a House Armed Services Committee hearing featured notables such as Adm. William F. Halsey, Adm. Thomas Kinkaid, Adm. Chester Nimitz, Adm. Ernest J. King, and Capt. Arleigh A. Burke. In support, Robbie Robinson flew admirals around the country and gave speeches defending naval aviation to VFW meetings;

veterans' groups; chambers of commerce; and Rotary, Kiwanis, and Lions Clubs. Their collective efforts became known as the Revolt of the Admirals. Regardless of the good feelings the Blue Angels demonstration team inspired, these were scary times for the Navy.

It was against this backdrop that Swede got to work at flat, desolate Edwards AFB. "Al Carder was the company project chief on base at the time and was a most capable director with whom I enjoyed the finest rapport," Swede fondly recalled. Ignoring the enmity playing out in Washington, coordinator Al Carder oversaw an unwritten, cooperative competition between the Navy and Air Force. Initially their mutual objective had been to pierce the sound barrier with the latest rocket planes and turbojets. By October 1947, well before Swede arrived on the scene, Air Force captain Chuck Yeager had done just that. Since that accomplishment, both the Navy and the Air Force had pressed for new speed records, eager to expand their understanding of how aircraft might respond during and after penetrating Yeager's sonic portal.

"I recall watching most of one flight in which Yeager's plane went out of control and seemed doomed to crash. However, Chuck stayed with it, taking a terrific beating, finally recovered, and landed on the dry lakebed. I saw Chuck the next day and he was black, blue, and purple with badly bloodshot eyes from being buffeted about against the sides of the cockpit and canopy at terribly high g loads. Chuck smiled good-naturedly and allowed it to having been 'a bit rough.' He was one tough cookie."

In some ways the business of exploring the frontiers of space was a boy's dream; attach a rocket to everything and see how fast it could go. Exhilarating, intoxicating stuff, to be sure, but these rocket jockeys took big risks and got beat up or worse in their daunting work.

On June 25, 1950, interservice enmity dissolved when North Korea invaded South Korea. The South Korean army, accompanied by U.S. advisory units, hastily retreated to a collapsing Pusan perimeter in the southeast corner of South Korea. Absent a Soviet Union Security Council veto, the UN responded with force. Only USS *Valley Forge* (CV 45), aka "Happy Valley," with none other than Rear Adm. Peg-Leg Hoskins embarked, currently held station in the western Pacific. She launched the first Navy strikes and provided close air support in a desperate effort to avoid the complete eviction of the Allies from the Korean peninsula.

This far-off war had big implications for the research and test piloting going on at Muroc. Aeronautical engineers found themselves scrambling to counter the prowess of Russian MiG-15 fighters. Test-piloting new designs proved highly dangerous. Over a period of nine months the Air Force lost sixty-two pilots testing aircraft earmarked for Korea.

Swede focused on the collaborative nature of his work. "I was much pleased as the Bureau of Aeronautics representative to be working with the prime contractors on new aircraft and also keeping up with the many Air Force projects. Air Force personnel were always helpful and considerate and provided me with an opportunity to check out in their jets and fly chase during project flights. We had a number of planes—Douglas A-3 Skywarriors, F3D Skyknights (later designated the F-10), and others—all doing test work at Edwards that I got to watch.

"I was the project officer on the Navy's jet rocket ship, the D-558-I, which I never flew. The D-558-II was different. That one held eight speed records at one time. They wanted to break the speed of sound, and of course, with jets and rocket power, the D-558 was designed to do just that.

"My job was to work with Douglas, the manufacturer, and make sure everything was on schedule. The rocket motors came from Rocket Motors Inc., produced in Germany. I was the overseer."

Swede was involved with a pool of aeronautical luminaries; whether they were Air Force or Navy didn't matter. Chuck Yeager often flew chase on Navy D-588 flights, and Navy pilots returned the favor during the Bell X-1 series. There was no rivalry; the goal at Muroc was to go beyond the known, shred the old boundaries.

"I well remember one of the first flights of the Skyrocket with pilot Gene May (the sixth man to fly faster than the speed of sound) at the controls, which went well, lasted eleven minutes, and in which the pilot's contract called for one thousand dollars a minute. I could hardly believe it." Beyond May's notoriety as the sixth human to pierce the sound barrier, he had outdone himself by flying Mach 1 at ground level. This was money earned at the edge!

"Bill Bridgeman, a former Navy pilot, followed Gene May, and after a number of flights the Navy procured a B-29, which was configured to carry the D-558-II to altitude for a drop in order to achieve more flight time. I signed for the B-29, designated a P2B-1S, with Georgie Jansen as pilot and myself as copilot. As ever, I was most fortunate to be associated with Georgie, a master pilot with vast World War II experience in multiengine bombers. His Purple Heart came as a result of flying his B-24 Liberator over Ploesti, and he'd survived many an attack by enemy fighters over Europe. Georgie went on to test-fly the Douglas A2D Skyshark. He was a patient instructor and soon had me maneuvering the monster drop plane with complete confidence. We made many successful flights dropping the D-558 Skyrocket at altitude with Bill Bridgeman at the controls. These flights contributed immensely to our knowledge of high-speed flight. Shortly after I left, Bridgeman flew a Skyrocket to 1.88 times the speed of sound, a short-term record."[3]

"NACA [the National Advisory Committee on Aeronautics] was also based at Muroc, California, and this fine group let me fly a number of their planes such as the twin-jet-powered Bell P-59 Airacomet on familiarization flights and chase. NACA eventually took over the Skyrocket for additional data collection flights." On October 30, 1949, Swede advanced in rank to commander.

The Stapp Strap

Air Force colonel Dr. John Stapp was testing acceleration and deceleration forces in an effort to discover human tolerances around the shocking decelerations experienced during high-speed jet pilot ejections. Channeling Jimmy Flatley, Stapp aimed to develop strapping that could better protect pilots against the blunt forces they would encounter. There was mutual admiration between Swede and Stapp. "The good doctor came to pick me up a number of times to witness tests and even offered to give me a ride."

Normally one to jump at the chance for a ride on anything, Swede politely declined. Swede had begged off a ride on Stapp's rail sled originally set up to analyze the dreadful World War II German V-1 "buzz bombs" that had terrified London and vicinity. Postwar the track had been converted to an acceleration laboratory and was critical to the study of g forces. No backbench engineer, Stapp had volunteered for thirty-five torturous sled runs during which he survived far higher acceleration and deceleration g forces than had been thought possible. This brutal regimen conferred a multitude of bodily insults, including fractures of his wrist and collarbone, blood-filled eyes, bruises, and abrasions—all relatively minor but painful injuries. It took a lot of guts to strap in for yet another bang-me-up sled ride. The "careful daredevil" with a serious sense of humor became known for Stapp's Law, the ironic paradox that stated, "The universal aptitude for ineptitude makes any human accomplishment an incredible miracle."

Swede, like many others, was in awe of the man. "Dr. Stapp never asked a man of his crew to take a test ride until he had made one first. He later became the world's fastest human in this type of travel when he rode the sled at NOTS China Lake at some phenomenal speed and survived very nicely. I say he earned his retirement."[4]

CHAPTER 16

———

No Easy Days

Air Boss on USS Essex

I f the testing regimen at Muroc had been invigorating and fun, Swede's next billet in the Sea of Japan would be anything but. "The Navy had an older carrier that had just been redone. It was coming out of the yard, and they had an air officer on board who had suddenly come up with some very bad physical problems and needed to be replaced. So they tapped me. This good duty at Muroc ended when I received orders to report to the USS *Essex* (CV 9) as air officer."[1]

Something like operations officer, the air officer, or air boss, is third in command behind the captain and executive officer. The position meant that Swede managed four squadrons: the pilots and crew of VF-51, flying F9F Panthers; VF-53, a Corsair squadron; VF-54 flying Douglas AD Skyraiders; and McDonnell F2H Banshee squadron VF-172. His responsibilities further included rescue helicopters, handlers, armorers, and maintenance crews—in short, anyone involved with flight operations.

Korean Drumbeat, Deadly Attrition

As air boss, Swede had to contend with the "carrier demons." Any sailor's list of demons had to include weather and the sea beneath. This theater of operations would challenge the crews with typhoons, polar fronts, blistering heat, ice and snow, and piercing winds—conditions that could demoralize any crew. The harsh Korean climate rendered ships, planes, and catapults vulnerable to breakdown or failure. In addition to these environmental stresses, pilots faced accurate, concentrated enemy antiaircraft fire and crews feared mines that sank many auxiliary ships; everyone was on edge. An inescapable demon was basic human error. Even the best machine can be undone by simple mistakes and oversights. The added pressures of war, extreme weather, and overwork made slip-ups far more likely.

Compounding all of this, morale among the mostly Reservist pilots was lousy from the start. A few short years before, these men had contributed to winning a world war, defeating Nazi Germany and Imperial Japan. They had served well and survived the horrors, and they wanted nothing more than to savor peacetime normalcy, get married, have kids, buy a home. Many had started new businesses. Suddenly they were back flying combat missions in an inconclusive "police action," deeply resentful of the lucky guys back in the States who had not been wrenched out of homes, families, and jobs.

Further fueling their resentment was the fact that this "Korean Conflict" was about foreign interdiction, not national security. The Koreans and Chinese had not invaded America. In this war, the Allies were the ones bombing and killing Koreans defending their own country. To make matters worse for the pilots, President Truman, anticipating a quick victory, had restricted their operations. Instead of destroying the Communists' ability to wage war, Truman had hoped to preserve Korea's infrastructure for a postwar recovery, a policy that had endangered a lot of pilots.

By October 1950 Gen. Douglas MacArthur had pushed North Korean troops back near the border with China. On October 25, after issuing warnings, China flooded close to 300,000 troops across the border to prop up its North Korean ally. Shocked by this development, Truman was forced to broaden the scope of Allied operations. Eventually the Chinese were stopped, but the resulting stalemate and going-nowhere peace talks to conclude an unending, unwinnable war stripped hope from any man's equation, created legions of cynics, and magnified the stresses already in play.

The morale problem ran deep.[2] Swede understood that poor morale was also linked to hardships back home. "The guys returning to service weren't making any money. I heard stories about how tough it was for these guys to pay for their homes bought in peacetime with peacetime salaries. Others told of little food at home. It was very difficult. Of at least four officers to serve with me, three committed suicide after they had detached. One had served as assistant flight deck officer, another as gunnery officer, and the third was hangar deck officer. All those positions were tough jobs—handling ordnance, loading bombs, napalm."

Swede's air group would contribute to an established order of battle. The faster and short-legged Panther and Banshee jets would swoop in to suppress AA fire, followed by Corsairs and ADs carting the heavier bridge-busting or rail-cutting bomb loads. The remarkable AD Skyraiders could haul the same bomb load as a World War II B-17 and remain four hours on station. Swede added, "We could strafe, drop napalm, fire rockets, or drop bombs. The AD was the right plane for this war." If MiG-15s showed up to disrupt these missions, pilots were instructed to dive away and head for Wonsan Harbor and let the Air Force F-86 Sabre jets tangle with the high-performance MiGs.

Swede's first Korean combat tour began in August 1951, and it wasn't long before things got nasty. They had not even reached their combat station when Typhoon Marge battered *Essex* and her escorts for three misery-filled days. Heavy swells had been damaging, but officers and crew alike were badly shaken when, in the black of midnight on August 21, 1951, *Essex* tipped a scary 25 degrees. Wave action and equipment breaking loose resulted in a long list of needed repairs. When she rendezvoused with Task Force 77, *Essex* sported a humbled crew.

On August 22, 1951, *Essex*, with Rear Adm. John "Blackjack" Perry, commander Carrier Division One, embarked, joined USS *Boxer* (CV 21) and USS *Bon Homme Richard* (CV 31) to form Task Force 77, under the overall command of Rear Adm. W. G. Tomlinson. Their mission was to support UN forces advancing north of the thirty-eighth parallel by providing close support, deep support, armed and photo reconnaissance, interdiction of enemy supply lines, and strikes against enemy installations.

In addition to *Boxer* and *Bon Homme Richard*, carrier roulette in that first year of the conflict had *Essex* rotating with *Valley Forge*, *Philippine Sea*, USS *Leyte* (CV 32), and *Princeton*. Once in theater, a roughly six-month tour was broken into four combat segments interspersed with replenishment breaks.

On August 23, 1951, *Essex* launched F2H Banshee jets, opening up a new chapter in carrier aviation. But any celebration of that accomplishment would be muted. That same day, before rotten weather canceled operations, Lt. (jg) Eugene Leo Frantz, piloting an F4U Corsair in instrument weather, became separated from his flight leader and was never seen again. The next day Ens. Gordon E. Strickland's AD-4 lost power on takeoff; he made a water landing ahead of the carrier and was rescued by a vigilant helicopter.

On August 25, twelve F2H-2s and twelve F9Fs escorted thirty Air Force B-29 Superfortress bombers. In a departure from the interservice acrimony of the late 1940s and its consequent Revolt of the Admirals, for the first time Navy aircraft escorted Air Force bombers on a strike. "That was unusual," Swede observed. "Our business was strikes."

A series of horrendous trials to come began a day later when an AD-4N burst into flames in the air and crashed, killing Lt. (jg) Lauren D. Smith and his crewman, Aviation Electronics Technician Airman (E-3) Phillip Kendall Balch. During a bombing run on that same August 26, one of VF-51's Panthers was hit by AA fire. As the pilot struggled to control his plane, he swept through a "clothesline" steel cable the North Koreans had strung between hills to bring down low-flying aircraft. That shocking intersection sliced several feet off his starboard wing. Somehow, he gained control and coaxed a very compromised Panther toward Pohang near a Marine airfield designated K-3, where he made his first ever ejection. In storybook fashion, no sooner had he landed than a Jeep pulled up and out jumped one of his flight school roommates. Two days later, young Ens. Neil Armstrong was back flying Panthers.[3]

The day after Armstrong lost his plane, two F9Fs crashed and burned, killing pilots Lt. (jg) Ross Kay Bramwell and Lt. (jg) James Joseph Ashford. On August 30, an F4U-5NL returning from a night heckler mission flew into the water; a screen destroyer picked up the pilot. On September 2, cracks were detected in the catapult hooks, and a Corsair caught fire en route to the target area; the pilot was rescued. On September 3, Lt. Frank N. Sistrunk, flying an AD, was lost fifteen miles inside enemy territory. On September 8, an F4U-4B went down to enemy action; a bombardment destroyer recovered the pilot. That same day Lt. (jg) Joseph Buford Parse Jr. was seen pressing home his bombing run when his AD suddenly burst into flames, crashed, and burned. Three days later when one of those new

Banshees landed without braking power and rolled off the side, the reliable *Essex* helicopter performed the rescue. The next day, September 14, a Skyraider was forced to ditch, the pilot again rescued.

In just a little more than two weeks the air group had lost seven airmen and thirteen aircraft to enemy action and operational accidents. A psychological demon began eating at the survivors who had gone out and done the killing their jobs required, and in so doing witnessed the deaths of good friends and trusted squadronmates. Now safely back on board, they were tormented by their own survival. Everybody knew somebody, "a better man than me," lost. They had failed to get him home. The invisible wounds of sorrow, guilt, and grief made for somber ready rooms. As air boss, Swede was getting hammered. It would get a lot worse.

September 16, 1951

Swede set the stage. "The CO, Capt. Austin W. Wheelock, had neglected to have the nylon barrier installed. We had undergone an extensive $40 million overhaul at Bremerton, Washington. It was a big job, lots of changes. A barricade was available, but one of the last items on a long list of things to be done. We were late, and we put to sea without one, heading down to San Diego. Defending his decision, Captain Wheelock decided that there was no need for the nylon. The pilots and I were adamant that we needed the thing. He replied that we were needed back on station off Korea. This was war, and he was anxious to continue operations. So we went without a nylon barricade, and September 16 demonstrated the price of that decision."

On September 16, 1951, VF-53 exec Lt. Clayton Fisher, a storied vet from the Pacific war, was waiting to land when F2H pilot Lt. (jg) John Keller was involved in a midair collision and requested an emergency deferred landing. Clay Fisher looked on as Keller made his final approach and touched down on the deck. At first glance it looked as though Keller had landed well, but as Keller continued down the flight deck, Fisher noticed that his tail hook was not extended. Whether Keller neglected to or could not drop his tail hook didn't matter; he failed to snag a wire. A nylon barrier would have arrested the runaway and prevented what happened next.

Swede watched the whole thing from vulture's row. "It was an accident of the type dreaded by all hands. He came in for a routine recovery, a little fast.

Then he jumped the regular wires. There was no nylon barrier. His plane then crashed into parked aircraft refueling and reloading. A tremendous fire broke out from ruptured tanks and spilled fuel. Of grave danger were the AD planes parked on the port side and all loaded with tanks of napalm. One jet was giving the firefighters much trouble in that it was lodged in the pack with the tail to port and turning up at 100 percent aimed at the napalm-laden ADs. All efforts to stop the engine by pumping retardant foam into the intakes failed, so the flight deck officer, Cdr. Al Bolduc, with quick reaction and good judgment, had the driver of the deck crane lower the boom and push the plane over the side. As it went under, it was still turning up 100 percent, making the sea boil. I never had to say a word. The deck crews, without regard to safety, went in and snaked the planes with the napalm tanks back and away from the fire.

"The helicopter rescued several men from the water, a crewman jumping in and attaching a sling so one of the injured men could be hoisted on board and returned to the flight deck. I watched one particularly outstanding effort in which the helo hovered over a burning patch where a hand had been seen groping above the surface. The flames were dispersed by the wind from the blades and a crewman leaped into the water and attached the sling. I was on deck when the helo arrived and was shocked to see my good friend and former squadronmate from F8F [Bearcat] days, Lt. Cdr. John Moore. Badly burned, John would nonetheless recover and fly again. The medical crews were on deck tending to the injured and taking others to the sick bay for treatment.

"But that was the worst fire I ever witnessed aboard a carrier. Not one of those threatened ADs caught fire. It could have been far worse. You can't get rid of napalm." In the event, three men died, four went missing, and twenty-seven more were injured. Two F2H Banshees and two F9F Panthers were destroyed.

How could such a disaster come to pass? "The captain was an aviator, but not a flyer. He hadn't kept up with the latest developments. He was a fine guy, stubborn, a damn capable CO. After the crash there was an investigation, but there were no repercussions. This incident never hurt his career; he made admiral."

Swede held himself partially responsible. "Wheelock and I argued about landing Keller's plane dangling a bent tail hook. Wheelock trumped with,

'We are at war.' I gave in on that. I could have improved my performance by being more stubborn." Of course, there was only so far an officer could press an issue, because his future in the Navy depended on positive officer fitness reports written by his superiors. In this instance Wheelock would be assessing Swede's performance.

Swede looked to his assistant air boss, who "got along better with the captain. He could tell the CO it wasn't going to work out his way. I let him deal with the old man without much argument."

Before *Essex* departed for Yokosuka, one more AD lost power on takeoff and sank, making for yet another grateful pilot offering a helicopter crew a bottle of scotch. Since entering the combat zone, Air Group 5 had lost nine airmen, plus the three known dead and four missing in the deck crash. Materially, the air group lost six ADs, four Corsairs, five Panthers, and three Banshees, totaling eighteen aircraft.

This first combat segment had provided Swede with a hellish introduction to the air boss business. Captain Wheelock's report blithely concluded, "In view of the recent casualty suffered by this vessel, when an F2H aircraft bounced and went over all barriers, it is strongly recommended that a higher barrier be installed on the flight deck to prevent any repetition of this type of accident." Certainly higher than the one he had refused to install.[4]

Continued Operations

After ten all-too-brief days in port, *Essex* resumed station off Korea for her second period of combat operations. Swede and everyone else hoped the rest and reflection would improve performance outcomes. On October 3, Rear Adm. J. J. "Jocko" Clark relieved Tomlinson and took brief command of Task Force 77. Shortly thereafter Rear Admiral Perry relieved Clark.

The summer's mix of oppressive heat and destructive typhoons had passed. October was marked by beautiful, clear autumn days featuring dramatic views of the Taebaek Mountains interspersed with fits of atrocious weather presaging the harsh winter to come. In that month, three pilots—Lt. Cdr. Irad Blair Oxley, Lt. (jg) Cordice Isaac Teague, and Ens. Richard Alan Bateman—and four planes were lost to enemy action. Another plane was lost when an electrical problem cut off the catapult mid-shot. The unlucky Banshee pilot had no opportunity to brake, dropped overboard, and added another name to the list of aviators fortunate to be recovered.

Breakdowns of the catapults essential to launching Panther and Banshee jets spelled big trouble for tactical planners and pilots alike. With only one of the two catapults working, form-ups took longer. For short-legged jets, this meant less time over target dealing with North Korean or Chinese AA gunners. Catapult repairs became urgent. A hastily repaired catapult signifying a return to full combat operations meant one thing to an admiral, quite another to the next pilot set for launch. "Sure, it's fixed," might sound less than reassuring when measured against the consequences of catapult failure: crashing out of control into the water directly in front of an onrushing carrier. In that event, only agile conning could prevent the ship from running over a shocked and terrified pilot. In a way, arresting cable and catapult failures were worse than Korean AA fire. Pilots up flying combat missions felt they had some measure of control.

Swede, in charge of air operations, wanted his airmen to know he had their backs. No sooner was a pilot in the water than a helicopter was right there to pluck him out of the unforgiving ocean. To wit, on October 25, Lt. (jg) Leonard Doss, a Banshee jockey, was in the water only one minute and fifteen seconds before the vigilant *Essex* helicopter picked him up. Within three minutes he was back on deck. But not everyone was rescued. The loss of three pilots and five planes stung, but Air Group 5's second month in the combat zone had gone much better than the first.

Swede's endless duties precluded personal indulgences like buckling into a plane and roaming the skies. "I did no combat flying in Korea; I was mostly deckbound. I did occasionally get up in an A-1, the prop job. I didn't have any time. Operations there were demanding, even in summer. We had typhoons, hailstorms, snowstorms, high winds, all of which were tough on our pilots and ship's crew."

Meanwhile, the North Koreans had plenty to say about Air Group 5's attacks. The Koreans' sophisticated AA batteries included machine guns, 37-mm cannons, and larger radar-controlled guns, all registered on the only possible approaches to or egress from predictable targets such as bridges or tunnels. They shot up, crippled, and downed a lot of Panthers and Banshees, and even more of the slower prop-driven ADs and Corsairs.

Pilots in shot-up and no longer airworthy planes faced the unwelcome choice of bailing out or trying to ditch in the relatively calm but heavily mined waters of Wonsan Harbor. Never a pleasant prospect, ditching took on a far more ominous tone as the temperatures dropped. Even if a pilot survived the ditching, successfully exited his sinking plane, and loyal squadronmates overhead summoned rescuers, survival time in the frigid Sea of Japan was about eight minutes. To counter hypothermia pilots wore woolen underwear, a g suit, inch-thick quilted underwear, three pairs of socks, and over all this a rubberized Mark III exposure suit dubbed the "poopy suit."

David Sears wrote evocatively,

> The poopy suit was at once the pilot's most vital and most loathed piece of gear. A neck-to-toe, one-size-fits-all, galvanized-rubber affair, the suit—just as often called a poofy suit or poopy bag—had the smell, inflexibility, and texture of an inner tube or pair of galoshes. The poopy suit's discomfort—a blend of sweat, odor, and claustrophobia—was only made worse by the reality that gave the suit its name. As pilot Lt. Ray Edinger ruefully recalled years later, "either you couldn't do anything that your body may want to do for four and a half hours—or you did it in the suit."[5]

On the flight deck, suave pilots climbing into the suits morphed into clumsy penguins waddling toward their planes. And in a frigid ocean a poopy suit provided no guarantee. Sears continued, "The poopy suit was supposedly watertight. If the seals held, the poopy suit could be the salvation of a pilot ditched and adrift in the Sea of Japan; any leakage, however, could quickly make it a death trap."[6]

If the relative safety of Wonsan Harbor was out of reach, a pilot's remaining option was to bail out. There were many sound reasons why bailing out over enemy territory gave pilots pause. In the act of exiting an aircraft, a pilot might collide with some part of the plane. Entangled chute lines were another threat. Once the pilot was safely away from the aircraft, a parachute landing came with its own perils in the form of trees, cliffs, lakes, or rivers. A pilot arriving safely on the ground risked being shot or badly roughed up by outraged villagers, who received bounties for turning their captives over to North Korean forces. For those unlucky pilots, life in a cold, brutal POW camp would follow. While helicopter rescues could and did happen, no pilot cared to bet on one.

In late October, partisan units had determined that senior Chinese, North Korean, VIP military, and political leaders would attend a conference at Kapsan near Manchuria. Clay Fisher led eight VF-53 Corsairs and eight VF-54 ADs on a top-secret bombing mission intent on wiping out the leadership elite. The surprise raid succeeded in killing several hundred top officials. The North Korean press labeled the pilots butchers. The *Essex* combat action report on the mission, on the other hand, beamed, "*Essex* Special Strike Group today outperformed the man who wrote the book. Well Done."

Despite successes of that nature, the oncoming winter in the Sea of Japan presented Swede's air group with a harsh new adversary. The intense cold created fuel problems, hydraulic systems failures, and jammed guns. Exposure to Korea's wicked windchill rendered normal watches or shifts untenable, and ice-slicked decks made for countless bruises and broken bones. Officers scrambled to adjust duty rosters, and available deckhands were forced to work overtime.

Swede came to realize that the World War II *Catch-22* mentality was still operant. "I felt for these guys trying to put fuses in the bombs; they had no gloves, their hands were freezing. To help them out I drew some pilots' gloves, but the supply officer says, 'You can't do that, they're not for that purpose.'"

Wind chill dove deep into negative numbers as wind speeds often rose well into the ninety miles per hour range. "We strung twenty-three wire cables to tie down one AD. If we positioned a plane with the tail extended over the catwalk, it might lose its tail. There was snow on the decks, lots of it, so we had to shovel it off. It was a real challenge to keep the flight deck clear of snow. We even cranked up an F9F and swept it around hoping to melt the snow and ice with the exhaust blast. Of course the ice immediately froze up again."

During their third action segment of the tour, pilots Lt. William Arnold Bryant Jr. and Lt. (jg) Eugene Brewer Hale and eight planes were lost before *Essex* detached for two weeks of Christmas R&R. Against an unfavorable wind and a narrow channel into Yokosuka, Captain Wheelock conjured up "Operation Pinwheel." Reluctantly supported by *Essex* CAG Cdr. Marshall U. Beebe, Wheelock ordered the prop-driven F4Us and ADs be chocked down along the port side and revved to full power in order to assist docking the big ship. The prop squadrons' COs rightly protested that running the engines at full power while chocked in place could easily burn out the engines.

The evening before their arrival in port, Cdr. Herman J. Trum, the Corsair squadron skipper, and Paul Gray, CO of VF-54's Skyraiders, appealed to Beebe. "You realize that those engines are vital to the survival of all the attack pilots. We fly those single-engine planes three hundred to four hundred miles from the ship over freezing water and over very hostile land. Overstressing these engines is not going to make any of us very happy." Gray continued, "Marsh [Beebe] knew the danger; but he said, 'The captain of the ship, Capt. Wheelock, wants this done, so do it!'" Resentful pilots dubbed the notion "Operation Pinhead" or "Operation Wheelchock."[7]

To preserve those engines, Trum and Gray quietly advised their pilots to give no more than half power, and if engine temperatures started creeping up, to take them back down to idle. The ship docked without incident, but when their subversive half-measure came to Wheelock's attention, he ordered Beebe to restrict pilots of both squadrons to the ship. After thirty hard days on the line and in desperate need of R&R, they now languished in hack for three miserable days. Admiral Perry got wind of it all and ordered them released immediately. Such assaults on sensibility only worsened morale.[8]

Three days after Christmas 1951, *Essex* reentered the combat zone along with the carriers USS *Antietam* (CV 36) and *Valley Forge*. Continuing disasters plagued this combat segment. On January 3, owing to a broken breech lock, a Banshee 20-mm cannon discharged. The round exploded among a crew replenishing a Panther parked forward, wounding five crewmen, one critically. As air operations continued over twenty-four of the next thirty-six days, *Essex* lost ten aircraft and four more pilots killed in action.[9]

However they were lost, pilots viewed each death as yet another sacrifice in an abysmal game of inconclusive interdiction. This police action without end offered no strategic victories or exit. Hope was not in season.

As winter deepened, the tragedies continued. On January 6, Ens. Glen Howard Rickleton was killed when his Panther crashed and exploded. Three days later Ens. Raymond Gene Kelly's AD-3 was hit over enemy territory, crashed, and exploded on impact.

Forces beyond enemy action were in play for at least one pilot's loss. *Essex*'s action log for January 11, 1952, noted, "Lt. (jg) Joseph Henry Gollner executed a normal takeoff, jettisoned his 1,000-pound bomb, abruptly climbed to an estimated nine hundred feet, made three shallow turns to the right, the last steepening into a nose-down diving spiral. The plane sank immediately after striking the water. Two helicopters conducted a fruitless search for the pilot. No radio transmissions were received from the pilot at any time. Cause Unknown. Pilot listed as killed in the line of duty."

It couldn't come quickly enough for Air Group 5, but on January 13—some called it lucky thirteen—Capt. Walter Rodee relieved Captain Wheelock. A few days later, on January 19, 1952, U.S. Air Force major F. N. McCullum, an exchange pilot with VF-172, was shot down and killed. Over the next eight days of combat operations the air group lost five more planes and another Panther pilot, Lt. (jg) Leonard Ray Cheshire. The month's carnage totaled four pilots and ten aircraft in just twenty-four days of air ops.

The emotional rollercoaster—fear and loss compounded by simple boredom in off-duty time—demanded outlets. "One winter day," Swede recalled, "I watched two guys racing our plane-spotting tractors on an icy flight deck, the object of which was to see who would come closer to the edge. I caught up to them and observed, 'Good God guys, give it up, I don't want to lose you.' Still, in all my travels on the deck, I never heard a complaint and marveled at the fortitude of the American sailor."

Swede's responsibilities were beyond demanding. "Most of the time I was in the air boss shack supervising air operations. I did that for over two and a half years. I know I went through five COs while I was there. It was a really high-pressure operation as we had to refuel continuously, we had to rearm continuously, and this was often done at night. The COs had me on the bridge there to keep the carrier alongside the oiler or ammo ship and getting everything aboard so I was real tired there part of the time."

On February 21, 1952, in the dark of winter, Lt. (jg) Francis Gene Gergen got disoriented in a snowstorm and disappeared with his Corsair. In this segment's nine days of actual flight operations an additional two ADs were lost to Korean AA guns, described in the captain's report as "mobile in every sense of the word."

On the way back from Clay Fisher's final VF-53 bombing mission, some of his group ignored radio discipline and began singing a ditty made up specifically for Swede, knowing he would be monitoring their radio channel. In character, Swede egged them on.[10]

On March 5, 1952, after nearly seven months of operations against bridges, trains, troops, and anything else of value to the North Koreans and Chinese, *Essex* detached for a well-earned rest and replenishment back in the States. This brutal combat tour had claimed a total of twenty Air Group 5 airmen and forty-three planes. Sharpshooting Korean AA crews had downed twenty-five of them. Eighteen fell victim to equipment breakdowns such as catapult failures or flameouts. All this translated to a lot of buddies lost and a big hit on airplane inventory. Welcome to Korea, where air superiority didn't much feel like it. For Swede, the man who never had time to sleep, this tour had been a nightmare.

As boss of the air department, Swede owned the task of analyzing air operations and summarizing hard-won lessons learned in the air and on board. One major plane-spotting problem had to do with the Banshee wings. The wings were precariously difficult to fuel and could not be folded up when the tip tanks contained any fuel, further frustrating plane spotters on both the flight and hangar decks. Maintenance suffered because planes could not be moved to the hangar deck immediately following recovery. Captain Wheelock's action report noted, "Flight and hangar deck crashes were caused largely by errors in judgment of personnel making fast re-spots under over-crowded conditions."

During their tour the crew had to manage a manpower shortage, endure horrendous weather, survive catapult and equipment failures, submit to leadership absurdities such as Operation Wheelchock, and fly missions of no strategic import, all while prospects for peace were slim to zero. The tour would have played havoc with the sturdiest of souls. Swede was worn out.

Robbie Is Down

Unbeknownst to Swede, Robbie Robinson, his buddy from Guadalcanal days, was also in theater. No longer a smart-ass ensign, Robbie currently commanded the VF-64 Freelancers, a *Boxer* Corsair squadron. *Boxer* had joined Task Force 77 a month before *Essex* rotated out.

Back in June 1950, when the North Koreans swept over South Korea, Robbie had been stationed at the Pentagon. Stymied for the past two years, he had finally wrangled his way through the pipeline and, for better and worse, gotten himself into the action.

Nearly a month into *Boxer*'s second combat segment, on another superstitious Friday the thirteenth, this one June 13, 1952, the *Boxer* action report noted, "Lt. Cdr. L. Robinson, Commanding Officer of VF-64, was forced to ditch his Corsair (F4U) in Wonsan Harbor after his engine failed. He was picked up by a friendly small boat after a short interval in his raft and transferred to LST 799 for treatment of bruises."

The report was a masterful understatement. North Korean gunners had achieved something two Japanese Zeros near Guadalcanal had not. Flak set Robbie's engine afire, but just as he had off Guadalcanal, Robbie managed to extinguish the flames. Nonetheless, it was soon evident that his plane would not get him home. He prepared to bail out, yanked open the canopy, and got a face full of engine oil and hydraulic fluid. He was still over enemy territory and blinded by oil, so bailing out was no longer an option. He figured he could make it to the mine-free waters near Yodo Island in eastern Wonsan Bay and ditch there. Robbie relied on his wingman, Ens. Ralph "Tweedy" Tvede, to guide his blind descent to the water. Tweedy's instruction to cut the engine came early, and Robbie slammed hard, tail first onto the water. The compression of the crash shredded multiple discs and fractured several vertebrae and his coccyx.[11]

Somehow Robbie hauled himself out of the cockpit and clambered through the Corsair's prop into the cold water of Wonsan Bay. Clearing his now-sinking Corsair, a shocked Robbie had the presence of mind not to deploy his easily targeted life raft. Instead, he inflated his Mae West life vest while his anxious squadronmates orbited overhead and radioed for help. Thus began a cold, painful wait for salvation, which came in the form of a muscular crewman who hauled Robbie's helpless form out of the water and into a small boat. Preferring his squadron not see him return via stretcher, he instead endured a painful ride over to *Boxer* seated in a breeches buoy.

Her segment completed, *Boxer* detached for Yokosuka, where Robbie's incapacitating wounds initiated an ordeal of spinal blood draws and rehabilitation. On a Friday the doctors informed him that on the following Monday there would be a Purple Heart ceremony acknowledging his serious injuries. Then they asked him whether he wanted to sit or stand for the rest of his life because they had decided to fuse his spine. For Robbie that was a no go. He arranged for his squadronmates to spirit him out of the hospital late that night. They dutifully returned him to *Boxer*, which departed Yokosuka the next morning to resume station off Korea.

Some days later, as combat operations geared up, Robbie convinced a metalsmith to fashion him a back brace so he could fly. When the brace sat him too high to fit under the canopy, Robbie simply discarded the parachute he normally sat on. He continued to fly missions until some higher-up got wind of it.

Robbie's flying and leadership during this *Boxer* combat tour resulted in a Purple Heart, two Air Medals, and a Bronze Star. The citation for his Bronze Star read in part, "Although he suffered a back injury during a water landing on 13 June 1952, Lieutenant Commander Robinson flew six strikes before the gravity of his injury was discovered and he was grounded for the remainder of the time in Korean operations." The citation concluded that the Combat Distinguishing Device was authorized, and was signed by Vice Adm. J. J. Clark, commander, Seventh Fleet.[12]

Second Tour

By the summer of 1952, Seoul, South Korea's capital, had changed hands four times, and the fight for the Korean peninsula had degenerated into a killing-field stalemate. Because the endless, futile negotiations had produced no movement toward a truce or cease-fire, Truman realized that his policy of limiting his forces to interdiction had failed. Overturning his prior restrictions, Truman released his forces to go after industries, commercial hubs, refineries, and hydroelectric power stations, targeting anything that might degrade the enemy's will or capability for war.

This had implications for Robbie, who had become a valued contributor to strikes and strike mission planning. Grounded for the time being, he assisted in the planning for a massive raid on the Sui-ho Hydroelectric

Complex spanning the border between North Korea and China. As Robbie assisted in planning raids and recovered from his injuries, *Essex* geared up for her second tour. Swede dreaded a repeat of the disastrous first one.

During the summer of 1952, before returning to combat operations, *Essex* and *Philippine Sea* carried out a photo-intelligence sweep along the Chinese coast. With all eyes on Korea, the concern was that China might invade Formosa (Taiwan). Swede's air group put on mass air parades over Formosa and conducted exercises over the strait, the latter fully visible to any interested Chinese observers. The tour was not without its perils. During refueling, the destroyer USS *Duncan* (DD 485) lost steering and rammed *Essex*, causing minor damage to the carrier.

It was late July when *Essex* rejoined Task Force 77 off eastern Korea. On August 1, Swede's air group opened their second Korean combat tour. It did not begin well. Shortly after 6 a.m. the first day after joining *Bon Homme Richard* and TF 77, an AD crashed ahead of the ship; the pilot was rescued. Five minutes later a Corsair did the same; the pilot survived but was pretty banged up. On August 4, in the ongoing carrier shuffle, *Boxer*, Rear Adm. Apollo Soucek embarked, replaced *Bon Homme Richard*.

The dangers inherent in carrier operations were by no means confined to *Essex*. On August 6, just two days after *Boxer* took station, a gas explosion in *Boxer*'s hangar deck involved fueled aircraft. Very quickly, .50-caliber and 20-mm ammunition and a 500-pound bomb cooked off. Up on the flight deck, the conflagration threatened fifty-eight fully armed and fueled planes. It took nearly five hours of dangerous, heroic firefighting before the mortal threat to the ship was past. The disaster cost eight dead, one missing, one critically burned, one seriously burned, and seventy overcome by smoke. Of the sixty-three men who went over the side to escape the flames, all were recovered and returned to the ship.

The next day *Boxer* took stock, transferred Rear Admiral Soucek and his staff by high-line over to *Essex*, and departed for Yokosuka for repairs. Thus Swede met the remarkable Apollo Soucek. In 1930 Soucek had flown his single-engine Curtiss Hawk biplane to an altitude of 43,166 feet, far higher than many commercial jets of the modern era. Later he had served admirably as *Hornet*'s air boss during the Battle of Santa Cruz. There was a lot they could discuss.

On August 8 an *Essex* AD-4N lost oil pressure near Yangdo Island and was forced to ditch. The destroyer USS *Ozbourne* (DD 846) plucked the pilot and crew from the water and high-lined them back on board *Essex*. Ten days later Typhoon Karen began a two-day battering of TF 77. Eleven more days of air operations without a casualty brought their first combat segment to a successful close. No pilots and only three planes were lost, very satisfying for Swede and a vast improvement over the previous year's disastrous introduction.

During their second combat segment, Swede's air group coordinated with the Air Force on joint strikes. Otherwise it was pretty much back to the dangerous business of attacking North Korean infrastructure. Threats to health and safety were not restricted to combat action. One of those terrifying catapult breakdowns forced *Essex* to withdraw for a week and a half of repairs.

On November 20, during their third segment, yet another catapult failure resulted in another traumatized pilot and the loss of an F2H-2P. Repairing the extensively damaged machinery would require two and a half weeks in Yokosuka. Sheltered from the Sea of Japan's brutal weather and relieved from operational dangers, the *Essex* crew gratefully took in the city.

Back on station just two weeks later, an *Essex* aircraft accidentally released a bomb over the American 10th Corps front lines, killing one friendly and wounding three others. On January 10, 1953, *Essex* and Air Group 5 completed their second tour. At the conclusion of their fourth and last combat segment the air group could celebrate a victory. They had lost a lot of their naiveté but not one pilot.

Atom Games

As air boss, Swede was aware that *Essex* carried one atomic bomb and a modified F2H aircraft to deliver it. "We had special training on nukes—very, very thorough briefings. We were told what they were, what they did, means of delivery, and operational policies. We attended a number of classes, not only Navy people, civilians too. They instructed us on a bomb's capability for a variety of target considerations. The Navy contingent included lieutenant commanders who had handled technical assignments; most were commanders or captains."

Late in this posting, Swede was advised that the Washington brass were considering the use of an atomic bomb in Vietnam, where the French were struggling to retain vestiges of their fast-dwindling colonial empire. "In total secrecy, a Marine pilot had trained to deliver the bomb. He would fly a McDonnell twin-engine F2H whose front landing gear had been extended to accommodate the bomb slung below the plane. The modified Banshee sat in readiness on the hangar deck. The long legs made the squat plane a bit taller. At the last minute, I think, Admiral Radford, commander of the Pacific Fleet, decided against the hush-hush plan. I never saw the bomb, and I never knew where it went. In Yokosuka, there was a top-secret ordnance material transfer one night from the *Essex* to another carrier. I was pretty sure that was the bomb. We let out no information; Japan had no use for those things in her ports. We didn't want Japan suspicious."

Though Swede was headed elsewhere, the fighting in Korea would continue for another bloody six months. As he departed for his new billet, Swede harbored one overriding question, "What are we doing here?"

CHAPTER 17

—

Grooming

There would be shooting at Swede's new assignment, just not at people. Even better, the new posting meant Swede could regularly climb back into a cockpit. "Following the Korean action, for two enjoyable years [April 1953–April 1955] I was commanding officer of the naval air facility at China Lake, California, the premier site for weapons development whether they be guns, rockets, or propellants. Here I had a chance to fly many types of aircraft carrying out numerous projects and testing various ordnance developments by the scientists at that base. The Sidewinder infrared air-to-air missile, which proved to be one of the most successful air weapons of all time, was an ongoing project. The Mk-16 computing gun sight was being tested and developed, as were numerous rockets and new concept bombs. It was a privilege to be a part of the research and development program at that time. Tasked with adapting rockets to aircraft, we used homing devices, put them on the plane, and tested them in the air."

Flying a Douglas A-4, under development at the time, Swede was the first to shoot down a radio-controlled drone and subsequently shot down drones with smaller rockets fitted onto F2H aircraft. Bombs were upgraded. Fueled by memories of hardened German submarine pens in French harbors, the work also focused on guidance bombs and resulted in a bomb capable of penetrating seven feet of reinforced concrete before detonating.

Dugway: A Curious Interruption

The Korean shooting war finally gave way to a ceasefire, and the Cold War took its place. The roots of this new "war" could be traced to a little-known

Allied operation begun just before the end of World War I. In September 1918, two months before the November 11 Armistice, an Allied expedition of U.S., Canadian, British, and French troops conducted a campaign far in Russia's frozen north to defeat the Red Army. The venture, intending to reverse the Communist government in Moscow, continued until late spring of 1919, well after the "War to End All Wars" had concluded. The Allies were eventually forced to withdraw, but the Russians had been appalled by this bold-faced imperialist gambit and chafed at the memory. Their justified resentment and suspicion fueled a new kind of war, one without pitched battles. U.S. and Soviet military-industrial complexes competed in a high-stakes arms race and began to conduct proxy wars of liberation or colonialism.

At the conclusion of World War II, the Soviet Union had captured Japanese officers involved in biological weapons research. To counter any potential Soviet biological weapons development the United States enlisted the talents of notorious Japanese major general Ishii Shiro. During World War II, Ishii had supervised human subject experiments with a variety of biological and chemical agents in Manchuria's infamous Unit 731. Following Japan's surrender, the United States offered Ishii immunity from war crimes in exchange for his assistance in developing and countering such weapons. Biological bombs were subsequently developed and were shipped to Dugway Proving Ground, west of Salt Lake City, to be tested for accuracy and efficacy.

Swede suddenly found himself in the middle of it. He was transferred from his China Lake posting, partnered with the Air Force, and tasked with dropping "poison" bombs in an effort to determine the agents' dispersal range. It was late in Swede's piloting career to reprise his dive-bomber skills, and it remains rather odd that he was chosen for this assignment.

"They had me there because they wanted a dive-bomber pilot. It was a big program aimed to develop lots of bombs that affect humans and animals. I dropped a bunch of those—biological agents. I was responsible for dropping a bomb that killed a whole herd of sheep. I was flying an AD, but I didn't know what the bomb was. There was a wind shift up there in the mountains [Granite Peak], and it blew all this poison, agents, onto the sheep; killed a bunch of them. They must have paid the guy 'cause I never heard any more. It's not secret; people knew about it, it just wasn't advertised." Their targets were regular markers to provide an aiming point surrounded by instruments recording each weapon's dispersal.

In Swede's case, the poisoned sheep were an accident. In subsequent experiments, live animals were tethered within the presumed range of bioweapons. Swede was not proud of the work that certified him as a member of RATS (Registry of Atmospheric Testing Survivors). The group's logo portrayed a lineup of members, all unidentifiable in their biohazard masks.

Carrier Operations Officer

Beginning in April 1955, Swede spent fifteen months as operations officer on board various carriers planning and executing sea operations under Commander of Carrier Division 5 Rear Adm. Bill Davis, an old associate of Swede's. In the 1920s Davis had been a member of the Three Sea Hawks, the Navy's first stunt team. In 1950 Davis assumed the prestigious command of the carrier USS *Franklin Delano Roosevelt* (CVB 42). It turned out that back in 1949, he and Swede had worked together on the D-558-II Skyrocket. During that billet Davis became the second naval aviator to fly faster than the speed of sound. Familiarity and shared interests made for a very workable relationship.

"While in Japan, Bill Davis would invite various Japanese naval officers aboard to discuss World War II actions. It was here I met Saburo Sakai, the great Japanese ace, and others who had participated in many of the battles. I talked with him at length a number of times. He was a great conversationalist. He had a hell of a lot of experience. Some interesting times were spent poring over charts and getting the other point of view."

During the year-and-a-quarter billet, the primary focus was on cruises and air operations. "We spent a lot of time qualifying aviators, and they were damn good. This was a time of international tension between China, Taiwan, and Japan. We operated with the Japanese Self-Defense Forces. During a cruise down between Taiwan and China, the Chinese made flights to check us out, but they did not go near us."

Swede followed the carrier ops posting with a year ashore in Newport, Rhode Island, attending the Naval War College. "This was a wonderful idea. It came at the proper time and involved international government personnel. We got lectures from some very learned men on Ukraine and

Russia that were absolutely great. There were classes on Warfare I and II. In Warfare II every student worked on a project developing a problem dealing with current situations and solving it."

Not everyone viewed the Naval War College experience with the same enthusiasm. "I had classmates, friends, that would go out, give some guy fifty dollars for prepared papers, and made no effort to succeed on their own. This was just so much time wasted for those who did not apply themselves."

Swede next served a two-year stint as director of the Research and Development Division, where he developed air weapons systems for the Bureau of Ordnance. "I was back with the advanced Sidewinder, smart bombs, more rockets, and guns, which were again coming into favor. Some German developments were unique, and a lot of testing was done; however, the Gatling gun was favored and installed in most of our fighters after that time."

On October 8, 1956, the Department of Defense issued a startling release announcing that "the famed aircraft carrier *Enterprise*—the "Big E" to her crew—has been declared 'unfit for further naval service' and will be sold for scrap purposes soon." The notice included a 1945 quote from former secretary of the Navy James Forrestal: "Time has accomplished what the enemy failed to do in four years of desperate and costly effort: The USS *Enterprise* must be taken out of service because modern planes cannot be flown in combat from her flight deck."

Swede was flabbergasted. "When I got that news, I couldn't sleep for a week. I wrote letters to protest. They were so stupid. Why not preserve the greatest carrier of all?" (Years later Swede treasured his three mounted sections of the *Enterprise*'s Douglas-fir flight deck.)

The next month, on November 1, 1956, Swede advanced to captain. Almost a year later, while *Enterprise* awaited her demise, on September 14, 1957, the keel was laid for one of two new *Kitty Hawk*–class super carriers capable of handling jet fighters and bombers.

Command at Sea

Before Swede could aspire to a coveted carrier command, he would first need to manage a supply ship. Accordingly, from July 1959 until August 1960 Swede was assigned command of USS *Firedrake* (AE 14). Commissioned December 27, 1944, she began as *Winged Racer*, a 459-foot, 15,295-ton merchantman, before her conversion to an ammunition ship. *Firedrake* had served honorably late in the Pacific war, most notably enduring kamikaze attacks at the Kerama Retto anchorage near Okinawa.[1]

"I got good practice and experience, and spent a lot of time handling ordnance. Out of San Francisco, we went on a number of missions to dump all our old ammunition, rockets, bombs, and torpedoes now deemed unusable. This was great training for the guys, and it took a couple of days to crane the stuff overboard. Kinda bothered me. We never had any incidents since nothing was fused. I had heard of the World War II *Port Chicago* ammo ship explosion, and that story kept us on our toes."

Elsewhere, in winter of 1959, the heroic and now obsolete *Enterprise* had been ingloriously towed to a shipyard in Kearny, New Jersey, where the dreary process of dismantling the ship and reducing her to scrap would begin. Sounds simple. Just cut the thing apart and be done with it. The reality, however, was that this was a very delicate process, carefully balancing and counterbalancing weight as portions of the ship were removed. Any oversight, such as rainwater caught in now-exposed compartments, could easily upset this delicate deconstruction geometry. In the event, it took nineteen months for reluctant torch cutters to accomplish what the Japanese never could, despite their six claims of having done so.

Firedrake, meanwhile, from October 19, 1959 until January 15, 1960, underwent an overhaul at Mare Island. In April, Swede set out for a western Pacific tour, during which *Firedrake* would steam between Japan and the Philippines, with occasional stops in Hong Kong and Okinawa's Buckner Bay. "Notable and well remembered," Swede recalled, "was riding out a typhoon in Subic Bay, Philippines, a place where these storms get particularly vicious."

Given their cargo, Swede was told to keep his distance. "On our West-Pac cruise they put us out and away from everything in case we blew up. We were very isolated. I got plenty of practice ship handling. When we got ahead of schedule we might stop and let crewmen handle the ship. It was a good cruise."

Fleet Ops

Following that less-than-glamorous sea billet, Swede served for the next two years as fleet operations officer on the staff of Adm. Harry D. Felt, CinCPac.

Stationed in Hawaii, Swede was the aviation voice for the flag director. Among a bewildering array of duties, the posting required that he produce operations orders, connect directly with squadron commanders, schedule exercises and inspections, and decide who needed more training. It was a busy job juggling shore and carrier-based squadrons, but it did leave time for swimming and surfing in the warm, seductive Hawaiian waters. "I'm not keen on staff duty. A lot of people like it because they have time off. It's easy, but I much prefer doing something active."[2]

Preferences aside, Swede was being groomed for a prestigious major command.

CHAPTER 18

———

USS *Constellation*, "America's Flagship"

On December 19, 1960, three years after *Kitty Hawk*–class *Constellation*'s keel had been laid, and with construction of the new super carrier 90 percent complete, a catastrophic fire on board required the assistance of the Brooklyn Fire Department. *Constellation*'s $400 million (in 1961 dollars) price tag was immeasurably inflated when 50 people were killed and 323 injured in the fire. During the twelve-hour effort to extinguish the blaze she took on 15,000 tons of water. Heavy damage delayed her commissioning nearly ten months.

Commissioned finally on October 27, 1961, she was nicknamed "America's Flagship"—"Connie" to her crew. The super carrier stretched 1,062.5 feet, provided 4.5 acres of flight deck, displaced 82,200 tons fully loaded, and could muster speeds in excess of 30 knots. With a crew of 2,900 and an air wing of 2,480, she was home to 85 aircraft. Her surface-to-air defense boasted three RIM 2 Terrier missile systems complemented by three 20-mm Phalanx CIWS Mk 15s, rapid-fire Gatling guns capable of firing three thousand uranium rounds per minute. Though still powered by fuel oil, USS *Constellation* (CVA 64) was a state-of-the-art aircraft carrier.

In December, a year after the devastating construction fire, Connie's first CO, Capt. Thomas J. Walker III, took her out for sea trials several miles off New York City. A broken oil line in Connie's boiler room sparked a fire that killed two crewmen, a civilian shop worker, and a civilian design engineer, and injured nine more. The star-crossed *Constellation* headed back to New York for repairs.

By the summer of 1962 repairs had been completed, and *Constellation* was transferred to the Pacific Fleet. Captain Walker would deliver her to her new homeport in San Diego. Connie's size ruled out a Panama Canal transit. Instead she would make the two-month trip around Cape Horn beginning with a July 25 departure from Mayport, Florida.

By October 1962 Swede had served as air boss on board *Essex* and had spent just over a year commanding *Firedrake*. Most recently he had logged extensive experience on CinCPac's staff, which provided an inside look at Pacific Fleet operational strategy. "Without a doubt one of the real high spots and something I had hoped mightily for was command of an aircraft carrier. With almost fifteen years on board this type of vessel, I felt well qualified for command."

Seemingly out of the blue, without having been designated prospective CO of anything, Swede was given his dream command: *Constellation*. "I couldn't believe it, being assigned command of the largest, finest, most current, up-to-date combat vessel in the world. They had a CO. I knew the guy, never thought I'd get the spot. It was a complete surprise." At 10 a.m. on November 19, 1962, Swede relieved Captain Walker and began his yearlong captain's billet.

Swede was eager for the opportunity, though the statement of *Constellation*'s officially prescribed role might have intimidated most mortals:

Her mission is to support and operate aircraft, to engage in sustained operation against the enemy. To accomplish this, she can provide all the elements of airpower necessary for control of the seas and defense of our country: nuclear or precision, conventional attack, reconnaissance, air superiority, interdiction and close air tactical support.

Mobility, flexibility and versatility are her trademarks. The ability to protect United States military forces overseas—unrestricted by foreign landlords or influence since she operates outside territorial waters—is as important as her ability to move six or seven hundred miles daily across the vast ocean areas of the world.

Flexibility and versatility also play an important role in her life in that she is not limited to a single purpose use as are intercontinental bombers. She can peacefully show the flag, perform armed reconnaissance, or launch deft attacks in small or large scale assaults with conventional or nuclear weapons. Her tentacles reach out and embrace the sea, its shores and most of the world's large land targets.

This huge carrier will provide a major contribution to deterring all-out war. It has the enemy over a barrel. If he decides to strike at this carrier and its forces, he will lose the vital element of surprise—or he can choose to ignore the carrier and be annihilated.

Regardless, our naval forces will be the forces-in-being after an exchange due to their dispersal, mobility and concealment capabilities. Carrier striking forces led by *Constellation* will be the residual power, which will control the situation at the end of any war.[1]

Mission statement bluster aside, Swede was comfortable with his new responsibility. "During Korea I'd had a lot of ship handling aboard the *Essex*. We had to replenish, frequently in bad weather. This got very tiring for the CO, who would look for a break. As air officer I was around a lot, and during night ops or changing course, the CO would turn to me, 'Swede, take her in.' I'd done a lot of it; I was confident of my ship handling."

Constellation's structure compromised some of Swede's ship-handling confidence. Her island had been set well aft, and her long bow made for blind docking. Swede wisely deferred to harbor pilots and tugs when he brought her into Pearl Harbor.

While *Constellation* was primarily a combat vessel, Swede viewed the ship as a seaborne city, and he made it his business to visit every neighborhood on board. As he familiarized himself with the carrier's many departments, Swede's authentic enthusiasm and empathy charmed his crew. Photos of those meetings reveal a genuine affection for their engaging captain.

In the Heat of the Cold War

Swede's prestigious command began a mere three weeks after the terrifying Cuban Missile Crisis. Beyond the dramatic Khrushchev-Kennedy stare-down, an American U-2 spy plane had been shot down over Cuba, and one brave Soviet officer had barely prevented the firing of his submarine's nuclear torpedo at harassing U.S. destroyers above. The world had very narrowly avoided nuclear confrontation. While the crisis had been defused, tensions had not passed.

A mere four hours after Swede assumed his highly sensitive command, on November 18, with Carrier Air Group 14 embarked, Swede steamed

Constellation to the mid-Pacific for training operations. In the warm waters off Hawaii, the task group conducted elaborate exercises simulating the delivery and handling of nuclear weapons. Their performance left Swede highly pleased with both the air group and *Constellation*'s crew. Following a brief provisioning stop back in Pearl Harbor, *Constellation* departed for her first western Pacific cruise. Swede set course for Subic Bay in the Philippines.

Correctly anticipating a strong Russian interest in this newest state-of-the-art weapons platform, Swede requested a screen of four destroyers from CinCPacFlt. "In Hawaii, I had occasion to visit with my former boss, Adm. John "Savy" Sides. [Considered the father of the guided-missile program, Sides had played a role in the development of the Terrier missiles currently stockpiled on board *Constellation*.] He provided me with a four-ship escort of his best destroyers." Because Soviet bombers had overflown sister carrier USS *Kitty Hawk* (CV 63) during multithreat exercises off northern Japan in the latter part of January, the destroyers would provide advance warning of the Russian aircraft expected to overfly and observe *Constellation* and her air group.

"We left Hawaii early. I wanted the destroyers two hundred miles out in front to pick up Russian planes. When, on March 16, 1963, the Russian planes did approach we were six hundred miles southwest of Midway. Not one of the destroyers picked them up; our radar did. We launched VF-141 Vought F-8E Crusaders, VF-143 McDonnell F-4B Phantoms, RF-8A Crusader reconnaissance planes, and A-4Ds, which intercepted them one hundred miles out.

"I was on the radio the whole time to CinCPacFlt. Three huge Tu-95 four-engine turbo-prop, extreme-range bombers flew 2 passes at 30,000 feet, then dropped down for 7 passes under 3,000 feet. They flew around us for forty minutes, their contra-rotating props purring like sewing machines. I wanted as many pilots as possible to get up close and personal with the bombers. But it was very quiet up there. The Bear gunners were inactive; nobody swung guns or pointed them at us. There was nothing unusual about this; the Russians had frequently overflown our carriers.

"It wasn't publicized, but we had expert interpreters aboard. When our Phantoms intercepted the Bears, one of the bomber crew was said to exclaim,

'I see the big, ugly bastards.' As we could monitor all their frequencies, we knew what was being said both within and beyond their aircraft.

"Of course, they were interested in photographing our new carrier, radar data, frequencies we used with our transmitters and receivers. Every plane we put up had cameras; the larger tandem Phantoms took up ship's photographers. One of the bombers had a refueling probe, which we were very curious about. The two others did not, and we never figured out how they flew so far without some replenishment. The Bears dwarfed our interceptors.

"Finally, apparently on signal, the Bear pilots added power and climbed steeply away. Intelligence later informed us that these same bombers returned to a snowy base in faraway Siberia. We recalled our planes, took them aboard, and debriefed them. Much time was spent viewing the photos and preparing a packet for Admiral Sides, which we delivered by aircraft to Midway Island."

An exciting incident, but sobering, too. Russian bombers had casually observed America's flagship from high above and boldly flown close aboard. Anyone bearing witness had to wonder, "Just how vulnerable are we?"

Swede's command of the world's most advanced warship did not escape the notice of Swede's hometown *Circle Banner*. The March 29, 1963, edition proudly featured a full-page spread on Swede and *Constellation*. The piece included a biography of Swede, an essay on the role and power of the ship, photos of *Constellation*'s aircraft, and images of Terrier missile shots.

With the overflight excitement concluded, *Constellation* continued on to the Philippines, where Rear Adm. Ralph H. Shifley, commander Carrier Division Seven, and his staff embarked. Following that upgrade to flagship and five days in Subic, they made for the South China Sea. There, on April 5, Swede's dedicated crew hosted *Constellation*'s first flag change of command when Rear Adm. Thomas W. South relieved Shifley. After five days in Hong Kong, *Constellation* headed toward her homeport at Yokosuka, Japan. Upon their April 26 arrival, Rear Adm. L. J. Kirn, commander Carrier Division Five, and his staff embarked.

In 1942, Swede had been out to destroy anything and everything Japanese. Twenty-one years later he warmly hosted local visitors at several Japanese ports of call. This visit was a two-way exploration. Not far from Yokosuka, the peaceful seaside town of Kamakura lured men from *Constellation*. The Daibutsu, an exquisite forty-foot-tall bronze Buddha, offered any crewman who made his way there a rare opportunity for contemplative serenity, something not often available within *Constellation*'s city limits.

On June 1, *Constellation* experienced her second flag change of command when Rear Adm. R. B. Moore relieved Admiral Kirn as commander Carrier Division Five. Their two weeks docked in Kobe made for good public relations as hundreds of visitors toured the carrier.

Iwakuni was the next stop on their tour of Japan. Not many miles from that lovely port of call, Hiroshima still struggled to recover from atomic devastation. The Hiroshima Peace Memorial Museum was still under construction, but A-bomb slums were fully developed. Here was Swede, a man already convinced of the folly of atomic war, commanding the world's most advanced nuclear-tipped attack carrier visiting ports of the former enemy. It is difficult to know if the local Japanese felt more protected or threatened. Swede bought a packet of Hiroshima photos as a reminder that atomic war was nothing short of hell on earth. Much more to his liking, Captain Swede oversaw the first wedding performed on board.

Constellation returned to Yokosuka prior to further operational exercises. She spent a week at Sasebo, then set sail for Buckner Bay, Okinawa. There, on July 11, forty-six midshipmen embarked for a summer training cruise. A few days later *Constellation* docked at the Japanese resort city of Beppu in a call aimed at enhancing public relations. Crewmembers painted a local orphanage while the locals toured the enormous carrier.

As *Constellation* next steamed south toward Taiwan, Rear Admiral Moore proved to be a continual thorn in Swede's side. "The admiral distanced his own staff. He ordered the supply officer to procure a new washing machine. It was for the admiral's exclusive use, and this made for more difficulty for me." Then "the admiral decided that the skeet shooting should be his own personal province. He had his own boys set it up for him. I made an issue of that. I told him, 'It's not in the spirit of things for you to be using ammunition reserved for the pilots.' They relied on the range to develop their own deflection shooting. Every base had a skeet and trap range. It was a fine piece of training for interceptor pilots. Active pilots should have first call for gunnery practice." The guy just didn't get it. Swede noted that black crewmembers in particular had no fondness for the admiral.

Chiang Kai-shek

The Taiwan visit was to be a show of solidarity. "During our 1963 west-Pac cruise, the Chinese were acting up. So to avoid being tracked by the Chinese we did a speed run at night and dropped the hook the next morning off the north coast of Taiwan. Generalissimo Chiang Kai-shek; his wife, Madame Chiang; Gerald Wright, the U.S. ambassador; and his wife helicoptered over, as did the commander U.S. Seventh Fleet, Vice Adm. Thomas H. Moorer, who stayed until the end of the meet-and-greet. We put on a two-hour air show for them all, launched a full squadron, demonstrating bomb and napalm drops, and performing supersonic speed runs as pilots described the action. From the bridge they could watch recoveries, launches, everything.

"After lunch Admiral Moorer introduced the generalissimo, who addressed the crew. This was a very special day, and I reflected at the time on the superior abilities of our executive officer, Cdr. Ray Volpi, and the officers and crew of the *Constellation* in handling and coordinating the myriad details required for such an occasion.

"They stayed on board for many hours, and to the disgust of Admiral Moore, the generalissimo spoke with me alone for some thirty minutes. He was happy to report that during a recent mix-up with the Communist Chinese, the Sidewinder missiles had been impressive. All but one had hit their targets. I didn't realize that our Sidewinder technology had been released to the Taiwanese. As his air force consisted primarily of U.S. Air Force planes, training, and equipment, he was very interested in our naval capacities.

"I had hoped to speak to his wife, Madame Chiang, who spoke English better than most of us. She had been a great friend to the American Volunteer Group, later known as the Flying Tigers. She'd befriended Tex Hill and Don Jones, but I didn't get the opportunity to talk with her. Meanwhile, the Chinese were running air probes daily, and we were on alert all the time. None of our pilots engaged the Chinese."[2]

Constellation steamed back to Yokosuka, where to Swede's satisfaction, the irritating Admiral Moore disembarked. More training exercises ensued, and on August 6 Swede hosted the Honorable Fred North, Secretary of the Navy. A couple more weeks in and around Yokosuka completed their tour. After six months at sea, Swede set course for home.

Upon returning to San Diego on September 10, 1963, Swede summed up some of his feelings. "We had a fine group of officers and a crew that was unbelievable. I don't know how those people could work like they did. It's a big job keeping a carrier clean and operating properly, but they did. It was beautiful, beautiful. The ship was clean as a whistle." There was more to the story.

What Just Happened?

Despite the happy travelogue above, this was not an uneventful cruise. Three operational accidents marred Swede's year commanding *Constellation*, horrific reminders that the dangers inherent in carrier operations applied to ship's crew and airmen alike. With regret coloring his voice, Swede reflected on the painful memories and responsibilities of command. "An AD came in and snapped an arresting cable. It whipped across the deck and a plane handler lost both legs just below the hips. I visited him in a hospital in Oakland. These terrible injuries had a bad psychological effect on him."

The second incident involved the ship's RIM-2 Terrier missiles. With a range of ten to twenty miles, this system was specifically designed for shipboard defense. "We had launching platforms starboard and port aft. These were radar-guided antiaircraft rockets. We spent quite a lot of time training on loading, making sure everything worked. The problem was we needed targets, and the drones were hard to come by. We got very little actual firing."

The accident occurred on a track dedicated to bringing the Terrier missiles up from storage to a launching pad. "The crewman got caught in the mechanical train and was killed. He was badly torn up; we couldn't save him. This was a very difficult thing to lose a man like that; it bothered the hell out of me. How does something like this happen?" The weapons officer was devastated. "He was very capable, very alert, but it was his man that was killed. He took it badly. He had a marvelous record as shipboard officer. He was passed over for captain, likely because of this death."

During training off Okinawa a third and worse accident involved a recently replaced arresting cable. "We hadn't 'teched' out the primary recovery wire. After a plane or two you've got to stop, pull the wire, take tension out of it, or it'll wrap up. Hadn't been done. The wire had formed a loop before it goes down into the catapult wheels. When the plane caught the wire, it snapped. The Phantom F4H did not even slow down. The plane tore apart as it shot over the side. There was no time to eject; we lost the pilot, the radio/intercept officer [RIO], and the plane."

Swede, observing from vulture's row, turned to his air boss, Bill Spell, and said, "What just happened?"

"We both knew because we had watched it unfold. That bothered me considerably. Losing that plane, pilot, and crew ruined what had been a very successful cruise. Our Hawaii stop was canceled, the crew missed out on R&R, and we enjoyed no real homecoming. Instead we had a low-key return. I convened a board of inquiry. Even though accidents are something you have to expect, it all reflects on the CO. You don't question the responsibility."

After a year of carrier command that began with the Cuban Missile Crisis and concluded with Kennedy's assassination, it was time for Swede's next assignment. The timing of his relief proved highly fortunate. During *Constellation*'s 1964 westPac tour, she responded to reports that North Vietnamese naval units in the Gulf of Tonkin had attacked the destroyer USS *Maddox* (DD 731). In the ensuing action, *Constellation*'s air wing suffered two firsts for the Vietnam War. Lt. (jg) Richard C. Sather was the first Navy pilot killed when his A-1 Skyraider was downed by AA fire. Lt. (jg) Everett Alvarez Jr.'s A-4E Skyhawk was shot down, and he became the first Navy POW.

CHAPTER 19

Do Not Pass Captain

When it came time to evaluate his candidacy for admiral, Swede was passed over. Upon reflection, this should have been no surprise. The Navy desires flag officers who are also good politicians. Any questionable incident could easily sour a selection board.

Looking back, elements of Swede's résumé raised eyebrows. He was not a product of Annapolis, and he had outraged Jimmy Thach while training in 1942 when he challenged the accepted wisdom of Thach's "Weave" maneuver. At Santa Cruz, Swede had publicly criticized Admiral Kinkaid's decision to send off a strike group. Then, in March 1943, Swede rejected Vought's F4U Corsair for carrier duty. Most recently, during his *Constellation* westPac cruise he had lost a crewmember, a plane, and its pilot and radar intercept officer. And Swede had taken vocal issue with Admiral Moore's leadership style.

Perhaps his compulsion to speak truth to power worked the most against his promotion. But having so recently commanded "America's Flagship," this rejection made no sense to Swede and many others.[1] Robbie and Whitey were disgusted to learn Swede would not advance to admiral. It was just another case of promotion politics that had more to do with who was doing the evaluating than with the candidate's capabilities.

Though shocked, Whitey could understand the rebuff. "Swede was an iconoclast. Swede always told it like it is. So the upper ranks disliked his lack of deference or his impertinent truths. The junior officers, of course, wanted to know everything he could tell them. Swede wasn't out to make himself popular. He had very little respect for his seniors."

Swede stolidly carried on. "Every officer should have a tour in the Pentagon! Shortly after the return of the *Constellation*, that is where I found myself, ensconced in an office in one of the many corridors." For the next year and a half, from December 1963 until July 1965, Swede worked in the Office of the Chief of Naval Operations (CNO) in Washington, D.C., where he served as head, Air Strike and Carrier Warfare Branch, Strike Warfare Division, Office of Deputy CNO (Fleet Operations and Readiness).

During Swede's CNO billet Southeast Asia heated up. On June 7, 1964, Lt. Charles F. Klusmann, flying an RF-8A photoreconnaissance plane off of *Kitty Hawk*, was shot down over Laos. He was captured by the Pathet Lao, managed to escape, and after two days eluding his captors was able to reach a government camp, one of a very few ever to escape captivity. Busy with staff duties, Swede had not heard anything about Klusmann's troubles.

The corridors of power were not for Swede. "Some officers enjoy the great shuffle with the layered organization, little understood by most folks. I am afraid I will never see the need for such a large organization. I wondered, 'How can I get out of here?' and was most pleased when good fortune took me elsewhere."

Miramar: Top Gun

The escalating war in Vietnam had demonstrated that aerial rockets had limited application. Swede worked up a plan to dedicate ComFair Miramar to advanced tactical training. Following some political wrangling, he snared the command. "I almost didn't get CO."

For the next three years, from August 1965 until June 1968, with the Vietnam War raging, Swede served as commander, Fleet Air Miramar. Ever the pilots' advocate, "I'd set up Miramar while I was in the Pentagon. Something was missing; we had new planes, pilots, bombs, rockets, guns, everything. All this new stuff could be better handled if we established a ComFair Miramar to oversee our preparations for Vietnam."

Essentially, Swede's organization would be an enabler for pilots and squadrons headed into harm's way. He described his work's urgency and complexity. "My job was to be of assistance to some six or seven very independent squadrons. Training was intense, and pressure on the squadrons was great as they were engaging in combat in a new environment with many new weapons both offensive and defensive. Radar-guided surface-to-air missiles were a major threat and called for electronic warning systems and countering devices to be installed in the aircraft on a continuing basis and, as well, the development of tactics to best evade and counter the enemy under all conditions. North Vietnamese antiaircraft was downing a lot of our aircraft. So we needed to improve our air-to-ground capabilities. Everybody was consumed with working on missiles, rocket work, and new operations for every type of jet. To get them ready to deploy I tried to coordinate training and exercises with NAS San Diego. But we had to work within a tight budget; there was a lot of concern about that—not just jet fuel but all our training materials. Jets drink fuel, so we tried to plan every flight to get the most out of training."

With the rapid development of missile technology, which could target aircraft miles away, dogfight training—or aerial combat maneuvering (ACM)—had been considered obsolete, dangerous to those engaged, and a waste of precious fuel. Now MiG pilots were mixing it up and posing serious challenges for Navy and Air Force pilots. With Swede's encouragement, ACM got reemphasized. It was not without risks.

A collision during an exercise resulted in the deaths of one pilot and RIO and prompted an investigation that questioned the need for this high-stakes training. In his endorsement of the panel's findings, Swede wrote, "The aircraft accident described in this investigation . . . is of course most regrettable. In considering this particular air combat maneuver, thoughtful consideration was given relative to its value in the training syllabus because of the high potential danger it presents. The training of replacement pilots in air-to-air tactics is a necessity, albeit the high risk of mishap, and such training must continue."[2]

During Swede's first year at Miramar, Lt. Cdr. Dan Macintyre and his rear-seat man, Lt. (jg) Alan Johnson, rotated through, having just returned from Vietnam. Flying a Phantom off USS *Coral Sea* (CV 43), the two had downed a MiG-17 and secured the first air-to-air victory for their carrier. Despite their authentication of the event, they were denied credit for it. During their stay at Miramar, Macintyre appealed to Swede for help in receiving proper credit. Their victory, if approved, would result in a Silver Star for both Dan and Alan.

Macintyre also wrote to a Florida senator for his help, to no avail. When Swede pressed the case from his position as ComFair Miramar, he ran into roadblocks put up by both the CIA and the Defense Intelligence Agency. The appeal was denied. Mystified by the cloak and dagger, Swede never understood what made the case so controversial. Swede noted the implications for Macintyre: "A Silver Star was looked upon with favor and would likely lead to command of a squadron."

How times had changed! In October 1942 Swede was credited with seven victories and one probable at Santa Cruz, for which he was awarded his third Navy Cross. Now, during the Vietnam War, downing one plane merited a Silver Star, the country's third-highest combat award.

Swede recalled how a medal might be scripted. "An Air Force captain, Steve Richie, shot down five MiG-21s over Vietnam. EC-121 radar picket planes were providing radar images of when MiGs were sent aloft, thus setting up an opportunity for aerial combat. It was damn well done. Another guy with four down didn't get the same help, never got a chance for his fifth victory."

During his Miramar billet, an obviously impressed Swede and his father were photographed flanking a bemedaled lieutenant. Swede considered the man a true hero. "I was at Miramar when Dieter Dengler came through. He was the only U.S. pilot, *to my knowledge*, who had escaped from a prison camp in Laos after being shot down while on a mission in that area. Dieter was sighted by an Air Force pilot, rescued, and returned to us. Dieter was a young man of unusual ability and courage, and his full story is most fascinating."

During Swede's second year at Miramar he was abruptly summoned to Subic Bay in the Philippines to participate in a board of inquiry investigating a disastrous October 26, 1966, fire on board USS *Oriskany* (CV 34) that killed 44 officers and men and injured more than 150. The seven-week inquiry carried out a high-paced investigation that involved twelve interested parties, six law specialists, and the interrogation of more than one hundred witnesses. All this resulted in a nearly two-thousand-page record. Rear Adm. V. P. de Poix, commander Carrier Division Seven and future head of the Defense Intelligence Agency, sat as senior board member. Not a man to be taken lightly, de Poix had earlier worked in aviation fire control and more recently had commanded USS *Enterprise* (CVN 65), the first nuclear-powered aircraft carrier.

After the inquiry de Poix wrote a letter of commendation in which he eloquently praised Swede's performance, contributions, and consummate professionalism. "During the period of extreme pressure noted above," de Poix wrote to Swede,

> your performance was most outstanding. Your impeccable conduct, continuous display of superior professionalism and unflagging energy and interest, particularly during the many successive late hour sessions, your many valuable suggestions, and your calm, human and accurate analytical approach were essential elements in the generation of a record which has been judged by higher authority to be extremely thorough and of high quality. The many ideas you offered for modifications or improvements in procedures and equipment are of inestimable future value to the Navy. Your personal contributions in the fields of aircraft carrier operations and naval ordnance were particularly valuable. It is a pleasure to commend you most strongly for your performance while serving with me as a member of the Board.

Closer to home, Swede's aviation career path was about to flame out. "I was flying, very busy training squadrons during the Vietnam War. One day the secretary had a message for me. It says, in no uncertain terms, 'Stay out of airplanes. You can't even get in the backseat.' No reason given. I told the doc I just had a flight physical; this is crazy."

Men of action eventually know when to step aside; Swede felt swept aside.

> They said, "There was a discrepancy of long standing in your EKG." All they did was go on and on about this discrepancy. That gets down to the end—retirement. They had to throw me out. I'd done thirty years. So they threw me out.
>
> Before that, they kept me on indefinitely, subject to health checks, wouldn't clear me health-wise. They kept me on for five years. At the end of those five years, not a goddamn thing different. Eventually they looked at my old EKG, taken early in my combat career. One look at that and their response was, "Ground this guy immediately," which they did. I never got

cleared from that. At the end of five years they retired me. They never came up with any reason for it. I had to get a Navy attorney to sit up there with me at meetings of the board to investigate my EKG. They gave me stress tests every six weeks.[3]

Swede's retirement really began as he concluded his three fruitful years at NAS Miramar, where his efforts were recognized with a Legion of Merit. Beginning in June 1968, Swede's next (and final) billet was chief of staff for the Eleventh Naval District, work related mostly to civilian interests. "I was a good candidate. It was a lot of liaison work involving liberty for sailors, police work, and plans for the development of the waterfront."

According to a March 26, 1970, Headquarters Eleventh Naval District news release, Swede received the Meritorious Service Medal for promoting new and improved programs throughout the district. Journalist 3C Sam Bordeaux explained, "Some of those programs pertained to the prevention of water, air, and sound pollution, minority group relations, and Navy cost reductions." Closest to Swede's heart was the Casualty Assistance Calls Program, which would "provide assistance to families of servicemen who may die, become prisoners of war, or missing in action."

After two years as chief of staff, on July 1, 1970, Swede recognized the inevitable and stepped away from his remarkable naval career. Whether flying heroically, overseeing the development of new aircraft and weapons systems, or commanding the world's most advanced carrier, there was very little about carrier aviation that Swede Vejtasa did not know. "I was retired long before I felt ready to take that step; however, thus ended the saga of one Navy dive-bomber and fighter pilot whose only regret is that I could not have been more a part of the action."[4]

In his unsought retirement Swede worked for the Rey River Ranch, an outfit owned by a group of doctors. The ranch promoted outdoor activity, hunting, and fishing—"a nice place to take the family," as Swede put it. They hired Swede as a secretary, someone to handle stockholder business. He would research stock interests and negotiate with attorneys. "I spent twenty years as secretary and retired in 1991 at the age of seventy-six."

But for an occasional *Enterprise* reunion, and in Whitey's case, at Aces gatherings, Swede, Whitey, and Robbie seldom enjoyed opportunities to interact in their later years. But they would always share sharply honed memories of pivotal days in October 1942.

A few years before his second retirement, Swede made a trip to Patriots Point Naval and Maritime Museum in Charleston, South Carolina, where he boarded *Yorktown* to be inducted into the Carrier Aviation Hall of Fame. Former inductees, familiar to students of carrier history, had all played significant roles in the development of naval aviation. Swede's class of 1987 included Lt. Cdr. Godfrey deC. Chevalier, the first aviator to land on a ship under way; Admiral J. J. "Jocko" Clark, commander of *Yorktown* during Swede's VS-5 days; Rear Adm. John Crommelin, Swede's old air boss at Santa Cruz; and Capt. Art Downing, a renowned and highly decorated dive-bomber pilot. Fabled carrier aircraft designer Ed Heinemann, who designed the Dauntless dive-bomber and the A-4 Skyhawk among others, rounded out that year's distinguished inductees.

Swede's citation read:

> Sole WWII carrier pilot to receive Navy Crosses for dive-bombing and aerial combat: VS-5 in *Yorktown* CV 5 at Coral Sea his SBD bomb helped sink a carrier and his fixed guns shot down three Zeros. VF-10 Grim Reapers in *Enterprise* CV 6 at Santa Cruz his F4F Wildcat in one CAP flight shot down seven dive bombers and torpedo planes saving "The Big E." Air Officer *Essex* CV 9 Korean War, Jan. '51–Apr. '53. Commanding Officer *Constellation* CV 64, Nov. '62–'63.
>
> Elected to Carrier Hall of Fame in 1987.

This was high company, and no accident. He very much belonged there.

CHAPTER 20

Afterthoughts

"My favorite plane in combat? That would be an SBD-3. It was a great airplane, despite being belittled for its lack of guns. There was no trouble with those two .50-caliber machine guns, only restriction. There was no volume of fire. You just had to point them in the right direction."

The last plane he flew? "Oh, that would be a Phantom F-4B. It was 1968 down at Miramar."

His most difficult decision? "That would be when I was ordered to fly out on that Goose Chase. As I passed Jim Thomas on my way to the flag plot to bitch about the mission, he says, 'Don't be so hasty.' I paused, and decided then to go on the mission."

Which of his medals and decorations meant the most to Swede? "The Navy Cross, by all means. That requires some dedication and performance. I have three of those. I feel that there were some pretty close calls there. I could have easily become another statistic. The Navy Cross should be an example of maximum performance."

Prominent among Swede's decorations is a Bronze Star with the Combat V, signifying valor. Asked to differentiate between valor, courage, and bravery, Swede preferred the term "valor." "That means a bit more. You expose yourself during difficult missions to enemy fire. Sure, that refers to me."

Whitey Feightner admired Swede's intensity. "Swede was pretty laid back, but he was very intense in his beliefs. Swede had a lot of combat experience; he knew more than most everyone. He got pissed with those who didn't know what they were talking about, and he had little patience with paperwork. He was an aviator's aviator. A superb combat pilot. That was it. He was a different breed. He was always his own man. People respected Swede for who he was and the expertise he brought to any mission."

Robbie Robinson acknowledged his great affection for Swede and didn't hesitate to tell him. During an April 26, 2011, visit, the author sat in while Robbie engaged Swede in a phone conversation.

"Hey, you old son-of-a-gun, how the hell are you?"

Pause.

"Ninety-six? I didn't know you were that old!"

Silence as Swede made some response.

Robbie blurted, "You were the best damned flier. I always felt safer when you or Joe Foss were up flying escort."

Again Swede made some reply.

As the conversation wound down, Robbie confessed, "I don't usually tell men 'I love you.' I love you Swede." Wearing an easy smile, Robbie sat back and savored what had been a great moment for both.

Swede reflected on his naval aviation career and beyond. "I wanted to be successful. I flew in war and held very responsible positions. In combat you evaluate yourself, make comparisons with others, and see what improvements are needed. I participated in operations with Poles, Italians, Spaniards, training fighter tactics, individual combat training. I was involved with the breaking in of new weapons. Rockets were new, and we had to figure out how to use them and how to hang them.

"At China Lake I helped adapt rockets to aircraft, which was very satisfying. Back in 1954 I shot down the first drone while flying a Douglas A-4, and later flying a Grumman F9F. I experienced a profitable time there. China Lake was the premier weapons development center in the U.S. We worked on everything from guns and rockets to propellants—broad fields of endeavor. And these weapons were designed for the Navy, Air Force, anybody who can use them. We developed the Sidewinder missile there."

Such professional achievements bore little relation to what Swede wanted people to know about him, what was important to him.

"Not Navy stuff. My early life. We were a pioneer family. What a terrible, tough experience, especially for my mother. She never got to town; there was no place to shop. We had no fences, and so few visitors. Same thing for my dad. He was a very hard worker, a strong laborer. He built a homestead, did everything himself. He did dry land farming; to produce a crop was almost impossible. His workday went from daylight to ten at night. Later he became clerk of the district court because he had a college education. But before that, he had the pioneer spirit. He thought it would be easy. He did prove he could homestead and make a living, but we had none of the niceties—no running water, no telephone, no car, no postal service. Both parents homeschooled us, which was great. But we had no lights, not even a kerosene stove; these were disadvantages we had to cope with. There weren't many people like that. Most didn't stay; many were broken by the experience."

Swede's thoughts regarding an afterlife circled back to his upbringing. "I don't really have any positive conclusions on what happens. Pretty generally, a person is just so much protoplasm, and he's gone. It's nice to have religion and think of spirits. That part is good. They're gone and they're not coming back. It's just a memory, really. I want to be cremated and have my ashes scattered at sea from an aircraft carrier, a ceremony unavailable to civilians. I practically lived with Indians in Montana. I'll become one with the Great Spirit."

On January 23, 2013, Swede Vejtasa, the man Rear Adm. Whitey Feightner described as a "pure flyer," passed on. Though Swede was justly famous for his superb combat proficiency, his pioneering contributions to the development of naval aviation and his career dedication to pilot training and safety continue to inspire those under his command. Swede has gone from us, his indomitable spirit now entwined with the Great Spirit.

Epilogue

Bill Burch

William O. Burch Jr. was promoted to rear admiral in 1956, retired in 1962, and along the way was awarded a Navy Cross with two gold stars (in lieu of a second and third Navy Cross), the Legion of Merit, a Distinguished Flying Cross, and a Purple Heart. He passed away on January 21, 1989, at age eighty-five.

Whitey Feightner

Following his World War II service, Whitey Feightner flew the F7U Cutlass for the Blue Angels and was the only man to take the F7U-1 on board ship for its initial carrier qualifications. He also served as a test pilot, captained two Navy ships, and honorably retired in 1974 as a rear admiral. His decorations include the Navy Commendation Medal, Legion of Merit (2), Distinguished Flying Cross (4), and Air Medal (12). Whitey wrote the 2012 testimonial letter included in Appendix 4 supporting a review of Jimmy Flatley's 1942 recommendation that Swede be awarded the Medal of Honor.

Jimmy Flatley

An astute pioneer of fighter pilot doctrine, Lieutenant Commander Flatley was a tactical analyst par excellence. Continuing his military career after World War II, Flatley rose to the rank of vice admiral prior to his untimely death at age fifty-one. Flatley's awards include the Navy Cross, Distinguished Service Medal, Legion of Merit, Distinguished Flying Cross, and Bronze Star.

Adm. Thomas C. Kinkaid

Kinkaid's black-shoe talents helped to redeem him later in the war. In late 1944 the Japanese formulated a complex plan to disrupt the American landings in the Philippines, resulting in the Battle of Leyte Gulf. Kinkaid commanded Adm. Jesse Oldendorf's Bombardment and Fire Support Group opposing the Japanese Southern Force in the Surigao Strait, during which Oldendorf annihilated Admiral Nishimura's southern threat to the Philippine landings. Admiral Kinkaid died on November 17, 1972, at the age of eighty-four. His awards include the Army Distinguished Service Medal, the Navy Distinguished Service Medal with three gold stars, and the Legion of Merit.

Robbie Robinson

After his Korean adventures, Robbie served as a test pilot, retired as a commander, and in 1961 went to work for Lockheed. Robbie's awards include a Bronze Star with Combat V, Distinguished Flying Cross, Air Medal, Air Force Commendation Medal, and presidential unit citation. Until the day he passed away Robbie could be heard to say, "To hell with rank." That day came on January 2, 2012. At ninety-one years of age, Robbie joined the slipstream.

Gus Widhelm

Acknowledged master of the flamboyant, Gus walked the walk. During World War II Gus was awarded a Distinguished Flying Cross and two Navy Crosses, the first at Midway and the second at Santa Cruz. For his outstanding service during the war he was awarded a Legion of Merit. Later, in the Solomons campaign, he commanded the first night fighter squadron, VF (N)-75, flying F4U Corsairs. Captain Widhelm died in a T-28 accident at age forty-six on July 19, 1954.

APPENDIX 1

Goose Chase Controversies

The tragic events of October 25, 1942, demanded some explanation. A comparison of Flatley's after-action report, Admiral Kinkaid's serials, Captain Hardison's report, *Enterprise* deck logs, and interview transcripts reveals a number of controversies: the decision to send Air Group 10; the number of escorts; who flew those escorts; the altitude flown by the strike group; the assigned search leg distance; an empty Point Option; the absence of YE, radar, or radio contact; and the resultant loss of aircraft.

Given the distance to *Kidō Butai*, historians have been mystified by Kinkaid's impulsive decision to send off an attack group in the first place, flouting his carrier's duty status, and then to select for the mission his untried *Enterprise* attack group over *Hornet*'s experienced air group.[1] Providing a dubious rationale for Kinkaid's inexplicable decision, Captain Hardison, in his November 10 report to Admiral Halsey via Kinkaid, wrote that "the need for getting them off promptly in order to prevent their being caught on deck by an imminent air attack, and also to get them out to the attack before the enemy carriers opened out too far, were undoubtedly factors in the O.T.C's decision." A puzzling interpretation since those in flag plot knew that U.S. land-based patrol planes had spotted the Japanese carriers 350 miles away.

Needing to explain the Goose Chase, in which he had no part, Jimmy Flatley included in his extensive after-action report Enclosure A: "Comments on Attack Mission during Evening of October 25, 1942, by USS *Enterprise* Air Group."[2] In it Flatley wrote:

During the early afternoon of October 25, 1942, a contact report was received which indicated the Jap CVs were then about 350 miles away. We immediately headed in their direction and at 1500 launched a 200-mile search. At 1530, we launched a composite attack group with orders to proceed 200 miles and if no contact was made to return to base. Sixteen escort fighters were assigned this mission. The flight proceeded out and immediately climbed to 17,000 feet. This altitude was maintained for three and a half hours, both on the outgoing leg and on the return. This group should have returned to their base at sunset, 1835. Instead of that, they returned at 1930, long after dark. They failed to locate the enemy.

On the question of how many escorts flew the mission, Flatley wrote that sixteen escort fighters were *assigned* to the mission, but he did not specify how many actually flew the mission. Kinkaid, in his undated Serial 0077 to Admiral Halsey, incorrectly stated that eleven VFs flew escort. Lt. John C. Eckhardt wrote in the Fighting Squadron Ten log that twelve fighters were launched for escort, but three failed to rendezvous and returned to base, still leaving nine flying escort. Swede and Whitey, of course, understood that eight actually flew the mission. Such confusion was not limited to escort numbers. Kinkaid's serial also stated that the strike group included twelve scouting bombers instead of the five that actually flew.

Flatley did not identify the pilots flying escort. Lieutenant Eckhardt's Fighting Squadron Ten report for October 25 is vague and, according to Swede and Whitey, erroneous. Eckhardt wrote that "Lieutenant Commander Kane's flight consisting of Lieutenant Faulkner, substituting for Lieutenant Eckhardt, Lieutenant Frank D. Miller, and Ensign Wickendoll; Lieutenant Vejtasa's flight consisting of Ensign Feightner, substituting for Lieutenant Harris, Ensign Dowden and Ensign Leder, composed the escort VF. Ensigns Long, Gordon, and Slagle took off, but were unable to rendezvous and returned to base." Eckhardt also wrote that Miller was seen to crash in the water rather than bailing out as Whitey had witnessed. The report concluded, "The remainder of the group of VF-10 landed aboard at 2000." Eckhardt failed to mention Coalson's simultaneous landing with Swede, presumably because Coalson was not officially part of the escort. But Swede knew Coalson as "a really exceptional pilot and very good friend," not a likely source of identity confusion during such a dangerous moment. Eckhardt's report provides a perfect example of how records may verify an event but often contain errors in fact. Better to rely on the participants' version of events.

Substitutions and the fact that three pilots aborted lent further confusion to the situation. Eckhardt implied that Kane led one flight, but in Swede's narrative, Kane had not come along at all. If he had, then as senior officer Kane would have assumed escort command. Swede was also convinced that Fritz Faulkner did not fly. Perhaps Fritz was one of the pilots who returned to base after failing to join up. The records provide no clarity on this issue. Thus, we rely on Swede and Whitey for the truth regarding who flew escort.

Regarding the altitude flown, Flatley continued, "The reasons this particular flight is being discussed in this report are that several lessons were learned: (1) The flight altitude of 17,000 feet was maintained much too long. Many of the VF exhausted their oxygen supply. The proper procedure would have been to let down during the return flight, which would have conserved gasoline and would have shortened the return flight."

In his unpublished memoir Hoot Gibson wrote that they flew at 21,000 feet and remembered freezing in his unheated cockpit.[3] Against that, Swede and Whitey insisted that they never flew above 10,000 feet. Swede recalled flying at 7,200 feet. Whitey supported the lower altitude, noting, "I never wore my oxygen mask during the flight."

While Group Commander Gaines' supplemental gas supply allowed for periodic higher-altitude searches, there was no gas-saving gain for the rest of them flying at 17,000 feet. And it should be remembered that the strike group included a number of experienced pilots well practiced in fuel conservation.

Flatley's report on the length of the search legs is at odds with Kinkaid's. According to Flatley, the strike group had been directed to search out to two hundred miles, and if no contact was made to return promptly to Enterprise. Kinkaid's after-action report states that the pilots were to search 150 miles out, which makes little sense when the Japanese fleet had been initially spotted more than 300 miles away. An officially shorter search leg would return them before nightfall, however, and vindicate Kinkaid's decision to send them in the first place.

As for the likelihood of contact, Flatley got to the heart of the matter. "When the flight was ordered off, there was practically no hope of success because of the distance. However, if the ship had continued on toward the enemy at high speed and then at 1730 an attack group had been launched, the chances of success would have been increased a hundredfold. There was a full moon, rising about 1930."

That speculation involved some large *ifs*. Flatley realized contact could be remotely possible only if the Japanese held to their original course and if TF 61 conducted a two-hour high-speed run, which would be seriously compromised by the need to constantly reverse course to launch and recover aircraft. Further, Kinkaid had learned late that afternoon that the Japanese had turned north.

Aircraft Losses

In his Serial 0077 Kinkaid finally acknowledged the shocking operational aircraft losses on October 25. "As pilots were not qualified for night landings, the group was landed with difficulty and with the loss of six planes through deck crashes and water landings. This was a serious loss as earlier in the day five planes had been damaged on deck by the first deck crash which had occurred since Group Ten came on board." In fact, the night's losses totaled not six but eight planes. It began with Miller's F4F, followed by four SBDs, of which two were perforated by the bomb blast at Point Option and ditched. Carroum's wreck cost two more. While the deck was being cleared, fuel exhaustion forced three TBFs to ditch.

In his Serial 0052 to Admiral Halsey dated November 3, "Preliminary Report of Action, October 26, 1942," Kinkaid opened with his version of the October 25 Goose Chase. In paragraph two he wrote:

> On 25 October at 1250, our shore based patrol plane reported sighting two enemy carriers and supporting ships, distant 360 miles on course 145, speed 25. Course was changed toward the contact and speed increased to 27 knots. No further reports were received. Evidently the patrol plane was not tracking. If enemy maintained the reported course early contact could be expected. Therefore, the afternoon search from the *Enterprise* was made by a search and attack group. *Hornet*'s attack group stood by on deck.

Shortly after this search was launched a report was received that enemy carriers were on course north and it was evident that if they remained on this course no contact would be made. The *Enterprise* attack group returned and was landed after dark with considerable difficulty as pilots were not qualified for night landings. The *Hornet* striking group stood by during the night, the plan being to launch a moonlight attack provided a position within striking distance of enemy carriers could be reached. At the suggestion of Commander Task Force 17, *Enterprise* retained duty carrier status and again made the morning search on 26 October.

Kinkaid recognized the impossibility of contact when the Japanese turned away, but he made no effort to contact Swede's now-pointless strike group. He further acknowledged the difficulty with landings on the evening of October 25, referenced a veteran *Hornet* strike group spotted for launch, and noted that *Enterprise* retained duty carrier status, which should have limited air operations to CAP and searches.

Silent YE, Empty Point Option, and the Nature of Zeal
Three days later, in his November 6 Serial 0056, Kinkaid commented on Murray's "USS *Hornet* Report of Action," in which he only obliquely referenced his abandonment of Point Option. "Late return of the attack group was not due to the difficulty of keeping Point Option but to the *zeal* of the striking group commander in pressing on beyond the scouting line in an endeavor to find the enemy." Kinkaid did not bring up a malfunctioning YE-ZB homing signal; nor did he account for the single day's loss of two Wildcats, eight SBDs, and three TBFs without a shot being fired. Kinkaid's phrase "considerable difficulty," however, reveals a flair for understatement.

It was not until Captain Hardison's November 10 report that correspondence vaguely touched on the silence of YE equipment and the difficulty of holding Point Option:

Point Option, as a result of YE-ZB equipment, has lost something of its importance. This equipment has failed at critical moments. Therefore, it is desirable to keep near Point Option if circumstances permit. Probably the chief reason for wide separation is the effort to maintain a relatively fast moving Point Option in a down wind direction. With light winds and frequent launchings and recoveries incident to patrols and searches, this is almost impossible. Therefore, estimates as to its travel under such conditions should be conservative.

Hardison provided no specific incident of YE-ZB breakdown, but he clearly implied that a signal's absence would be due to a breakdown. If on October 25 the YE-ZB homing equipment did critically fail, then, having learned that the Japanese had steamed away to the north, what sense did it make to vacate Point Option at night?

Whitey recalled, "The YE wouldn't reveal their position; they only needed to leave that on. Not one squawk. I'm sure the YE was off. It worked well on other occasions; sure didn't that night."

In his Serial 0077 to Admiral Nimitz via Admiral Halsey, Kinkaid reiterated much of his previous report, revealed the morning's loss of five aircraft, and redefined "zeal":

The attack group was ordered to proceed out on the median line of the search to 150 miles then return if no contact was made. Shortly after the search and attack group was launched another report was received indicating that the enemy carriers were on course north, and it was evident that no contact would be made. The search group returned on time and was landed. The striking group, through *excess zeal* [author's italics] of its leader, proceeded out to two hundred miles and then searched eighty miles to northeastward in the hope of making contact. They returned to the *Enterprise* after dark and low in fuel. As pilots were not qualified for night landings, the group was landed with difficulty and with the loss of six planes through deck crashes and water landings. This was a serious loss as earlier in the day five planes had been damaged on deck by the first deck crash which had occurred since Group Ten came on board.

Despite the fact that he had ordered the group out on an impossible mission, failed to recall them when advised the Japanese had turned away from any possible contact, and vacated Point Option after dark, Kinkaid sought to shift the blame for these losses to pilot deficiencies.

In this more detailed summary, Kinkaid qualified the strike commander's zeal as excessive zeal. Zeal is equal parts enthusiasm, passion, keenness, and positivity—all desirable traits in combat pilots. Without a recall from Kinkaid, by nature and training skipper Jim Thomas would have done his utmost to locate and attack the Japanese task force. As Kinkaid saw it, the responsibility for the evening's disaster lay not with his initial decision to send the group out but with the overzealous Jim Thomas.

Hardison tried for a more positive approach. "When night landings became necessary on the evening of 25 October, results were disappointing, especially during the short period between dusk and moonrise. As soon as the moon rose sufficiently to clear some low clouds on the horizon, landings improved materially. However, had it not been for landing crashes which tied up the deck for considerable periods, there is no doubt that several planes which landed in the water due to fuel exhaustion, would have gotten on board."

The full moon rose at 7:30 that evening, and Eckhardt's report has them landing at 8 p.m. There is little evidence that landings improved with moonlight. Carroum's disregard of Lindsay's wave-off and his subsequent crash, however, did substantiate Hardison's implicit criticism.

Hardison's report contextualized some of the problems and provided recommendations: "The *Enterprise* Air Group went into action some ten days after departure from Pearl Harbor. It had never before been embarked as a group in a carrier and its carrier experience as a group consisted only of the qualification and refresher exercises conducted over a period of some five days immediately prior to departure. The fast passage to this area did not permit as much training as was desirable."

Hardison then inverted Kinkaid's caustic interpretation of the term "zeal." "Considering the inexperience of many of the group, their performance was in general very good and in some cases excellent. In courage, zeal, and determination they were outstanding."

Having softened Kinkaid's "excess zeal," Hardison appeared to place the blame for their "difficulties" on pilots' inadequate navigation and lack of night-landing skill.

However, it is very evident we must never let up in the training of our groups, especially replacement groups. They must be expert in communications and gunnery (including bombing). Navigation must be stressed continuously, both for homing (radio silence and breakdown of ZB equipment must be considered) and, more important still, because it is only by good navigation that accurate contact reports can be made and attack group[s] led to their objectives. Groups should be thoroughly indoctrinated in night landing procedure. If possible the pilots should be qualified on board, and in any event, they should be carefully checked out ashore in night carrier landings by a qualified carrier signal officer. This checking out should include the full procedure required when a group returns to a carrier after nightfall.

It is unclear how any of this applied to Air Group 10, given that navigation had not been a problem, and it was widely known before the mission that most of the pilots had not yet qualified for night landings. Focusing on pilot shortcomings, imagined or real, merely shifted blame away from Kinkaid's questionable decision making.

On the issue of night landings, Flatley defended his pilots. "The flight as originally planned and ordered, would have returned the planes to their base at sunset. It so happened that only a few of the pilots had ever made a night carrier landing. However, if a night landing had been planned and the pertinent points gone over with the new pilots, they would have been better prepared for the experience."[4]

These were leadership failures. No one addressed the matter of how an absent YE-ZB homing signal or vacating Point Option might have contributed to the evening's chaos.

Flatley's last point in Enclosure A: "One VF pilot, Lieutenant Frank D. Miller, U.S.N., failed to return from this flight. He was seen to crash after dark about 45–50 miles from the ship. The cause of his crash is undetermined. He is listed as missing." Though Miller did not crash, but bailed out, his needless loss was on Kinkaid.

Whitey found the whole episode appalling. "In the first place, it was a stupid idea to send us out there. Really dumb. I can't believe they did this, and we got not one word from them. Radio silence. Swede was outraged, rightly so. I don't think anyone consulted him about the mission. After Gaines and Thomas, the two senior guys, Swede led the fighters. Gaines in his unarmed, gas-loaded TBF flew up and behind the bombers.

"They expected us back early, but we flew those extra legs. We stayed out an hour and a half beyond expectation. Maintaining radio silence, we were very isolated in the growing dark. Radio silence from the *Enterprise* was another stupidity. To shove off leaving that many folks out there with no word . . . ?"

Having foreseen nothing but calamity from Kinkaid's plan, Swede was harshly critical. "Kinkaid was not an aviator. He didn't know what a plane was. Some of the things he did—the day before the Battle of Santa Cruz—unbelievable. We knew where the Japanese forces were located. He ordered a search and destroy when our SBDs had no chance to find the Japanese fleet."

Up to the day he died, Swede viewed Kinkaid's abandonment as "Criminal!"

APPENDIX 2

Mission Myths Deconstructed

Swede figures to a greater or lesser degree in nearly every account of the Battle of Santa Cruz, and noteworthy historians have produced many rousing accounts of what transpired on October 26, 1942. Curiously, no two of them are alike. In *History of United States Naval Operations in World War II*, volume 5, *The Struggle for Guadalcanal, August 1942–February 1943* (1950) Samuel Eliot Morison describes Swede's two dive-bomber victims as already in their dives. Later, Swede was ready and waiting as "dark-green Kates (torpedo bombers) came in from the south. He led his wingman into the thick of them, expertly destroyed six and then ran out of ammunition." As for the plane that crashed into *Smith*, "While guns were still spitting, one torpedo plane charged in for a suicide try, curiously picking on destroyer *Smith*. Carrying his torpedo under his belly this 1942-style Kamikaze hurtled into the destroyer's forecastle."[1]

Cdr. Edward P. Stafford wrote in *The Big E* that Swede's second Val had dropped his bomb and was retiring. Swede next downed a solitary Kate before closing on three Kates entering a cloud. After downing them, "Vejtasa saw the shadow of another Kate and he pulled up hard in a low side run but failed to knock him down. He followed him out of the cloud where the task force AA at once took over. Swede could see the enemy was too high and fast for an effective drop and let the AA have him. It was this plane that crashed the *Smith*."[2]

Brothers James and William Belote, coauthors of *Titans of the Seas* (1975), wrote that Swede downed two retiring dive-bombers. Quoting Swede's after-action report, they described his subsequent destruction of three Kates in *thin* cloud cover. Swede took on another Kate but "missed him badly"; that plane crashed into the destroyer *Smith*. Swede shot off the last of his ammunition on another retiring Kate, which finally geysered into the sea after a five-mile pursuit.[3]

Peter Mersky's *The Grim Reapers* (1986) has Swede shooting down seven bombers that day. The first of two Vals was said to be running for home following a strike on *Hornet*. After restarting his engine in a high-speed dive, Swede downed a Kate, then shot down a section of three Kates; Mersky did not mention clouds. Swede finally damaged the Kate that crashed into *Smith*. Lastly, he downed yet another Kate for an unprecedented tally of seven. Mersky included that Jimmy Flatley, a man who did not believe in awards, recommended Swede for the Medal of Honor.[4]

In *Guadalcanal: The Carrier Battles* (1987), Eric Hammel characterized Swede's first two shoot-downs as diving and retiring dive-bombers. Swede then closed on three torpedo planes (Kates) entering a cloud and shot down all three. Back in the clear, and dodging friendly antiaircraft fire, he failed to finish off the Kate that plowed into *Smith*. Lastly, Swede dropped an outbound Kate many miles after setting it aflame, for a total of seven down.[5]

In *Guadalcanal: The Definitive Account of the Landmark Battle* (1990), Richard Frank offered an ambiguous tally and an account quite at odds with Swede's version. "This plane was the first victim of a Wildcat flown by Lieutenant Stanley W. Vejtasa or his wingman. Vejtasa pursued one group, perforating four with gunfire; one blew up and two others appeared to catch fire. He chased the fourth—which he thought he missed—in the clouds, but the plane dived down to plow into the forecastle of destroyer *Smith*."[6]

In *The First Team and the Guadalcanal Campaign*, John B. Lundstrom wrote that Swede dispatched one Val in a dive and a second with Tex Harris. Regarding the Kate torpedo bombers, Lundstrom wrote, "Although he felt certain he finished all three aircraft, they kept on going toward the task force." As for the last Kate torpedo bomber in that group, "Either Vejtasa or the AA had tagged this kanko (Kate or Type 97)." Swede's last kill was the widely cited retiring Kate downed after a lengthy chase.[7]

Barrett Tillman's *Wildcat Aces of World War 2* (1995) says that Swede downed two Vals and then went after the others: "Chasing the green-painted Nakajimas in and out of clouds was hard enough, without the added danger of having to dodge 'friendly' flak, but Vejtasa persisted. In the next several minutes he rode up close to five B5Ns and sent them burning into the choppy grey seas." Adding to the confusion, the caption beneath the accompanying photo of Swede has the victories reversed: "The VF-10 aviator claimed five 'Vals' and two 'Kates,' possibly saving *Enterprise* from destruction."[8]

Steve Ewing's *Reaper Leader: The Life of Jimmy Flatley* (2002) gives Swede's remarkable ace run sparse coverage. "Swede Vejtasa and Lt. Leroy Harris quickly downed one enemy aircraft, and then Swede proceeded to shoot up three others, possibly downing one. These aerial victories, the disruptive effect of other Reaper attacks, effective AA batteries and effective conning of the carrier and evading nearly a dozen torpedo tracks saved *Enterprise*."[9] Ewing failed to acknowledge Swede's official tally of seven down and, curiously, never mentioned Flatley's recommendation for the Medal of Honor.

In *Wings of Gold* (2005), Gerald Astor quoted extensively the after-action report attributed to Swede that was included in Flatley's report. The scenario: Swede downed one Val prior to his pushover, and a second one in retreat. A wing tank problem forced his temporary retirement from the action. Then, in the clouds,

> I followed very close a three-plane section [Kates] and blew up the number-two man with two short bursts. Next I fired at the leader and shot the rudder off before the plane caught fire. The third plane started a shallow turn and caught on fire after I fired a rather long burst into it. These attacks were no-deflection runs from directly astern in a heavy cloud. I observed no return fire from the planes. Pulling up, I saw another enemy plane above me and I tried a low, side attack, but missed him badly. Following him out of the clouds, I saw he was too high and much too fast for an effective drop on our carrier. The A.A. guns opened up in one direction, so I broke away. The torpedo plane continued on in almost a straight line and hit a destroyer. There was tremendous explosion near the No. 1 turret forward.[10]

Finally, Swede is said to drop a last, retiring, Kate after miles of pursuit. Astor observed that despite Flatley's recommendation for a Medal of Honor, "the decoration was reduced to a Navy Cross."[11]

Pacific Air, by David Sears, also credits Swede with seven victories and continues the fiction of Swede breaking off from the Kate that crashed into *Smith*. As for the last victory after *Smith* was hit, "Vejtasa chased and emptied his magazines into one plane, which caught fire and staggered a few more miles before finally crashing."[12]

Barrett Tillman, in Enterprise: *America's Fightingest Ship and the Men Who Helped Win World War II* (2002), wrote that Swede "shot two of them [Vals] apart" and later added that Swede was "credited with downing five torpedo planes for an American record of seven kills in one mission. However many he splashed, he undoubtedly helped save *Enterprise*."[13]

In addition to the literary accounts, the History Channel's popular video docudrama *Battle 360°* (2008) details *Enterprise*'s battle history through World War II. In the docudrama we are informed that Admiral Kinkaid, owing to his former command of cruisers, was the perfect choice to lead *Enterprise* into the Battle of Santa Cruz. The narrator further informs us that Swede, "determined to avenge the damage done to *Enterprise*," was credited with shooting down seven bombers that day. The series' presentation of Swede's mission is an exercise in confusion. First, he is said to have ambushed four dive-bombers, then he downed a Kate that cartwheeled into the water. His sixth victim was a Kate that crashed into the destroyer *Smith*, and the seventh was a retiring bomber.

Why this perplexing historical disunity? Part of the answer lies in Jimmy Flatley's "Fighting Squadron Ten Action Reports for October 25 and 26, 1942," the primary reference supporting the many incomplete or inaccurate historical accounts.

Flatley's Fallacy

Flatley's Enclosure D, "Narrative of Events by Lieutenant Stanley W. Vejtasa, U.S.N., Leader of One Combat Patrol Flight on October 26, 1942," presents many familiar elements of the historical accounts and is reproduced here in its entirety:

At 0930 on October 26, 1942, it was announced that an enemy attack group was approaching the task force from the northwest, distance sixty miles.

Eleven available F4F-4s on deck were launched immediately to augment the combat air patrol of twelve fighters already on station. My flight known as Red Seven made a running rendezvous immediately after takeoff and we climbed under full power proceeding toward the *Hornet*, which was about ten miles bearing 270 degrees from the *Enterprise*. We were then vectored out on a bearing of 230 degrees, distance five miles, and instructed to look for bogies reported at seven thousand feet. By this time, we were at 12,000 feet and still climbing. Looking up, I saw six or eight enemy dive bombers in a loose column, making a high-speed glide to their pushover point, which was about 12,000 feet. The *Hornet* was already under attack by another group of dive bombers, which had approached from a slightly different angle.

One of the approaching bombers dove beneath a cloud and came out at our level. By executing a steep wing-over, we got into position for a high side run and [it] went down in flames. The other bombers passed over us about two thousand feet and made their attack. We received no further instructions, so we dropped to a lower level and picked up two enemy dive bombers, which were retiring and shot them both down in flames. They attempted no defensive maneuvers.

Thus far, I had been draining gas from my wing tank to get as much use from it as possible. My engine suddenly cut out and I observed the fuel pressure gauge to be reading zero. I shifted to the main tank and the engine caught. Seeing a stream of gas spewing from beneath the trailing edge of my right wing, I knew that the tank had been punctured or the fuel line connection had come loose in the dive. After several unsuccessful attempts, I finally released it by pulling with both hands on the release toggle.

We climbed back to 10,000 feet and reported our position to Reaper Base. We were instructed to orbit and look for torpedo planes. While circling, I heard Reaper Base vector other sections out to intercept enemy bombers coming in. We flew out on these vectors a short distance, but again the enemy bombers came in over us. I saw two F4F-4s intercept them close to the screen and follow them into their dive and into the AA fire which was exceedingly heavy and apparently quite effective as several dive bombers caught on fire on the way down. Others pulled out as high as seven thousand feet and left.

Shortly, I heard Red Four vectored out on course 330 degrees. Reaper Base stated that bogies may be friendly planes returning from their attack. When about ten miles from base, I heard Ensign Leder give a "Tally-Ho, nine o'clock down." We were then at 13,000 feet, and I sighted the enemy torpedo planes below at about 7,000 feet. They were very easy to distinguish by the smooth dark paint on the wings and fuselage. I believe there were eleven planes in this group flying in a step-up column of three 3-plane sections and one 2-plane section. My second section, Lieutenant Ruehlow and Ensign Leder, who had pulled away and dove on two Zeros a few minutes before, already were attacking the torpedo planes. We picked up about 350 knots in our dive and were able to place ourselves in position for a steep, high side run. I estimated the torpedo planes to be making about 250 knots. They were already in a high-speed approach about to deploy beneath a large cloud and attack the task force. Lieutenant Harris and I attacked one three-plane section and each set a torpedo plane on fire. As I broke away, I saw another F4F-4 attacking. The formation then broke up and instead of going under the cloud they flew into it. I followed very close behind a three-plane section and blew the number two man with two short bursts. I then fired at the leader and shot the rudder off before the plane caught fire. The third plane started a shallow turn and caught fire after I had fired a rather long burst into it. These three attacks were no deflection runs directly from astern in a heavy cloud. I observed no return fire from the torpedo planes.

Pulling up, I saw another enemy plane above me and I tried a low, side attack, but missed him badly. Following him out of the clouds, I saw he was too high and much too fast for an effective drop on our carrier. The AA guns opened up in one direction, so I broke away. The torpedo plane continued on in almost a straight line and hit a destroyer. There was a tremendous explosion near the No. 1 turret forward.

Circling around the screen, I saw two torpedo planes come through the anti-aircraft fire and start to retire flying close to the water. I saw another F4F-4 coming down, so I attacked the nearest one. My ammunition was about gone, so I emptied my guns into the plane. As I fired, the Jap pilot skidded his plane violently in an attempt to evade my fire. The plane caught on fire, but proceeded about five miles before diving into the water.

Lieutenant Harris, who had lost contact with me in the cloud, joined up, as did Lieutenant Ruehlow and Ensign Leder. As we were all out of ammunition and low on gas, I asked to pancake. The ship had no opportunity to land or launch planes as another attack was coming in. We circled just outside the screen for an hour and twenty minutes, out of ammunition and low on gas. While circling we observed an F4F-4 pilot parachute from his plane at about seven thousand feet, and land in the water about twelve miles from the carrier on a bearing of 320 degrees. At about 1320, all Reapers were told to pancake and my flight landed aboard the *Enterprise*.

The report includes all the familiar elements. The retiring bombers, the balky gas tank, the number of torpedo planes in the cloud, shooting the rudder off the leader's Kate, the "missed him badly" comment, the Kate that crashed into *Smith*, and downing the last retiring torpedo bomber all derive from this one narrative.

Many fine historians, exercising due diligence, have reasonably relied on "Swede's" after-action report. These were Swede's own words, so why bother the man with questions?

"No, not at all," Swede insisted. "I never wrote that report, it was filled with errors, and I never signed off on it."[14]

Someone, it seems, fabricated a compelling mission narrative, and in the process created a pool of misinformation. Historians, understandably, have relied on this convincing official document. The report's "facts" have provided the details of nearly every incorrect account of Swede's intercept. Historians then selected details to suit their respective narratives, resulting in a range of accounts—each unique, some stirring, and none of them accurate.

Swede time and again avowed that the account in this book, not Flatley's version, is the mission he flew. So, who authored the imaginary account? Air Group Commander Gaines? Flatley? Hardison? And what might be gained by tampering with the specifics of Swede's mission?

If Flatley *did* write the account of Swede's mission, which he did not witness, he likely used secondhand snippets from a number of pilots to piece together a semblance of the action. The pilots would not be reading these accounts; there was no need to dispute the details so long as Swede's record officially stood at a record seven downed with an additional probable.

How to reconcile Flatley's report with what Swede experienced? It's about the details. Exactly how many planes did Swede shoot down? Did his engine cut out? Was the second Val dive-bomber retiring? How many Kates did he down in the clouds? What about the rudder he shot off one of the Kates? Was his last victory of the day a retiring Kate or the Kate that devastated *Smith*? During an April 2011 interview and over many hours of phone follow-up, Swede, eager to clarify, recounted his flight and addressed each of these questions.

According to published accounts, Swede was still carrying his balky auxiliary wing tank and suddenly needed to restart his gas-starved engine. Swede vividly recalled numerous wing tank problems. "The tanks never fit right; sometimes they would rip right off. The fuel pumps should have done the job, but they would leak. Our auxiliary pumps, located on the upper right-hand corner of the instrument panel, were designed to handle the problem, but they always seemed to leak. And they were slow to pump. Your hands got sore and you'd wear out gloves." But there was no wing tank problem that morning. What good were auxiliary tanks when an overhead intercept was imminent?

Swede steadfastly affirmed that he downed not three but four planes in that cloud. Furthermore, "I didn't write about the leader's rudder, I didn't shoot any rudder off. He snapped upward and came back at me. I jerked away to avoid him." And none of those Vals or Kates he shot down was retiring.

Swede was quoted as saying, "I missed him badly." The only thing he missed badly at that moment was more ammunition. Swede's supposed lament more likely reflected some anguish over not being able to finish the last Kate that ravaged *Smith*.

While Flatley's account certainly provided the source material for the many flawed accounts, the mystery of who actually authored the report will likely persist. Until his passing, Swede wondered where it came from.

APPENDIX 3

Crisis in Leadership

KINKAID'S FAILURE

There can be no question that the aggressive Admiral Halsey had thrust Kinkaid into a highly challenging command situation. Marked by the searing horrors he had personally witnessed at Eastern Solomons, and perhaps preoccupied with his own mortality, Kinkaid's command devolved into unreasonable battle directives. There was no disguising the fact that his leadership failures at Santa Cruz contributed to the loss of *Hornet* and the near-fatal damage to *Enterprise*. Further, he wasted airmen and planes in the process. And after the battle, Kinkaid's reports seemed intent on shifting the responsibility for these disasters away from him.

View from Above

Historians have not praised Kinkaid's leadership at Santa Cruz. Thomas Miller identified two tactical errors Kinkaid committed during the battle. His first was "to send the carrier attack groups against the enemy piecemeal."[1] Richard Frank contextualized that decision, saying that it "stemmed from Kinkaid's explicit decision to try to hit first rather than hardest by saving assembly time."[2] Kinkaid's second error was his "assignment of fighter direction for both task forces to *Enterprise*" and its inexperienced FDO. Unfortunately, Kinkaid's misguided decisions were not limited to the two Miller identified. I have identified eight. In chronological order they are:

1. Deciding to send a search/strike against the Japanese despite the impossible distance involved, especially since launching aircraft required the task force to reverse course.

2. Despite the fact that *Enterprise* had duty carrier status, and with a battle-tested *Hornet* strike already spotted on deck, Kinkaid chose to send off elements of his inexperienced Air Group 10.

3. After sending off his strike group, Kinkaid learned that the Japanese fleet had turned away to the north, thus negating any possibility that Swede and company could find them, but he made no attempt to recall the group.

4. At nightfall, Kinkaid vacated Point Option without contacting his strike group. (Until his death in 2013, Swede steadfastly maintained that Kinkaid's departure from Point Option, made worse by the silent YE, constituted criminal neglect.)

5. Rather than taking advantage of *Hornet*'s experienced FDO, Kinkaid decided on the recently arrived Lt. Cdr. John H. Griffin from *Enterprise*, a man out of his element and who subsequently infuriated pilots with misguided, confusing intercept instructions.

6. On October 26 the *Enterprise* strike group was instructed to proceed without *Hornet*'s strike group, thus diluting a combined strike force and exposing smaller groups like Flatley's to devastation.

7. That same morning, Swede's CAP was left waiting on the flight deck until after *Hornet* was attacked. This was a part of an overall failure to unify the air defense around Task Force 61.

8. After the battle, rather than reflecting on and learning from his own errors, Kinkaid blamed the Goose Chase debacle on Jim Thomas' "excessive zeal" and spread the blame to the pilots in general for their lack of navigation and night landing skills.

Regarding the events of October 25, Swede wanted the record to show that "Kinkaid had no concept of how to organize a strike group, or to direct an attack on Japanese task forces. Kinkaid had not bothered to ask Flatley or Thomas, experienced combat pilots, for their advice. We had just finished the buildup of Air Group 10, and our group had never had one squadron or group practice at this; we certainly had no prior action. Kinkaid was disorganized and had no schedule for combining two carrier forces. He was primarily interested in creating a combat situation."

During the following day's battle, Kinkaid's inexperience commanding a carrier task force resulted in loose CAP arrangements, which many blamed for the loss of *Hornet*. Even Gerald Wheeler, Kinkaid's biographer, wrote, "No naval aviator would have left *Hornet* so poorly defended by the fighter cover available."[3]

A ninth misguided decision occurred after the battle when Kinkaid downgraded Flatley's recommendation for Swede's Medal of Honor to a Distinguished Flying Cross.

A strong case could be made that Thomas Kinkaid was suffering from posttraumatic stress disorder, or battle fatigue as it was called at the time. At Eastern Solomons, Thomas Kinkaid had personally experienced the horrors of war when *Enterprise* took a terrific beating. He and his staff had been thrown about the bridge, and he had seen the shattering consequences of those bomb hits. At Santa Cruz, a mere two months later, he was in overall command for the first time and had every reason to be terrified of another Japanese attack. Those deep fears could easily generate irrational or reactive decisions of the sort Kinkaid made at Santa Cruz.

APPENDIX 4

———

Medal of Honor MIA

The official record shows that Swede Vejtasa downed seven Japanese planes with an additional probable during a single mission. As we have seen, Butch O'Hare, credited with five downed planes early in the war, was awarded the Medal of Honor. During the Battle of Coral Sea, Bill Hall helped sink *Shōhō* and shot down three Japanese planes with his SBD dive-bomber, sustaining wounds in both ankles in the process. Hall was awarded the Medal of Honor. At Coral Sea, Swede was credited with having done the same thing while bringing himself and his plane back intact. He was awarded a second Navy Cross.

Months after the Battle of Santa Cruz, in April 1943, Marine first lieutenant James Swett shot down seven Vals in his first mission and was shot down in the bargain. He was awarded the Medal of Honor. While Swede's stirring defense of *Enterprise* had not ensured victory, he had played a pivotal role in staving off defeat. As a matter of style, Swede's sorely needed fighter required only gas and ammunition for the next mission.

An account by Arnold House in *Wings* magazine describes Jim Swett as having "made history when he shot down seven Val dive bombers during his first combat on April 7, 1943, at the end of the Guadalcanal campaign. Feat was the most ever for a Wildcat pilot in a single day."[1]

Why was Swede overlooked? Months before, at Santa Cruz, Swede had more than matched Swett's accomplishment with seven confirmed kills and one probable. Furthermore, Swede had managed this in the first year of the war, when highly skilled Japanese pilots flew superior aircraft. Later in the war, American aces-in-a-day flew better aircraft and faced lesser-skilled Japanese opponents.

And just what might have befallen the U.S. war effort had the Japanese sunk America's last operational carrier at Santa Cruz? Faced with nightly Japanese fleet bombardments, a Japanese landing, and little opportunity for resupply or reinforcement, the Marines on Guadalcanal would likely have been overwhelmed.[2] Historians Jon Parshall and John Lundstrom, among others, now regard Guadalcanal as the decisive battleground of the Pacific war, and at Santa Cruz, Swede arguably played a crucial role in foiling a strategic Japanese victory.[3]

Reflecting nearly seventy years later, Swede allowed, "Yes, I might have earned the Medal of Honor that day; seven confirmed down was real significant for the defense of the *Enterprise*. Dave Pollock saw Flatley's write-up and spread the word; I was surprised to some extent. I had complained bitterly in the ready room before the Goose Chase, but considering O'Hare, I should have been given consideration. I saved all those pilots and planes the night before. That was a miracle, and Flatley had been affected. When I got recommended instead for the Distinguished Flying Cross, I was disappointed by comparison to other events."

Flatley's Recommendation Revisited

Early in our relationship Swede announced firmly that he did not want to talk about medals or promotions. However, as I came to understand how the Medal of Honor humiliation unfolded, Swede gave me permission to revisit Flatley's Medal of Honor recommendation. How did such a powerful recommendation get significantly downgraded to a Distinguished Flying Cross only to be bumped back up to a Navy Cross?

I contacted Swede's representative in Congress, Brian Bilbray, to pursue the matter and included a supporting letter from Rear Adm. Edward "Whitey" Feightner (see below). A young Army lieutenant in charge of veterans' issues took notes on the case and for his boss and wrote the Navy a somewhat insipid letter that included no strategic context for what Swede had done. Many months later Bilbray received a letter, dated May 24, 2012, from Secretary of the Navy Council of Review Boards signed by R. Claussen. It languished for three weeks before being stamped "received" by Bilbray's office on June 12, 2012.

Justifying the decision to take no further action, the Navy Department wrote to Swede via Bilbray:

> Previous Secretarial award decisions [Swede's Navy Cross citation was signed by Secretary of the Navy Frank Knox] of this kind are final, and cannot be reconsidered unless new and relevant material evidence is presented that was not available at the time of the original decision or sufficient evidence is presented to demonstrate that a material error was made in the processing and approval of the award. The documentation accompanying your letter of March 2 was excepted [sic] from the official reports of the battle mentioned above. Therefore, this information was available to Admiral Halsey when he approved the Navy Cross.
>
> The official reports of the battle contain many recommendations for awards of various levels to other officers and sailors. At least one other pilot was recommended for the Medal of Honor [Lt. Stockton Birney Strong for his audacious attack on *Zuihō*] but in the end was also awarded the Navy Cross. It is not at all unusual, whether during World War II or today, for the level of the final approved award to be different from that recommended by a squadron or battalion commander. There was no evidence in the records of any irregularities with the processing of this case. Further, the award of the Navy Cross to you was entirely consistent with awards made to other World War II aces who had more than five kills in a single day.

Swede's accomplishment surpassed those other heroic deeds, both in planes downed and in terms of his mission's strategic significance. Swede and I anxiously awaited some word on the case.

On June 18 Bilbray sent a nearly word-for-word rewrite of Claussen's letter to Swede. Bilbray concluded with a standard dismissal, "Mr. Vejtasa, I want to thank you for your service to our country, and for contacting me regarding this important matter. I regret that a more favorable outcome was not available in this case. This completes the Congressional action on this matter. Please feel free to contact my office in the future should you have any questions regarding another federal matter. As always, it is a pleasure to serve you."

On June 21, nearly a month after Claussen's letter was written, Swede and I received copies of Bilbray's letter. In light of the fact that on July 27,

2012, Swede would turn ninety-eight and faced serious health issues, the delay seemed to me unconscionable. The tone of cavalier dismissal left both of us feeling deflated.

How might it have gone? It would be easy to justify a Silver Star for bringing home his abandoned strike group and preserving all those planes, much as Lindsey had done in his own manner. Naturally, no captain or admiral wanted to reveal his own flawed leadership in a medal citation. That Goose Chase Silver Star would be in addition to the Medal of Honor Flatley recommended for Swede's unprecedented intercept. Thus, the citation for Swede's third Navy Cross must bear a large asterisk, signifying that by every right this one ought to have been the Medal of Honor.

LETTER IN SUPPORT OF SWEDE'S MEDAL OF HONOR FROM REAR ADM. EDWARD "WHITEY" FEIGHTNER (RET.), MARCH 12, 2012

On 25 October 1942, I was a fighter pilot assigned to VF-10 stationed on board USS *Enterprise* in the South Pacific. We were operating in an area about three hundred miles east of Guadalcanal when we were alerted that two Japanese aircraft carriers, the *Zuikaku* and the *Shōkaku*, were located approximately 360 miles to our northeast and headed in our direction. It was decided that we should immediately launch a search and attack group at about 1500 in the afternoon.

Visibility was excellent and we could see for approximately fifty miles in all directions. Upon reaching the position of the last sighting we had nothing in sight so we altered course 20 degrees to the right and flew for fifteen minutes and with still nothing in sight we again altered our course another 20 degrees to the right. At the end of this leg, and with nothing in sight, it was decided to return to the ship.

At this point we were all at minimum fuel state and about fifteen minutes later the leader of the second fighter division dropped out of the formation and opened his canopy and leaped out of his plane. I saw his chute open before we lost sight of him but we never heard from him again.

When we arrived back at our rendezvous position there were no ships anywhere in sight. We were told later that they had had a submarine contact and that they left the rendezvous point headed west. At this point the sun had set and we had some very low clouds forming between one to two hundred feet.

I was the wingman for Swede Vejtasa and he was flying right down on the surface of the water and using the light on his wingtip to look for an oil slick that he had observed being left in the ship's wake. We were headed straight west, and a few minutes later we came into sight of the task force dead ahead. I saw Swede lower his landing gear at this point and I quickly followed suit. I looked at my fuel gauge and it was sitting on zero. I made a small turn to the left in order to allow Swede to get clear of the landing area and when I turned back I saw another F4F right behind Swede. Both of them landed and caught separate wires. Fortunately I was able to delay my landing long enough to land without going around again. The rest of the fighters also made it aboard safely.

If Swede Vejtasa had not come up with his amazing solution to our problem, none of us would have made it back aboard ship. I am certain that I was very fortunate in surviving those early experiences because of what I learned from Swede Vejtasa.

The following morning [October 26, 1942] the Japanese found us before we found them. As our strike group was departing the Japanese shot down one division of F4Fs and three TBDs. Those of us who had flown on the previous day were assigned as Combat Air Patrol over the fleet and under the control of the *Hornet* radar controller. I was assigned as a wingman and we were directed by the *Hornet* fighter control to intercept a group of dive bombers who were attacking the USS *Hornet*. My flight leader's guns jammed and I was able to shoot down only one bomber before they started their dives on the *Hornet*.

Meanwhile Swede, after shooting down two Val dive bombers, was sent to intercept a flight of torpedo planes that were headed for the USS *Enterprise*. Swede managed to shoot down six of the torpedo flight before they were able to release their torpedoes and his wingman got three more.

Skipper Jimmy Flatley recommended Swede for a rightly-earned Medal of Honor but the award was demoted to a Distinguished Flying Cross allegedly because the USS *Hornet* was lost in the battle.

Rear Adm. Edward L. Feightner, USNR (Ret.)
Washington, DC

APPENDIX 5

Decorations and Citations Awarded to Swede Vejtasa

S wede was awarded the following decorations and citations in the course of his U.S. Navy career, listed here in chronological order.

Navy Cross

The President of the United States of America takes pleasure in presenting the Navy Cross to Lieutenant, Junior Grade Stanley Winfield Vejtasa, United States Navy, for extraordinary heroism in operations against the enemy while serving as Pilot of a carrier-based Navy Scouting Plane in Scouting Squadron Five (VS-5), attached to the USS *Yorktown* (CV 5), in action against enemy Japanese forces near Salamaua and Lae, New Guinea, on 10 March 1942. In the face of heavy anti-aircraft fire, Lieutenant, Junior Grade, Vejtasa dived and skillfully attacked one of three Japanese aircraft tenders or transports and obtained a direct hit on one of the hostile vessels. By his superb airmanship and outstanding courage he contributed to the destruction of the three enemy ships and upheld the highest traditions of the United States Naval Service.

Action Date: 10-Mar-42

Service: Navy

Rank: Lieutenant, junior grade

Company: Scouting Squadron 5 (VS-5)

Division: USS *Yorktown* (CV 5)

Second Navy Cross

The President of the United States of America takes pleasure in presenting a Gold Star in lieu of a Second Award of the Navy Cross to Lieutenant, Junior Grade Stanley Winfield Vejtasa, United States Navy, for extraordinary heroism in operations against the enemy while serving as pilot of a carrier-based Navy scouting plane in Scouting Squadron Five (VS-5), attached to the USS *Yorktown* (CV 5), in action against enemy Japanese forces at Tulagi Harbor on 4 May 1942, and in the Battle of the Coral Sea on 7 and 8 May 1942. On 4 May, Lieutenant, Junior Grade Vejtasa participated in dive bombing attacks on the enemy in Tulagi Harbor which resulted in the sinking or damaging of at least eight enemy vessels. On 7 May, he took part in a dive bombing attack on an enemy carrier in the Coral Sea, which resulted in the sinking of that vessel. On 8 May, while on anti–torpedo plane patrol, he engaged enemy bombing and torpedo planes heavily supported by fighters, which attacked our forces. The attacks on 4 and 7 May were pressed home in the face of heavy anti-aircraft fire with no regard for personal safety. Lieutenant, Junior Grade Vejtasa's conscientious devotion to duty and gallant self-command against formidable odds were in keeping with the highest traditions of the United States Naval Service.

Action Date: May 4, 7, and 8, 1942
Service: Navy
Rank: Lieutenant, Junior Grade
Company: Scouting Squadron 5 (VS-5)
Division: USS *Yorktown* (CV 5)

Third Navy Cross

The President of the United States takes pleasure in presenting a Second Gold Star in lieu of a Third Award of the Navy Cross to Stanley Winfield Vejtasa, Lieutenant, U.S. Navy, for extraordinary heroism in operations against the enemy while serving as pilot of a carrier-based Navy fighter plane and leader of a combat air patrol of four fighters of Fighting Squadron Ten (VF-10), embarked from the USS *Enterprise* (CV 6), during the engagement with enemy Japanese naval and air forces near the Santa Cruz Islands on 26 October 1942. As great numbers of enemy dive bombers and torpedo planes launched a vicious attack upon his carrier, Lieutenant Vejtasa unhesitatingly challenged and shot down two Japanese dive bombers and then gallantly led his patrol in an attack on a group of enemy torpedo planes with such daring aggressiveness that the formation was completely broken and three of the hostile bombers jettisoned their torpedoes as they fled. Lieutenant Vejtasa then personally shot down five of the remaining Japanese planes, making a total of seven enemy aircraft destroyed in a single flight. His superb airmanship and indomitable fighting spirit were in keeping with the highest traditions of the United States Naval Service.

Navy Commendation Ribbon

For meritorious achievement and outstanding performance of duty as Air Officer of the USS *Essex*, the first modernized aircraft carrier employed in combat operations. Discharging his many responsibilities with diligence and ability Commander Vejtasa participated in operations in the Korean combat area from 22 August 1951 to 12 January 1952. Thoroughly understanding the complex techniques required in operating advanced types of aircraft and equipment, Commander Vejtasa executing his many duties, showed great skill and foresight. By his judgment, outstanding professional skill and conscientious devotion to duty, he contributed materially to the damage and devastation inflicted on the enemy and his conduct throughout the period was in keeping with the highest traditions of the United States Naval Service. The Commendation Ribbon with the Combat Distinguishing Device is authorized.

Legion of Merit

The President of the United States of America takes pleasure in presenting the Legion of Merit to Captain Stanley Winfield Vejtasa, United States Navy, for exceptionally meritorious conduct in the performance of outstanding services to the Government of the United States as Commander Fleet Air, Miramar from 15 August 1965 to 7 June 1968. Captain Vejtasa played a vital role in the supervision and training of all Naval Air Force Pacific Fleet Fighter Squadrons deployed in carriers in Southeast Asia and in the indoctrination of replacement pilots, naval flight officers and maintenance personnel for those squadrons and our allies. His outstanding foresight enabled him to make vital contributions to future design and development of fighter aircraft and resulted in advanced weapons systems, armament and electronic warning devices for both the presently operational and the future fighter aircraft. His keen employment of Naval Air Force Pacific Fleet Fighter Aircraft contributed significantly to the anti–air warfare readiness of the surface forces in the U.S. Pacific Fleet. He originated and supervised the trans-Pacific flight of replacement jet fighter aircraft, a program essential to the timely support of deployed units. Captain Vejtasa's personal interest and concern for the welfare of all personnel in the fighter community and their families resulted in an exceptional Esprit de Corps within the military and an exceptionally fine rapport with the civilian community. His outstanding leadership, judgment and inspirational personal example were in keeping with the highest traditions of the United States Naval Service.

Action Date: August 15, 1965–June 7, 1968

Service: Navy

Rank: Captain

Bronze Star: Twice, both with Combat V

Meritorious Service Medal

Presidential Unit Citation (2) (USS *Enterprise*) (USS *Essex*)

Campaign and Service Medals:

Asiatic-Pacific

American Theater

American Defense

World War II Victory

China Service

Korea Service

United Nations

National Defense

Navy Occupation

Korean Presidential Unit Citation

NOTES

——

Author's Note

1. Unless otherwise cited in the text, Stanley W. "Swede" Vejtasa's quotes date from interviews with the author, April 21 and 22, 2011.
2. Edward "Whitey" Feightner's quotes came from an interview with the author, October 16, 2011, at the Army-Navy Country Club in Washington, D.C.
3. Bill Shinneman, "Interview of Swede Vejtasa, October 2, 2000" (hereafter cited as Shinneman interview); Barry Basden, "An Interview with Mr. Stanley W. 'Swede' Vejtasa," October 1, 2000 (hereafter cited as Basden interview).

Chapter 1. "The Admiral Is a Stupid Ass"

1. Ewing, *Reaper Leader*, 128.
2. Buell, *Dauntless Helldivers*, 156.
3. Don "Flash" Gordon, letter to Robert L. Lawson, *Hook*, July 11, 1979.
4. VB-10 war diary, October 25, 1942, courtesy of Steve Moore.
5. Commanding Officer USS *Enterprise* to Commander-in-Chief, U.S. Pacific Fleet, "The Battle of Santa Cruz, October 26, 1942."
6. Lundstrom, in *The First Team and the Guadalcanal Campaign*, writes, "Listening carefully to the YE [homing signal transmitter] signals, Faulkner, an experienced ex-SBD pilot, had plotted the correct course home" (351). Did Fritz go up late after Swede spoke with him on the flight deck, fail to join up, and return while the YE could guide him? The mystery of who flew this section endures.
7. Basden interview.

Chapter 2. Beginnings

1. Basden interview, 2–3. This chapter draws heavily from Basden's interview with Swede; the author's April 21, 2011, interview with Swede; and Swede's autobiographical essay.
2. Vejtasa, autobiographical essay, 1–2.
3. Ibid.
4. Ibid., 2–3.
5. Stanley Vejtasa, letters to Irene Funk, August 1937–September 1939.
6. Vejtasa, autobiographical essay, 5.

Chapter 3. Naval Aviator

1. Vejtasa, autobiographical essay, 6–7; many of the quotes in this chapter come from that essay. *Yorktown*'s activity comes largely from Cressman, *That Gallant Ship*.
2. Vejtasa, autobiographical essay, 5.
3. Ibid., 7.
4. Ibid., 8.
5. Ibid.
6. Cressman, *That Gallant Ship*, 47.
7. Ibid., 44–50.

Chapter 4. Pearl Harbor

1. Whether or not Japan played into Roosevelt's scheme to maneuver Japan into war in order to fight Axis ally Germany mattered not to those killed or wounded during the Japanese strike at Pearl Harbor. See Stinnett, *Day of Deceit*.
2. Vejtasa, autobiographical essay, 9.
3. Ibid., 10.
4. Ibid.

Chapter 5. Tulagi

1. Interview of Lt. Cdr. W. O. Burch, USNR, Commanding VS-5, USS *Yorktown*, in the Bureau of Aeronautics, September 3, 1942 (hereinafter Burch interview).

Chapter 6. Battle of the Coral Sea

1. Burch interview.

2. Swede Vejtasa, interview with the author, April 22, 2011.

3. Buell, *Dauntless Helldivers,* 159–60.

4. Years later during the Korean War, Swede had occasion to speak with some of the Japanese pilots who had attempted to land on *Yorktown.* When he asked why they didn't strafe, "They just smiled."

5. Buell, *Dauntless Helldivers,* 86–88.

6. Astor, *Wings of Gold,* 70; Cressman, *That Gallant Ship,* 108; Lundstrom, *The First Team,* 250.

7. For helpful detail, see Ewing, *Reaper Leader,* 82–98.

8. Commanding Officer to Commander-in-Chief, U.S. Pacific Fleet, May 25, 1942, "Battle of Coral Sea and *Yorktown* Air Group on May 8, 1942," Action Report, USS *Yorktown* (CV 5).

9. Lundstrom, *The First Team,* 277; Cressman, *That Gallant Ship,* 116.

10. Basden interview, 18–19.

11. Sherman, *Combat Command.* Captain Sherman later documented some of the hard-won lessons to be gleaned from this unprecedented unsighted carrier confrontation: "We learned that it was necessary to greatly improve the fire-fighting equipment on our vessels. We learned that our carrier complement should include more fighter aircraft. We learned that we must improve our fighter-direction methods and intercept attacking aircraft at greater distances from our ships" (117). Some of those shortcomings had to do with radar's inability to determine the altitude of incoming planes or to distinguish friend from foe. On the lesser scale of things, even the old Navy adage, "Don't clean it, paint it" became obsolete when it was learned that thick coats of oil-based paint burned stubbornly, greatly facilitating the spread of fire. And they learned that prior to an attack, fuel lines had to be cleared of aviation gas and filled with carbon dioxide.

12. Ibid., 114.

13. Wheeler, *Kinkaid of the Seventh Fleet,* 196, cited 2,685 men rescued; Sherman on page 9 of his after-action report gave a figure of 2,735. (In the bibliography this action report is included under David

Langbart's "The Death of a Lady: The USS *Lexington* [CV-2] at the Battle of the Coarl Sea, Part III: Battle Report.")
14. Wheeler, *Kinkaid of the Seventh Fleet*, 226.

Chapter 7. Intermission
1. Vejtasa, autobiographical essay, 15.
2. Ewing, *Thach Weave*, 89.
3. Vejtasa, autobiographical essay, 15.
4. Whitey has no memory of being hit by a bullet from another plane, "though I had been shot up by shrapnel from the ships' guns. Through sheer luck my only injury occurred when I caught a late wire, eight or nine, just short of the barrier. I stopped suddenly and my eye hit the gun sight. Some photos show me with a patch over my left eye." Whitey's experience was not lost on Flatley. He developed a harness arrangement designed to prevent needless head injuries incidental to trapping or ditching.
5. Ewing, *Thach Weave*, 89.
6. Basden interview, 37.
7. Foss and Brennan, *Top Guns*, 93.
8. Basden interview, 39.
9. Ewing, *Reaper Leader*, 119.

Chapter 8. Developments Elsewhere
1. Buell, *Dauntless Helldivers*, 156.
2. Wheeler, *Kinkaid of the Seventh Fleet*, 266.
3. Eugene Burns, "So Swede Helps Himself to a Big Platter of Japs," *Honolulu Star-Bulletin*, November 11, 1942.

Chapter 9. A Phantom Goose Chase Concluded
1. The VB-10 war diary says the two SBDs went down from fuel exhaustion. Scuttlebutt had it that a bomb brought down those bombers. Whitey thinks it might have been Scoofer Coffin who told him that. The exact circumstances that downed those two SBDs are still unclear. Steve Moore offered a credible scenario of shrapnel damaging the SBDs, leading to fuel loss and the need to ditch.

2. Gibson, *Slow but Deadly*.

3. Moore, Shinneman, and Gruebel, *The Buzzard Brigade*, has an excellent treatment of events of October 25 and has been very helpful in documenting personnel involved in the evening's events and the next day's battle.

4. Gibson, *Slow but Deadly*.

5. Feightner, interview with the author, October 16, 2011.

6. Burns, *Then There Was One*, 111.

7. Ibid., 113.

Chapter 10. The Battle of Santa Cruz

1. Burns, *Then There Was One*, 115.

2. Ibid., 120.

3. Notable historians have written about what follows. Curiously, no two versions are the same, and none matches Swede's recollections. Unless otherwise cited, quotes come from my interviews and phone conversations with Swede. Appendix 2 deconstructs this historical disunity.

4. Feightner, "Memoirs from an Aviator's Logbook," 74.

5. Burns, *Then There Was One*, 123.

6. Frank, *Guadalcanal*, 389, made a strong case that it was Batten's torpedo that struck *Porter*. Japanese records emphatically deny that it was one of their torpedoes.

7. This and other stories are based on personal interviews with Robbie in his home over many weeks. See also Edwards, *Leonard "Robbie" Robinson, Waxahachie Warrior*.

8. Jack Finrow later was awarded a Navy Cross for his bomb hit on the Japanese battleship *Musashi* during the Battle of Leyte Gulf, aka the Battle of Bull's Run. It was awarded posthumously because Jack was killed the next day participating in the sinking of the Japanese carrier *Zuikaku*, the last surviving Japanese carrier involved in the Pearl Harbor attack.

9. Burns, *Then There Was One*, 122.

10. Jim Daniels, letter to Lundstrom, April 18, 1985.

11. Burns, *Then There Was One*, 122.

12. Many historical accounts mention three Kates in the fog, and they all talk about Swede blowing the rudder off the leader's plane. See appendix 2 for a deconstruction of how these errors have defined the story.

13. Shinneman interview.

14. Regarding the last Kate, many accounts quote Swede as saying, "I missed him badly." Not so according to Swede.

15. Burns, *Then There Was One*, 123.

16. Years later, a *Smith* veteran told Swede of a fateful decision. "The sailor, a gunner 3c came to see me. His assignment had been in the forward gun turret, but he'd been very ill. The violent movements of the ship were making him worse. 'I'm dying here,' he told his commander. 'Okay,' came the response, 'we'll put you aft where there's less motion.' He was saved by that move. 'The whole thing was a miracle.'"

17. Daniels, letter to Lundstrom.

18. Barnes was never recovered. Whitey thought that a PBY had picked up both Barnes and Miller but had subsequently been shot down. Thus, while Whitey saw both pilots successfully exit their planes, neither was ever seen again.

Chapter 11. A Battle Concluded

1. Daniels, letter to Lundstrom.

2. Ibid.

3. Vejtasa, autobiographical essay, 15; and Vejtasa, interview with the author.

4. Wilcox, *First Blue*, 58.

Chapter 12. What Does Victory Look Like?

1. Dusty Rhodes went on to become the third flight leader of the Navy's exhibition flight team, the Blue Angels.

2. James H. Flatley, letter to Cdr. F. W. Wead, August 1943.

3. In many cases the after-action reports presented within Flatley's comprehensive report help sort out the battle. Appendix 2 clarifies the historical disunity around Swede's mission.

4. Flatley, "Fighting Squadron Ten Action Report for October 25 and 26, 1942," Enclosure H, p. 1. (In the bibliography this action report's author is Commander Fighting Squadron Ten to Commanding Officer, USS *Enterprise*.) See appendix 4 for some context regarding other Medal of Honor awardees.

5. Hal Buell, telephone interview with the author, July 3, 2011.

Chapter 13. The Naval Battle for Guadalcanal

1. As their exchange heated, Thomas snapped that Robbie could just stay behind. Robbie replied, "You SOB, you just implied I'm afraid to fly. I'll never fly on your wing again." However warranted, Robbie's petulant outburst would dog his aspiring naval career. Thomas thereafter declined to recommend medals such as the Distinguished Flying Cross, Silver Star, or Navy Cross that were typically awarded for the bombing accuracy Robbie had demonstrated that morning against Tanaka's convoy. Robbie always regretted his exchange with Thomas. His time flying wing on Thomas had forged strong bonds, and Robbie had considered him a good friend. They later repaired this breach in their relationship.

Chapter 14. On to Guadalcanal

1. Sherrod, *History of Marine Corps Aviation in World War II*, 110.
2. Vejtasa, autobiographical essay, 19–22.
3. Ibid., 22.
4. Feightner, "Memoirs from an Aviator's Logbook," 74.
5. Quoted in Wheeler, *Kinkaid of the Seventh Fleet*, 283.
6. Ibid., 283.
7. Feightner interview with the author.

Chapter 15. From Combat to Commander

1. Basden interview, 34.
2. Vejtasa, autobiographical essay, 23.
3. *The Lonely Sky*, by Bill Bridgeman, vividly portrays life at Muroc, the satisfactions as well as the maddening frustration of gearing up for a flight only to have it repeatedly postponed.
4. In 1954 Stapp got rocketed to 632 mph in 5 seconds, a 20-g experience and a new speed record. He further endured 42.6 gs in the 1.4-second deceleration, leaving him pretty beat up. Proclaimed the "Fastest Man on Earth" and arguably one of the bravest, Stapp wanted to apply what he had learned about jet ejection systems to automobile safety. To his everlasting credit, Stapp used his considerable national celebrity in a successful push to get seat belts installed in automobiles.

Chapter 16. No Easy Days

1. Basden interview, 29.
2. Writing dispatches from *Essex,* author James Michener heard these complaints firsthand and gave a human voice to a troubling issue in his acclaimed book and the memorable movie directed by Mark Robson, *The Bridges at Toko-ri.*
3. Sears, *Such Men As These,* 175–76, provides good context and evocative descriptions of carrier operations off Korea.
4. Later British innovations of a canted or angled deck and a mirrored landing system eliminated these sorts of disasters.
5. Sears, *Such Men As These,* 13.
6. Ibid., 14; Michener, *The Bridges at Toko-ri,* 70–71.
7. Gray, "Bridges at Toko-ri: The Real Story."
8. Sears, *Such Men As These,* 184–85. Whitey Feightner was stationed at Pax River at the time; he was working under Lt. Col. Marion Carl, flight-testing heavier Corsair bomb loads. Swede later related the Wheelchock incident to Whitey, who recalled, "Swede was incredulous at the idea of using plane engines to turn a ship and very vocal with his objection. It was a stupid idea, and fortunately short-lived."
9. *Essex* action report.
10. Fisher, *Hooked,* 223–24.
11. Robbie retained a balanced view on that Friday the thirteenth thing. "Yes, I got shot down that day, but I got rescued that day too." Edwards, *Leonard "Robbie" Robinson,* 66.
12. Robinson, personal records and papers.

Chapter 17. Grooming

1. With her complement of 23 officers and 244 enlisted, *Firedrake* continued to serve on up to the Vietnam War.
2. Basden interview, 31.

Chapter 18. USS *Constellation,* "America's Flagship"

1. "USS *Constellation,* CVA 64, Welcome Aboard," publicity packet, 1962–63.
2. As recounted by Swede during his April 22, 2011, interview with the author.

Chapter 19. Do Not Pass Captain

1. The up-and-comers had looked to Swede for his experienced outlook on the urgent matters of combat. The likes of Bill Hardy, Hal Buell, Robbie Robinson, and Whitey Feightner agreed that Swede was more than qualified for and certainly deserved flag rank.
2. Wilcox, *Scream of Eagles*, 89.
3. Vejtasa, autobiographical essay, 28.
4. Ibid.

Appendix 1. Goose Chase Controversies

1. John Lundstrom questioned Kinkaid's choice of attack group. "For some unexplained reason, he preferred to send the *Enterprise*'s inexperienced Air Group Ten on the afternoon attack instead of using the *Hornet*'s deckload strike already waiting in reserve" (*Guadalcanal*, 349). Lundstrom did not raise the issue of carrier duty status, which limited Kinkaid to CAP and searches.
2. Flatley, "Fighting Squadron Ten Action Report for October 25 and 26, 1942."
3. Gibson, *Slow but Deadly*.
4. Flatley, "Squadron Ten Action Report for October 25 and 26."

Appendix 2. Mission Myths Deconstructed

1. Morison, *The Struggle for Guadalcanal*, 211–12. Kamikazes did not make their dreadful appearance until late in 1944.
2. Stafford, *The Big E,* 186–87.
3. Belote and Belote, *Titans of the Seas*, 172–73.
4. Mersky, *The Grim Reapers*, 24–25.
5. Hammel, *Guadalcanal,* 406, 429, 430, 432.
6. Ibid.
7. Lundstrom, *The First Team and the Guadalcanal Campaign*, 421, 424, 425.
8. Tillman, *Wildcat Aces of World War 2*, 23.
9. Ewing, *Reaper Leader*, 136.
10. Astor, *Wings of Gold*, 130–32.
11. Ibid.
12. Sears, *Pacific Air*, 244.

13. Tillman, Enterprise: *America's Fightingest Ship*, 126.
14. As a matter of record, unlike the signed *Yorktown* VS-5 after-action reports, Swede's October 26 report is indeed unsigned. The after-action reports attributed to Dave Pollock, Steve Kona, Wick Wickendoll, and Don Gordon also lack signatures.

Appendix 3. Crisis in Leadership
1. Miller, *The Cactus Air Force*, 175.
2. Frank, *Guadalcanal*, 402.
3. Ibid., 286. Kinkaid's biography does not mention Lt. Swede Vejtasa at all.

Appendix 4. Medal of Honor MIA
1. House, "The Wildest Cat," 20.
2. Hornfischer, *Neptune's Inferno*, xix, describes the tripod required to hold onto Guadalcanal. Historian Lisle Rose noted, "If they lost too many planes to Japanese attacks, either ashore or at sea, if Henderson Field was overrun, or if Fletcher's remaining carriers were badly damaged or sunk, Guadalcanal would eventually fall" (*The Ship That Held the Line*, 181).
3. Bresnahan, *Refighting the Pacific War*. Both Parshall (180) and Lundstrom (186) acknowledged the vulnerability of U.S. troops on Guadalcanal had *Enterprise* been sunk at Santa Cruz.

BIBLIOGRAPHY

Books

Astor, Gerald. *Wings of Gold: The U.S. Naval Air Campaign in World War II.*
New York: Presidio Press, Ballantine Books, 2005.

Barlow, Jeffrey G. *Revolt of the Admirals: The Fight for Naval Aviation, 1945–1950.* Washington: Brassey's, 1994.

Belote, James H., and William M. Belote. *Titans of the Seas: The Development and Operations of Japanese and American Carrier Task Forces during World War II.* New York: Harper & Row, 1975.

Boyington, Col. Gregory "Pappy." *Baa Baa Black Sheep.* Fresno, Calif.: Wilson Press, 1958.

Bresnahan, Jim, ed. *Refighting the Pacific War: An Alternative History of World War II.* Annapolis: Naval Institute Press, 2011.

Bridgeman, William, with Jacquelyn Hazard. *The Lonely Sky.* New York: Holt, 1955.

Brown, J. D. *Carrier Operations in World War II,* edited by David Hobbs. Annapolis: Naval Institute Press, 2009.

Buell, Cdr. Harold L. *Dauntless Helldivers: A Dive Bomber Pilot's Epic Story of the Carrier Battles.* New York: Orion Books, 1986.

Burns, Eugene. *Then There Was One: The USS* Enterprise *and the First Year of War.* New York: Harcourt, Brace, 1944.

Caidin, Martin. *The Ragged, Rugged Warriors: The Heroic Story of American Pilots in the Early Air War against Japan.* New York: Ballantine Books, 1966.

Carl, Maj. Gen. Marion E., with Barrett Tillman. *Pushing the Envelope: The Career of Fighter Ace and Test Pilot Marion Carl.* Annapolis: Bluejacket Books, Naval Institute Press, 1994.

Cressman, Robert. *That Gallant Ship: USS* Yorktown *(CV 5).* Missoula, Mont.: Pictorial Histories, 1985.

Edwards, Ted. *Leonard "Robbie" Robinson, Waxahachie Warrior.* Felton, Calif.: FastPencil, 2010.

Elward, Brad. *Grumman F9F Panther/Cougar: First Grumman Cat of the Jet Age.* Forest Lake, Minn.: Specialty Press, 2010.

Ewing, Steve. *Reaper Leader: The Life of Jimmy Flatley.* Annapolis: Naval Institute Press, 2002.

———. *Thach Weave: The Life of Jimmie Thach.* Annapolis: Naval Institute Press, 2004.

Ewing, Steve, and John B. Lundstrom. *Fateful Rendezvous: The Life of Butch O'Hare.* Annapolis: Naval Institute Press, 1997.

Fisher, Cdr. Clayton E. *Hooked: Tales and Adventures of a Tail Hook Warrior.* Denver: Outskirts Press, 2009.

Foss, Joe, and Matthew Brennan. *Top Guns: America's Fighter Aces Tell Their Story.* New York: Pocket Books, 1991.

Frank, Richard B. *Guadalcanal: The Definitive Account of the Landmark Battle.* New York: Penguin Books, 1990.

Fry, John. *USS Saratoga CV 3: An Illustrated History of the Legendary Aircraft Carrier 1927–1946.* Atglen Pa.: Schiffer Publishing, 1996.

Gibson, Robert Douglas. *Slow but Deadly: A Navy Dive Bomber Pilot Makes a Pact with the Moon.* Self-published, 2001. Courtesy of Robert D. Gibson Jr.

Ginter, Steve. *Navy and Marine Fleet Single Seat F9F Cougar Squadrons.* Simi Valley, Calif.: Steve Ginter, 2006.

Halliday, E. M. *The Ignorant Armies.* New York: Award Books, 1958.

Hammel, Eric. *Carrier Clash: The Invasion of Guadalcanal and the Battle of the Eastern Solomons, August 1942.* Pacifica, Calif.: Pacifica Press, 1997.

———. *Guadalcanal: The Carrier Battles. The Pivotal Aircraft Carrier Battles of the Eastern Solomons and Santa Cruz.* New York: Crown, 1987.

Hara, Capt. Tameichi, with Fred Saito and Roger Pineau. *Japanese Destroyer Captain: Pearl Harbor, Guadalcanal, Midway—the Great Naval battles as Seen through Japanese Eyes.* Annapolis: Naval Institute Press, 1967.

Hargis, Robert. *US Naval Aviator: 1941–45.* Oxford: Osprey, 2002.

Henry, Chris. *Battle of the Coral Sea.* Annapolis: Naval Institute Press, 2003.

Hornfischer, James D. *Neptune's Inferno: The U.S. Navy at Guadalcanal.* New York: Bantam Books, 2011.

Hoyt, Edwin P. *Blue Skies and Blood.* New York: Pinnacle, 1976.

———. *Guadalcanal.* New York: Jove, 1983.

Johnston, Stanley. *The Grim Reapers.* Philadelphia: Blakiston, 1943.

———. *Queen of the Flat-Tops: The U.S.S.* Lexington *and the Coral Sea Battle.* New York: Ballantine Books, 1942.

Keeney, L. Douglas. *15 Minutes: General Curtis Lemay and the Countdown to Nuclear Annihilation.* New York: St. Martin's Griffin, 2011.

Lord, Walter. *Incredible Victory: The Battle of Midway.* Short Hills, N.J.: Burford Books, 1967.

Lundstrom, John B. *The First Team and the Guadalcanal Campaign: Naval Fighter Combat from August to November 1942.* Annapolis: Naval Institute Press, 1994.

———. *The First Team: Pacific Naval Air Combat from Pearl Harbor to Midway.* Annapolis: Naval Institute Press, 1984.

Marlantes, Karl. *What It Is Like to Go to War.* New York: Atlantic Monthly Press, 2011.

Marolda, Edward J., ed. *The U.S. Navy in the Korean War.* Annapolis: Naval Institute Press, 2007.

McGaugh, Scott. *USS* Midway, *America's Shield.* Gretna, La.: Pelican Publishing, 2011.

Meredith, Lee W. *Grey Ghost: The Story of the Aircraft Carrier* Hornet. Sunnyvale, Calif.: Rocklin Press, 2001.

Mersky, Peter. *The Grim Reapers: Fighting Squadron Ten in WW II.* Mesa, Ariz.: Champlin Museum Press, 1986.

———. *Whitey: The Story of Rear Admiral E. L. Feightner, a Navy Fighter Ace.* Annapolis: Naval Institute Press, 2014.

Michener, James A. *The Bridges at Toko-ri.* New York: Bantam Pathfinder Edition, 1965.

Miller, Thomas G. *The Cactus Air Force.* 1969. Reprint. New York: Bantam Books, 1981.

Moore, Stephen L. *The Battle for Hell's Island: How a Small Band of Carrier Dive Bombers Helped Save Guadalcanal.* New York: NAL Caliber, 2015.

———. *Pacific Payback: The Carrier Aviators Who Avenged Pearl Harbor at the Battle of Midway.* New York: NAL Caliber, 2014.

Moore, Stephen L., with William J. Shinneman and Robert Gruebel. *The Buzzard Brigade: Torpedo Squadron Ten at War.* Missoula, Mont.: Pictorial Histories, 1996.

Morison, Samuel Eliot. *History of United States Naval Operations in World War II.* Vol 5, *The Struggle for Guadalcanal, August 1942–February 1943.* Boston: Little, Brown, 1950.

Okumiya, Masatake, and Jiro Horikoshi, with Martin Caidin. *Zero: The Story of Japan's War in the Pacific—as Seen by the Enemy.* New York: Bantam Books, 1991.

Parshall, Jonathan, and Anthony Tully. *Shattered Sword: The Untold Story of the Battle of Midway.* Washington, D.C.: Potomac Books, 2005.

Rose, Lisle A. *The Ship That Held the Line: The USS* Hornet *and the First Year of the Pacific War.* Annapolis: Naval Institute Press, 1995.

Sakai, Saburo, with Martin Caidin and Fred Saito. *Samurai.* Annapolis: Naval Institute Press, 1957.

Sears, David. *Pacific Air: How Fearless Flyboys, Peerless Aircraft, and Fast Flattops Conquered the Skies in the War with Japan.* Philadelphia: Da Capo Press, 2011.

———. *Such Men As These: The Story of the Navy Pilots Who Flew the Deadly Skies over Korea.* Cambridge: Da Capo Press, 2010.

Sherman, Adm. Frederick C. *Combat Command: The American Aircraft Carriers in the Pacific War.* New York: E. P. Dutton, 1950.

Sherrod, Robert. *History of Marine Corps Aviation in World War II.* Washington D.C.: Combat Forces Press, 1952.

Smith, Peter C. *Fist from the Sky: Japan's Dive Bomber Ace of WW II.* Mechanicsburg, Pa.: Stackpole Books, 2006.

Stafford, Cdr. Edward P. *The Big E.* New York: Ballantine Books, 1962.

Stille, Mark. *Santa Cruz 1942: Carrier Duel in the South Pacific.* Oxford: Osprey, 2012.

Stinnett, Robert B. *Day of Deceit: The Truth about FDR and Pearl Harbor.* New York: Touchstone, 2000.

Symonds, Craig L. *The Battle of Midway.* New York: Oxford University Press, 2011.

Thomas, Evan. *Sea of Thunder: Four Commanders and the Last Great Naval Campaign, 1941–1945.* New York: Simon & Schuster, 2006.

Thompson, Warren. *F4U Corsair Units of the Korean War.* New York: Osprey, 2009.

Tillman, Barrett. *Clash of the Carriers: The True Story of the Marianas Turkey Shoot of World War II.* London: NAL Caliber, 2005.

———. *The Dauntless Dive Bomber of World War II.* Annapolis: Naval Institute Press, 1976.

———. Enterprise: *America's Fightingest Ship and the Men Who Helped Win World War II.* New York: Simon & Schuster, 2012.

———. *Hellcat: The F6F in World War II.* Annapolis: Naval Institute Press, 1979.

———. *U.S. Navy Fighter Squadrons in World War II.* North Branch, Minn.: Specialty Press, 1997.

———. *Wildcat Aces of World War 2.* New York: Osprey, 1995.

Toll, Ian W. *Pacific Crucible: War at Sea in the Pacific, 1941–1942.* New York: W. W. Norton, 2012.

Wheeler, Gerald E. *Kinkaid of the Seventh Fleet: A Biography of Admiral Thomas C. Kinkaid, U.S. Navy.* Annapolis: Naval Institute Press, 1996.

Wilcox, Robert K. *First Blue: The Story of World War II Ace Butch Voris and the Creation of the Blue Angels.* New York: Thomas Dunne Books, St. Martin's Press, 2004.

———. *Scream of Eagles.* New York: Pocket Star Books, 1990.

Wooldridge, E. T., ed. *Carrier Warfare in the Pacific: An Oral History Collection.* Washington, D.C.: Smithsonian Institution Press, 1993.

Journals, Pamphlets, and Periodicals

Bordeaux, Journalist Third Class Sam. "Chief of Staff Earns Medal." News release, Public Affairs Office, Headquarters, Eleventh Naval District, San Diego, Calif., March 26, 1970.

Carrier Aviation Hall of Fame. *USS* Yorktown *CV-10.* Pamphlet, 1987.

Deac, Wil. "Battle beyond the Horizon." *WWII History* 2, no. 3 (2003): 42–49.

Edwards, Christopher. "Prelude to Kamikaze." *Naval History* 21, no. 5 (2007): 28–33.

Feightner, Edward L. "Memoirs from an Aviator's Logbook: The Battle of Santa Cruz." *Flight Journal* 4 (April 1999): 273–74.

Gray, Capt. Paul N. "The Bridges at Toki-ri: The Real Story." USS *Bennington* web site, http://www.uss-bennington.org/non-benn-stories.html (accessed November 9, 2017).

"*Hornet*'s Last Day: Tom Lea Paints Death of a Great Carrier." *Life,* August 2, 1943, 42–49.

House, Arnold. "The Wildest Cat." *Wings* 28, no. 5 (1998): 8–39.

Lorey, Frank III. "Ace and Two Spares in a Day." Manuscript found in Vejtasa personal papers, proposed for publication in *Aviation History,* January 2000.

McFarland, Keith D. "The 1949 Revolt of the Admirals." *Parameters* 11, no. 2 (1980): 53–63.

Morgan, Lt. Cdr. Rick. "Where Are They Now? Whitey Feightner." *The Hook* 28, no. 3 (2000): 73–74.

Symonds, Craig L. "Guadalcanal II, October 1942–February 1943." In *Historical Atlas of the U.S. Navy.* Annapolis: Naval Institute Press, 1995.

Tillman, Barrett. "Where Are They Now? Swede Vejtasa." *The Hook* 14 (spring 1986): 10.

Letters and Unpublished Documents

Daniels, Jim. Letter to John Lundstrom, April 18, 1985.

de Poix, Rear Adm. V. P., Commander Carrier Division Seven. Letter to Capt. Stanley W. Vejtasa, USN, 081514/1310, Commander Fleet Air Miramar, March 10, 1967.

Flatley, James H., "Combat Doctrine, Fighting Squadron Ten." July 1942.

———. Letter to Cdr. F. W. Wead, August 3, 1943, excerpt.

Gordon, Don "Flash." Letter to Robert L. Lawson. *The Hook,* July 11, 1979.

Martin, Vice Adm. H. M., USN, Commander Seventh Fleet. Letter to Cdr. Stanley W. Vejtasa. Citation for the Navy Commendation Ribbon with the Combat Distinguishing Device, 1970.

Robinson, Leonard "Robbie." Personal records and papers, 2010.

"USS *Constellation,* CVA 64, Welcome Aboard." Change-of-command publicity packet with ship's history and photos, 1963.

Vejtasa, Stanley. Autobiographical essay on his naval career. No title, no date.

———. Letters to Irene Funk, September 1937–August 1939.

Action Reports

Commanding Officer to Commander-in-Chief, U.S. Pacific Fleet. May 15, 1942. "U.S.S. *Lexington* (CV2). Report of Action, The Battle of the Coral Sea, 7 and 8 May 1942." https://www.ibiblio.org/hyperwar/USN/ships/logs/CV/cv2-Coral.html

Commanding Officer to Commander-in-Chief, U.S. Pacific Fleet. May 25, 1942. "Battle of Coral Sea. Action Report: USS *Yorktown* (CV 5) and *Yorktown* Air Group on May 8, 1942." http://www.ibiblio.org/hyperwar/USN/ships/logs/CV/cv5-Coral.html.

Commanding Officer USS *Enterprise* to Commander-in-Chief, U.S. Pacific Fleet. "The Battle of Santa Cruz, October 26, 1942."

Commanding Officer USS *Essex* CV9 to Chief of Naval Operations. "Action Report for the period, 18 August 1951 to 21 September 1951." https://www.history.navy.mil/content/dam/nhhc/research/archives/action-reports/Korean%20War%20-%20Carrier%20Combat/PDF's/cv9a-51.pdf.

Commander Fighting Squadron Ten to Commanding Officer, USS *Enterprise.* "Fighting Squadron Ten Action Report for October 25 and 26, 1942."

Commander Scouting Squadron Eight and Bombing Squadron Eight to Commanding Officer, USS *Hornet.* 2 November 1942. "Action Report of 26 October [1942], with Enemy Japanese Fleet—Solomon Island Area."

Commander South Pacific Area to Commander-in-Chief, U.S. Pacific Fleet. "Preliminary Report of Action, October 26, 1942."

———. "Report of Action of *Hornet* Air Group 26 October 1942 in Carrier Action North of Santa Cruz Islands."

Commander Task Force 61 to Commander-in-Chief, U.S. Pacific Fleet. November 3, 1942. "Preliminary Report of Action, October 26, 1942."

———. November 8, 1942. "Report of Action, *Hornet* Air Group 26 October 1942 in Carrier Action North of Santa Cruz Islands."

Langbart, David. "The Death of a Lady: The USS *Lexington* (CV-2) at the Battle of the Coral Sea. Part III: Battle Report." *National Archives: The Text Message Blog* web site, February 11, 2016. (Includes Capt. Frederick C. Sherman's battle report.) https://text-message.blogs.archives. gov/2016/02/11/the-death-of-a-lady-the-uss-lexington-cv-2-at-the-battle-of-the-coral-sea-part-iii-battle-report/

Leu, Del. "The U.S.S. *Neosho* (AO 23)." DelsJourney.com, http://www. delsjourney.com/uss_neosho/neosho_home.htm.

USS *Enterprise*, After-Action Reports, 1941–1945. http://www.cv6.org/ship/logs/default.htm.

USS *Enterprise*, Deck Log: 25–26 October 1942. http://www.cv6.org/ship/logs/log19421026.htm.

VB-10 war diary, October 25, 1942. Graciously supplied by historian Steve Moore.

Interviews

"Interview of Lt. Cdr. W. O. Burch, USNR, Commanding VS-5, USS *Yorktown*." Bureau of Aeronautics, September 3, 1942.

Buell, Hal. Interview with the author by telephone, July 3, 2011.

Feightner, Edward "Whitey." Interviews with the author in person. October 16, 2011, and by telephone over a period of years.

Glass, Jack. Interview with the author by telephone, April 6, 2011.

Hardy, Bill. Interview with the author by telephone, May 8, 2011.

Robinson, Leonard "Robbie." Interviews with the author in person and by telephone over a period of many years.

Vejtasa, Brant. Interviews with the author in person and by telephone, September 21, 2016.

Vejtasa, Daniel. Interview with the author by telephone, September 19, 2016.

Vejtasa, Eugene. Interview with the author by telephone, September 16, 2016.

Vejtasa, Stanley "Swede." Interviews with the author in person April 21 and 22, 2011, and October 25, 2012, and by telephone on more than a hundred occasions from 2010 through 2013.

Vejtasa, Susan. Interviews with the author in person, February 5, 2014, and many times by telephone.

Oral Histories

Shinneman, Bill. "Interview of Swede Vejtasa, October 2, 2000." Oral History Archives of the American Airpower Museum in Midland, Tex.

Basden, Barry. "An Interview with Mr. Stanley W. 'Swede' Vejtasa, 'Ace' Fighter Pilot, United States Navy," October 1, 2000. National Museum of the Pacific War, Center for Pacific War Studies, Oral History Program, Fredericksburg, Tex.

Videos and Films

Long, Tony, dir. *Battle 360°,* season 1. History Channel. New York, N.Y.: A&E Television Networks, 2008.

Robson, Mark, dir. *The Bridges at Toko-ri.* Hollywood, Calif: Paramount Pictures, 1954.

Strickland, Jonathan, dir. *F4F Wildcat.* DVD. Charlotte, N.C.: Red Pepper Creative, Inc., 2003.

USS Hornet; *A Visual History of CV 8 and CV 12.* DVD. Task Force Films, 2005.

Victory at Sea. DVD. Minnetonka, Minn.: Mill Creek Entertainment, 2006.

World War Two: Crusade in the Pacific. DVD Box Set. Walnut, Calif.: Diamond Entertainment Corp., 2005.

INDEX

A6M Type 00 fighters, 54. *See also* Zeros
Abe Hiroaki, 124
Aces gatherings, 200–201
Admirals' Revolt (1947), 157–58
Aichi D3A dive-bombers (Vals). *See* Vals
Air Force, creation of, 157
Air Group 5, 168, 169, 173, 174, 176–78
Air Group 10: ashore at Guadalcanal, 131;
    Enterprise not at Point Option and, 81,
    86, 87; Flatley critique of after Santa Cruz,
    120; Flatley's focus on *Suzuya* and, 94;
    formation of, 38; Gaines' commendation
    for, 115; "group grope" over Hawaii by, 6;
    Kinkaid orders at Guadalcanal and, 5; on
    Kinkaid's disdain for, 88; lack of group
    cohesion in, 76; performance during
    Guadalcanal campaign by, 1; repaired
    and refitted *Enterprise* and, 75; training
    exercises in Noumea, 144. See also
    Enterprise; Vejtasa, Stanley W. "Swede"
    and Goose Chase
Air Group 44, 153
Akagi (Japan), 64
Akigumo (Japan), 114
Alvarez, Everett, Jr., 194
American Defensive Waters, 32
American Volunteer Group, 26, 140, 192
Anderson, 78, 112–13
Ansley, Harry Claude, Jr., 129
Antietam, 172
Arizona, 37
Armstrong, Neil, 165
Army, U.S., 32, 38
Army Air Corps, 18, 157
arresting cable failures, 169, 193–94
Ashford, James Joseph, 165
Astor, Gerald, 1, 54, 218
Astoria, 51, 73
Atlanta, 125
Atlantic, Battle of the, 29, 30, 32, 33
Atlantic City, New Jersey, training at, 150
atomic bombs, 153, 178–79

Ault, William B., 53, 54, 60
Australia, 49–50
Australia, Japanese strategy for, 38, 41, 46
Aviation Cadet Program, 24
awards: de Poix commendation for Vejtasa,
    199; for Vejtasa, 200, 202; for Vejtasa,
    Flatley on, 118, 120–21; for Vejtasa,
    Hardison on, 121–22; during World
    War II vs. Vietnam War, 197–98. *See also*
    Medal of Honor
Azumason Maru (Japan), 44

B-29 flight testing, 159
bailing out, in Korean Conflict, 170–71
Baker, John D., 48, 50–51, 52
Baker, Paul, 52
Balch, Phillip Kendall, 165
Barnes, Gordon, 75, 104, 116, 242n18
barnstormers, in Montana, 15–16
Barton, 78
Bateman, Richard Alan, 168
Batten, Richard "Dick," 93, 97–98, 116,
    241n6
Battle 360° (History Channel), 219
Bauer, Harold "Indian Joe," 131–32
Beebe, Marshall U., 172
Beedle, Robert Westfield "Bobbie," 70
Bell P-59 Airacomet, 160
Bell X-1 flight testing, 159
Belote, James and William, 216–17
Beneke, Albert C., 128
Berlin Airlift, 157
Betty bombers (Japan), 144–45
Big E, The (Stafford), 216
Bilbray, Brian, 228–29
Billo, Jim, 110, 116
biological weapons research, 181–82
Black Sheep Squadron, 28
Blair, Bill, 4, 5, 86, 87
Blue Angels, 154, 155, 158
Boeing F4B, 23, 24
Bolduc, Al, 167

ABOUT THE AUTHOR

———

Ted Edwards is a historian whose oral history work with World War II aviators and other veterans of twentieth-century war is driven by a desire to understand the events via firsthand accounts. Edwards has written on World War II aviators for *Naval Aviation News* and lives in Fenton, CA.

The Naval Institute Press is the book-publishing arm of the U.S. Naval Institute, a private, nonprofit, membership society for sea service professionals and others who share an interest in naval and maritime affairs. Established in 1873 at the U.S. Naval Academy in Annapolis, Maryland, where its offices remain today, the Naval Institute has members worldwide.

Members of the Naval Institute support the education programs of the society and receive the influential monthly magazine *Proceedings* or the colorful bimonthly magazine *Naval History* and discounts on fine nautical prints and on ship and aircraft photos. They also have access to the transcripts of the Institute's Oral History Program and get discounted admission to any of the Institute-sponsored seminars offered around the country.

The Naval Institute's book-publishing program, begun in 1898 with basic guides to naval practices, has broadened its scope to include books of more general interest. Now the Naval Institute Press publishes about seventy titles each year, ranging from how-to books on boating and navigation to battle histories, biographies, ship and aircraft guides, and novels. Institute members receive significant discounts on the Press' more than eight hundred books in print.

Full-time students are eligible for special half-price membership rates. Life memberships are also available.

For a free catalog describing Naval Institute Press books currently available, and for further information about joining the U.S. Naval Institute, please write to:

Member Services
U.S. Naval Institute
291 Wood Road
Annapolis, MD 21402-5034
Telephone: (800) 233-8764
Fax: (410) 571-1703
Web address: www.usni.org